FOLKTALE THEMES AND ACTIVITIES FOR CHILDREN, VOLUME 1

Learning Through Folklore Series

Norma J. Livo, Series Editor

Who's Endangered on Noah's Ark? Literary and Scientific Activities for Teachers and Parents. By Glenn McGlathery and Norma J. Livo. 1992.

Who's Afraid. . . ? Facing Children's Fears with Folktales. By Norma J. Livo. 1994.

Of Bugs and Beasts: Fact, Folklore, and Activities. By Lauren J. Livo, Glenn McGlathery, and Norma J. Livo. 1995.

Folktale Themes and Activities for Children, Volume 1: Pourquoi Tales. By Anne Marie Kraus. 1998.

Folktale Themes and Activities for Children, Volume 2: Trickster and Transformation Tales. By Anne Marie Kraus. 1999.

Folktale Themes and Activities for Children

pourquoi tales

Volume 1

Anne Marie Kraus

Calligraphy by Susan K. Bins

1998
Teacher Ideas Press
A Division of
Libraries Unlimited, Inc.
Englewood, Colorado

For Jenny and Michael,
for all that you are,
and all that you do.

Teacher Ideas Press
A Division of
Libraries Unlimited, Inc.
P.O. Box 6633
Englewood, CO 80155-6633
1-800-237-6124
www.lu.com/tip

Production Editor: Kay Mariea
Copy Editor: Diane Hess
Proofreader: Susie Sigman
Design and Layout: Pamela J. Getchell

Library of Congress Cataloging-in-Publication Data

Kraus, Anne Marie.
    Folktale themes and activities for children / Anne Marie Kraus ; calligraphy by Susan K. Bins.
        xv, 152 p. 22x28 cm.
        Includes bibliographical references and index.
        Contents: v. 1. Pourquoi tales.
        ISBN 1-56308-521-6
        1. Tales--Study and teaching (Elementary)   2. Folklore and children.   I. Bins, Susan K.   II. Title.
    GR45.K73   1998
    372.64--dc21   98-22419
                                                                            CIP

Contents

Preface

The explosion in the number and variety of folktales has been a welcome trend in the publishing of books for children. Libraries and bookstores increasingly enrich their holdings with lavishly illustrated single-tale picture book editions and thoughtful, illustrated collections for children. Teachers, school media specialists, public librarians, recreation specialists, storytellers, and parents are eager to use these multicultural stories with children. *Folktale Themes and Activities for Children: Pourquoi Tales* is a resource guide for planning children's folktale experiences. This guide offers an annotated bibliography and suggestions for grouping tales with common motifs, activities, and school curriculum connections. Whereas many of the activities focus on the school setting, anyone interested in folk literature will find this resource helpful as an organizational tool, a selection or purchasing tool, and an activity guide. Overall, *Folktale Themes and Activities for Children* may be used as a guide for choosing stories based on a culture or country or based on a topic, motif, or theme.

In my years as a school library media specialist, I have come to use and view pourquoi tales with wonder and ardor. As I read and tell these stories to children, their enthusiasm provides me with affirmation of these tales' enduring vitality. I have collaborated with creative and flexible teachers who further help bring these absorbing stories alive in the classroom. Students respond to some tales with laughter, with eager predictions, and with urgent requests for more. They listen wide-eyed and sober to other tales—for example, a tale that ends with a message of environmental consequences: "Perhaps through your own labor you will learn not to waste the gifts of nature" (Gerson 1992). Students also respond to these tales through creative outlets: writing, illustrating, and designing multimedia projects or puppet theater. Children demonstrate a strong memory for these stories and their messages, a testimony to the teaching potential of stories.

Today society in general displays a new awareness of cultural diversity. Educational and recreational institutions are infusing their programs with multicultural concepts; indeed, some see it as their duty to do so. With a rich body of folk literature available, the incorporation of multiculturalism flows naturally. These tales teach life lessons in a gentle way, expanding our view of humanity with their connections to the past and to other cultures. We often have a hard time cooperating—on both personal and global levels. Pourquoi tales provide needed perspective. I hope that those who sample folktales from this guide find refreshment and delight akin to a dipper of cool water on a hot day.

Acknowledgments

I would like to acknowledge the people who shared their time and talents, enabling this book to take shape. Many thanks to Paula Brandt of the University of Iowa Curriculum Lab for her initial and sustained encouragement, her discriminating ideas, and her invaluable knowledge of children's literature. Paula thoughtfully read the text and provided insightful feedback. I am fortunate to have worked with creative teachers who shared their classrooms and ideas with me, allowing us to explore folktales in collaboration: Chris Gibson, Wendy Deutmeyer, Chris Shope, and Andrea Keech.

Busy and talented author Robert D. San Souci took the time and care to pass on valuable information and experience. Storyteller and science educator Jo Anne Ollerenshaw Lewis shared her experience and ideas in her areas of specialization. Susan K. Bins added visual style with her calligraphy and accompanying art. Andrea McGann Keech drew the shadow puppet figures in Chapter 2 based on Paul Goble's illustrations from *Her Seven Brothers*, copyright © 1988 Paul Goble. They were used with the permission of Simon & Schuster Books for Young Readers, an imprint of Simon & Schuster Publishing Division.

I could not embark on a folklore project without an affectionate nod to the staff and participants at Folklore Village Farm, a community that keeps the joy of folk traditions alive and offered me the opportunity to field-test some of the activities in this book.

I am grateful for the kind help of Deb Green and Craig Johnson at the Iowa City Public Library, and Carol Sokoloff at Prairie Lights Bookstore. Robert M. van Deusen provided assistance with graphics and technical issues. Jean Donham of the University of Iowa School of Library and Information Science gave advice on launching this publishing project. I thank Ann Holton for her mentoring on all aspects of school librarianship. Author Linda Hogan provided thoughtful comments. Thanks to Jan Irving for helping me to connect with Libraries Unlimited. Juliana Pauley, Courtney Harris, Linea Bartel, Matt Maloney, Emily Molof, and Jonathan Launspach from Roosevelt Elementary School in Iowa City created the three student-produced graphic organizers included in Chapter 2. And thanks to my own children, and the children in my classes, for their bright-eyed enthusiasm. It keeps me going and firms my continued belief in the sustenance provided by folk literature.

In recent years, there has been a renaissance in the art of storytelling and a surge in publishing new, illustrated tellings of old tales for children. *Folktale Themes and Activities for Children: Pourquoi Tales* is a resource guide to help in the selection and planning of folktale-related experiences for children aged six through eleven. Folk literature, in single-tale editions and in collections, offers rich opportunities for read-aloud experiences, independent reading, group interactions, and individual activities.

Why is it important to provide planned experiences with folktales for children? Folktales constitute some of the world's oldest literature; they embody the concept of "story" while passing on the wisdom of a culture. Because these stories are so old, they provide a grounding upon which more contemporary experiences can be built. Familiarity with folktale themes is a measure of cultural literacy. Educationally, children benefit from these tales in many ways: They experience the sheer enjoyment of the story, they predict consequences, they apply critical thinking skills by comparing tales, they embrace environmental lessons taught through the tales, they create their own imaginative stories or plays based on these tales, and they experience multicultural contexts. In addition, they learn that ever since ancient times, people all over the world have had scientific wisdom, a sense of humor, and a reverence for nature.

Because folk literature is embedded in a cultural context, teachers need to understand some basic issues before using folktales. The background information in this introduction examines these issues and assists with choosing and presenting tales to children. Several criteria for selecting tales are provided. Finally, this introduction explains how this guide is organized, with suggestions for ways to use it.

BACKGROUND ON THE USE OF FOLK LITERATURE

The publishing of folktales raises issues of sensitivity to the originators of the stories. The originators of the stories are unknown. Their modern "authors" participate in a long tradition of "retelling." Some of these authors-retellers come from within the culture of the tales—for example, Native American storytellers Gayle Ross and Joseph Bruchac. Not every tale is published by someone from within the culture of origin, especially in language that speaks to children. Other storytellers have emerged, such as authors Robert D. San Souci and Verna Aardema, who dig stories out of dusty tomes or get them directly from the oral tradition and bring them alive for children. Children should be made aware that these stories have been passed down in the oral tradition over many, many years. They should understand that the "author" is someone who found or heard the tale and wrote or rewrote it so that we, too, can enjoy the story.

There is a strong need for sensitivity toward the cultural context of each story, which is often different from the background or cultural milieu of the author, reader, storyteller, or listeners. Every tale is tied to a culture's belief system and traditions. For example, among Native American peoples, certain tales are told only in a particular season, a fact that may be lost on nonnatives. Some aspects of a tale may have sacred significance unknown to a nonnative. In an African pourquoi tale, the creation elements may be part of religion. When possible, adults should research the culture that the story is from and take note of any background information provided by the author. But even when additional research is not possible, the adult's reverence and respect for the story will enhance the learning experience for children.

Representation of Native American culture in children's books has long engendered emotional discussion. Native peoples have been stereotyped as intellectually inferior or as noble, vanishing environmentalists. Fortunately, an increase in general awareness and in the number of native authors is helping to turn this situation around. However, with folktales coming from an old oral tradition, there are opportunities for misrepresentation. Many published folktales for children have come from written versions in English that were compiled by Euro-American anthropologists and other collectors in the latter nineteenth and early twentieth centuries. Translation is fraught with complexities because mere words are only part of the story; there are also vocal inflections, facial cues, idiomatic expressions, and the entire body of culture and belief systems embedded in the story. Children's versions of folktales are also criticized for the manner in which the tellers alter events to resemble those in familiar European fairy tales or to soften the edges of controversial issues (Stott 1995, 82–85).

Therefore, the selector relies on authors with a reputation for their research and familiarity with the field and on the documentation of authenticity in their books. In the 1990s, publishers are requiring retellers of folktales to research as many documented sources of a tale as possible and to locate the earliest known version if they can (Shepard 1996, 5). Betsy Hearne (1993, 25) urges librarians to use more stringent standards in evaluating folktales published for children. She is critical of vague source notes, preferring "the truly exemplary source note [which] cites the specific source(s), adds a description for cultural context, *and* describes what the author has done to change the tale, with some explanation of why." Distinguished Native American author Joseph Bruchac (1995, xiii), states, "My point is *not* that only Native people can write about Native Americans, but that deep knowledge is necessary for anyone (Native or non-Native) to write well about those essential building blocks of Native American cultures—the words of their elders, the traditional stories told to their children." Graciela Italiano (1993) agrees that scholarship and experience with a culture's traditions are more important in writing for children than being a member of that culture. Adults working with this body of literature would benefit from reading sections of Hearne's articles (1993), Slapin and Seale's *Through Indian Eyes* (1992), or Jon C. Stott's *Native Americans in Children's Literature* (1995) for additional background on this aspect of the literature.

While being mindful of these sensitivities to cultural contexts, we must also remember the children (and adults!) who are eager to hear these multicultural tales. We must also remember the spirit of the oral tradition in which these stories were conceived: the spirit of listening, sharing, and retelling the tale. The act of retelling implies a constant evolutionary process. Author-storyteller Aaron Shepard explains: "Stories originate with individual tellers and spread through a culture. Travelers carry them from that culture to another, where storytellers adopt them, adapt them, and spread them through their own cultures. Then travelers carry them on again. Few stories belong exclusively to the culture where they are found. Most are told in different versions all over the world." He goes on to say, "There should be room for retellings both by those within a culture and those without. Each brings different knowledge, perspectives, and insights" (Shepard 1996, 11). Betsy Hearne (1993, 33) proposes that when tales are adapted by authors outside the culture, "text adapted from folklore [should] be judged for its balance of two traditions: the one from which it is drawn and the one that it is entering." She warns against "fakelore," in which illustrations may imitate native art in a superficial way. These unresearched folk art designs may disregard cultural symbolism. She prefers new, original art for illustrations by nonnatives rather than generic "folk art."

In conclusion, I have used an inclusive approach tempered with care in selecting titles for the bibliography. Because I am a librarian and an educator with a philosophy of open access to literature, I have been as inclusive as possible while focusing on respect for the material, documentation of sources, background contextual notes, and authors' reputations. I have included stories in the same spirit that they originated: the spirit of sharing and spreading these tales. Because I love this literature, and because children respond to it with wonder and enjoyment, I believe it should be shared in a respectful and generous way. Children are fertile ground for planting the seeds of multicultural awareness and appreciation. As stated in a traditional ending to many African tales, "This is my story. If it be sweet, or if it be not sweet, take some and let the rest come back to me" (Aardema 1994, 30).

BOOKS INCLUDED IN THIS GUIDE

The books included in this guide were selected for their usefulness and appeal to children in first through fifth grade (ages six through eleven); in some cases, teachers may find the titles of use for kindergarten through sixth grade. Inclusion of books is based on their potential as read-alouds and for independent reading by children; most annotations include suggestions for age appropriateness. The teacher or librarian may assume that stories suggested for third- and fourth-grade independent reading are often good choices for reading aloud to younger children. However, the final decision on whether plot complexities or particular subject matter is suitable should rest with the adults who best know their groups of children. Suggestions for grade-level readability are approximate and are usually expressed as "primary grades" (first and second), "middle grades" (third and fourth), and "upper grades" (fifth and sixth). Again, these indications of readability are intended to give teachers a general idea of reading levels as a starting point, but the ultimate judge is the teacher.

Most of the books in the annotated bibliography are relatively recent publications; a few were published prior to 1988. Although there is a focus on illustrated, single-tale editions, several collections of folktale collections have been included for their usefulness. A majority of books in the bibliography are in print at the time of this writing, but the availability of books increasingly varies from year to year. Some titles are available in paperback editions, making multiple copies affordable for whole language reading classes.

In keeping with the foregoing discussion on authenticity, the included books, to the best of available knowledge, contain authentic, well-told traditional stories. Evidence of authenticity includes written documentation of story sources, the author's credentials or experience in the field, the illustrator's credentials, and recommendations in other selection guides or children's literature reviews. The annotated bibliography is intended to assist in selecting stories for use with children. The book list is not necessarily definitive or comprehensive but rather practical, reflecting a sincere effort to present quality literature.

WAYS TO USE THIS GUIDE

This guide is divided into four sections. Chapter 1 provides background on pourquoi tales. In Chapter 2 are activities and teaching plans for these stories. Chapter 3 contains an extensive theme and topic chart, and Chapter 4 is an annotated bibliography. The author-title index helps in locating full information on any book, and the general index assists with finding specific topics.

Folktale Themes and Activities for Children: Pourquoi Tales may be consulted in a variety of ways. A person looking for topics such as animals, food, weather, survival, and sky phenomena may browse Chapter 3, "Story Themes and Topics," or use the general index. Someone wanting a story from a particular geographical area may consult the annotated bibliography, which is arranged by continental area and further subdivided by individual cultures. One of the most fascinating aspects of folk literature is similar motifs (or similar plots, characters, origin explanations, or events) across cultures. For example, obtaining the sun or fire and the origin of star constellations are themes found in many cultures. Telling or reading two or more stories containing similar elements makes for cohesive programming for story hours or for "compare and contrast" skill activities for students. To plan a series of stories with similar elements, consult Chapter 3, "Story Themes and Topics." To provide students with a whole language reading or literature unit, Chapter 2 "Activities," offers lesson plans and student activities for reading classes or other curricular programs. Those seeking artistic extensions (for example, multimedia projects or shadow puppet theater) will find ideas in the "Creative Extensions" section of Chapter 2. Social studies and science tie-ins for pourquoi tales are also included in that chapter.

"I'd like some stories to integrate into our unit of study on weather (or astronomy or pond ecology or the rain forest)"; ... or ... "I'm fascinated with stories that have similar themes and would like to put some together to compare"; ... or ... "Our summer recreation program is called 'The Sky's the Limit,' and I need to come

up with some stories about the sky for the kids to hear and dramatize"; . . . or . . .
"There are a lot of neat folktale books out, and I'd like to have my students use them
for reading class, but I don't have the time or resources to get everything organized
and find enough different reading levels"; . . . or . . . "I need some ideas for infusing
multiculturalism into my curriculum"; . . . or . . . "My kids are studying the 50 states
and it would be nice for them to be able to find stories from those regions, you
know, learn more than the state bird and the industries." These are some possible
scenarios just ripe for the introduction of folk literature and for integrating multicultural awareness into the curriculum.

A FINAL THOUGHT

These stories come from a time before electricity and modern transportation,
when one of the main channels for passing down wisdom was stories. The gentle
lessons of these tales, the wisdom, the humor, are all old and yet still ring true
today. In today's world, where everything moves so fast and technology reigns,
folktales can ground us in our ancient past. There is a need to listen to the voices
of people who were closer to the rhythms of the earth and the power of nature than
we are today. A folktale "reminds everyone that we are all connected, like the
strands of Grandmother Spider's web" (Caduto and Bruchac 1989, 50).

REFERENCES

Aardema, Verna. 1994. *Misoso: Once Upon a Time Tales from Africa*. New York: Apple Soup Books.

Bruchac, Joseph. 1995. "Foreword." In Jon C. Stott, *Native Americans in Children's Literature*, xi–xiv. Phoenix, AZ: Oryx Press.

Caduto, Michael J., and Joseph Bruchac. 1989. *Keepers of the Earth: Native American Stories and Environmental Activities for Children*. Golden, CO: Fulcrum.

Gerson, Mary-Joan. 1992. *Why the Sky Is Far Away: A Nigerian Folktale*. Boston: Little, Brown.

Hearne, Betsy. 1993. "Cite the Source: Reducing Cultural Chaos in Picture Books, Part One." *School Library Journal* 39 (July): 22-27.

———. 1993. "Respect the Source: Reducing Cultural Chaos in Picture Books, Part Two." *School Library Journal* 39 (August): 33–37.

Italiano, Graciela. 1993. "Reading Latin America: Issues in the Evaluation of Latino Children's Books in Spanish and English." In *Evaluating Children's Books: A Critical Look*, ed. Betsy Hearne and Roger Sutton, 119–132. Urbana-Champaign: University of Illinois Graduate School of Library and Information Science.

Shepard, Aaron. 1996. "A Dozen Answers to the Multicultural Heckler." *Once Upon a Time* (Summer): 11.

———. 1996. "Researching the Folktale." *SCBWI (Society of Children's Book Writers and Illustrators) Bulletin* (February/March): 5–6.

Slapin, Beverly, and Doris Seale. 1992. *Through Indian Eyes*. Philadelphia: New Society.

Stott, Jon C. 1995. *Native Americans in Children's Literature*. Phoenix, AZ: Oryx Press.

Chapter 1

WHY THINGS ARE THE WAY THEY ARE

"In the beginning, . . ." or "Back in the old times, when the animals and the people spoke the same language, . . ." or "In the Dreamtime, . . ."—thus begin numerous fascinating stories of the origin of the world and its creatures. *Pourquoi tale* is the term given to stories that explain how things came to be. These stories come from people who spent time pondering the complexities, the details, the beauties, the awe-inspiring power of nature. *Pourquoi*, the French word for "why," is used for the body of tales sometimes called "origin" stories. These tales range from explanations for huge phenomena—the sky, the earth, human beings, death—all the way to those for small details of animals' physical markings—the cracks on the turtle's back, the rabbit's split lip, the colors on birds' feathers. Some stories explain the origin of plants and animals; others tell of the origin of things not always thought of as living, such as thunder and lightning or mountains. Some stories focus on natural phenomena such as stars, and others honor human activity, such as those on how weaving came to the Navajo people. The Navajo tale not only reveres Spider Woman as having taught the people to weave and keep themselves warm but also passes on some of the instructions for weaving and the values embedded in a good piece of weaving (Oughton 1994). The titles of these stories—"How the Ostrich Got Its Long Neck" (Aardema 1995) or "Why the Sky Is Far Away" (Gerson 1992)—arouse our curiosity. Sometimes humorous, sometimes hauntingly mystical, sometimes sobering, these stories continue to captivate.

CREATORS AND CULTURE HEROES

Included in the listing of pourquoi tales in Chapter 4 are many that are more often referred to as creation myths. Myths characteristically have creators, or gods and goddesses, whereas a pourquoi tale features a story line with a consequence resulting in a long-lasting trait (Clarkson and Cross 1980, 327). Creation myths often also feature one greater spirit who is in some way over all other creative agents. This spirit is sometimes known as the Great Spirit, the Sky God, the Supreme Being, the Blessed One. Some examples of creation myths in this guide are taken from Mayan, Aztec, and African cultures. This book focuses on the oral tradition of world cultures and does not explore classical Greek mythology or Biblical creation writings.

Many of the Native American origin tales feature creators who are known as "culture heroes." Culture heroes have power and stature beyond normal human beings but are not quite gods. They act for the benefit of the people or animals; sometimes they act more for their own personal benefit but still help others as a result. Some creator–culture heroes are also tricksters, such as Coyote (of the Southwest, who is more rascal than helper but does sometimes benefit others) and Raven (of the Northwest coast, who is generally more helpful and wise but still sometimes acts in his own best interest). Other culture heroes include Glooskap (or Kuloskap, of the Northeast coast) and Manabozho (or Nanabozho, of the northern woodlands of the Ojibwa). These latter two heroes are fairly human in form but have powers to transform themselves. They often act on behalf of creatures needing help and, in the process, also act as creators.

MOTIFS AND THEMES

A motif is "the smallest element of a tale having the power to persist in tradition" (Clarkson 1980, 4). One of the most compelling aspects of folklore study is the appearance of motifs across cultures. For example, there are many stories about how animals got, or lost, their tails. How the birds got their colored feathers and how Crow got his black coloring are motifs common in many tales. Stories of Turtle's cracked back or of Turtle flying with the birds are found around the globe.

In addition to motifs, broader themes are evident across cultures in pourquoi tales. One theme is the creation of human beings from earthly materials and the need for "spirit" or fine-tuning of their form and function. Several Native American tribes tell stories of the creation of the world that feature a similar theme: the earth-diver element. The world begins as water; a small animal dives and brings up a small amount of earth, which is usually placed on Turtle's back, and it grows into the earth. The origin of star constellations, especially the Big Dipper and the Milky Way, are other common themes found in different tales. An important theme in many Native American tales is the concept of parallel worlds: the sky world and the earth world. Children need a visual comprehension of these two worlds in order to understand this concept that is spiritual as well as physical. These parallel worlds exist in African tales as well.

REGIONAL INFORMATION

Because these stories explain the natural world, they in some ways become region-specific. Pourquoi tales of the Native Americans from the plains region are concerned with the buffalo and rain. Tales of the northern woodlands explain the animals, flora, and fauna of this region. Tales of the Southwest center around corn, the harvest, and the rocky, dry landscape. The people of the Northwest tell tales of ocean creatures and life at the shore. Because these tales present the wildlife and landscape of a region, they fit well in social studies classes covering regions of the United States (or other geographical areas or continents). The section in Chapter 2 titled "Social Studies Tie-In" explores these relationships between tales and regional studies.

SCIENCE AND POURQUOI TALES

When discussing pourquoi tales with children, teachers sometimes use a casual explanation, something like "People made up these stories to explain their world because they didn't have science yet to explain thunder or water lilies or why monkeys live in trees." But this attitude does a disservice to the culture; it can be condescending. These tales are not simply "quaint" or "entertaining" ways of explaining phenomena people did not understand. These tales *are* science—the science of their day. They reveal a wealth of scientific knowledge gleaned from primary sources—observation of the natural world. To belittle these stories as unscientific is to miss the point. They have multiple purposes: They pass on knowledge and information, teach lessons about danger or the power of nature, impart the culture's values and reverence toward the gifts of the earth, and give environmental warnings. Pourquoi tales are all the more amazing because they come out of premodern "scientific" times. Despite the "lack" of modern scientific methods, these earlier peoples learned, gathered, codified, and passed on a large body of scientific knowledge—without the written word! And they also lived by its environmental implications, adhering much more mindfully to sound environmental practices than the "modern scientific" population of today. Witness the message in "Loo-Wit, the Fire-Keeper," a story tracing the origin of Mount St. Helens: "If we human beings do not treat the land with respect, the people said, Loo-Wit will wake up and let us know how unhappy she and the Creator have become again. So they said long before the day in the 1980s when Mount St. Helens woke again" (Bruchac 1991, 25). The section of this guide titled, "Science Tie-In," explores these thoughts.

A WAY OF LIFE

In addition to containing scientific knowledge, these tales reveal a people who felt themselves to be very much a part of nature. For example, some Native American stories tell of people going into the sky to become stars or star people coming to earth. Jon Stott comments, "Whereas modern children are frequently told of the incredible distances between the earth and even the moon and the extreme unlikelihood of finding in the stars either landscapes or beings resembling those they know, the Native cosmos emphasized the links between the world around, the world above, and the world beyond" (Stott 1995, 58).

Some native peoples are sensitive about this literature being considered *folk*tales, preferring to think of them as *life* tales ("When I Talk Indian" 1996). The word *folk* is used in this book to indicate any tales coming out of the oral tradition and the traditional practices of world cultures. Erdoes and Ortiz (1984, xv) state the "life tale" view thus: "These legends are not told merely for enjoyment, or for education, or for amusement: they are believed. They are emblems of a living religion, giving concrete form to a set of beliefs and traditions that link people living today to ancestors from centuries and millennia past."

Pourquoi tales and creation myths reflect life with a creative perspective. These tales carry dignity and knowledge. They pass on information and culture. They are fascinating and belief-based. They leave their mark on the world. There are even pourquoi tales to explain the origin of stories, for example, "How Spider Obtained the Sky God's Stories," an Anansi story from the Ashanti people. When Anansi wins the stories from the Sky God, the Sky God proclaims, "No more shall we call them the stories of the sky god, but we shall call them spider stories" (Yolen 1986, 27).

REFERENCES

Aardema, Verna. 1995. *How the Ostrich Got Its Long Neck: A Tale from the Akambe of Kenya*. New York: Scholastic.

Bruchac, Joseph. 1991. *Native American Stories*. Golden, CO: Fulcrum.

Clarkson, Atelia, and Gilbert B. Cross. 1980. *World Folktales: A Scribner Resource Collection*. New York: Charles Scribner's Sons.

Erdoes, Richard, and Alfonso Ortiz. 1984. *American Indian Myths and Legends*. New York: Pantheon Books.

Gerson, Mary-Joan. 1992. *Why the Sky Is Far Away: A Nigerian Folktale*. Boston: Little, Brown.

Leach, Maria, and Jerome Fried, eds. 1972. *Funk & Wagnalls Standard Dictionary of Folklore, Mythology, and Legend*. New York: Funk & Wagnalls.

Norman, Howard. 1990. *Northern Tales: Traditional Stories of Eskimo and Indian Peoples*. New York: Pantheon Books.

Oughton, Jerrie. 1994. *The Magic Weaver of Rugs: A Tale of the Navajo*. Boston: Houghton Mifflin.

Stott, Jon C. 1995. *Native Americans in Children's Literature*. Phoenix, AZ: Oryx Press.

"When I Talk Indian, I Think Differently." 1996. Iowa Multimedia Workshop for Endangered Languages, panel discussion, University of Iowa, Iowa City, June 19.

Yolen, Jane. 1986. *Favorite Folktales from Around the World*. New York: Pantheon Books.

Chapter 2

USING POURQUOI TALES WITH CHILDREN

Pourquoi tales are compelling and thought-provoking; they draw children in with the topics and questions they explore. A planned literature experience, comprised of a thoughtful sequence of activities, provides the immersion and background children need to make connections across a spectrum of topics and cultures. This body of literature begs to be used to its best advantage, whether in a school setting, public library story series, or recreational program. The activities on the following pages can be adapted for use in a variety of settings with a variety of timelines. A story series in a park recreation program could feature a set of tales that have connections to one another. A public library storyhour might include a group of stories for children to act out with shadow puppets. A classroom teacher could plan an entire whole language reading/language arts unit based on the books and activities in this guide. A recreation leader or science teacher could launch an investigation or experiment with a pourquoi tale. A school library media specialist could plan sequenced literature classes and discussions based on this body of literature. A school library media specialist and teacher could collaborate on a student literature experience that integrates the classroom reading/language arts program and the library program. These tales and activities offer many opportunities to make connections among stories, among disciplines, and among the givers and receivers of stories.

Throughout this activities chapter, the reader may benefit from referring to other chapters in the book. Background on the stories is provided by the annotated bibliography in Chapter 4. Opportunities for making connections can be found in the themes and topics charts in Chapter 3. Perusing the chart may spark ideas or suggest new ways to use the tales. The activities on the following pages make use of a few of these themes as a model for children's discussions and creations.

The following activities are laid out as a whole language reading/language arts unit (but as stated previously, many activities could be adapted for other uses and other settings). The unit is geared toward third and fourth graders, since a good share of the tales work well with this age group in terms of listening skills, reading levels, and intellectual content of the stories. However, parts of the unit and many of the stories may be used with first and second graders, and most of this plan would work well with fifth and sixth graders. This unit of study spans four to six weeks and offers a balance of activities among teacher-led discussion, independent student work, and cooperative student work. Sections of it could be done in a shorter time frame. Following is the sequence of activities as presented in this chapter:

1. Read aloud a cluster of two to four stories that have a common element (i.e., stories about bat characteristics; consult chapter 3 for other ideas).

2. Conduct a whole-group discussion comparing the stories using a graphic organizer, such as a chart or Venn diagram. Estimated time: 30 to 40 minutes, during the same week the stories are read.

3. Repeat steps 1 and 2 with new clusters of stories as time allows (i.e., stories about fire, balance in nature). Both the classroom teacher and the library media specialist can read stories. The reading/discussion/graphic organizer sequence should be repeated at least once.

4. Students read selected tales independently. Suggestions are given for titles to purchase in multiple copies for reading groups.

5. Students participate in small group and independent response activities, including journal writing, small group discussion, small group charting, and Venn diagramming, drawing, and story webbing.

6. Students create original work: creative writing, multimedia production, and puppet theater.

7. Optional integration into science and social studies units of study: Teachers and media specialists integrate pourquoi tales into content-area studies. Specific titles are given for topics such as weather, astronomy, animals, land formations, and regional studies of the United States.

FOCUS AND GOALS FOR POURQUOI TALE STUDY

Focus statement: Throughout the years, from olden times, people have observed the natural world and told stories to help explain the origins of natural phenomena and aspects of the human condition. These stories have been passed down through the ages as a way for a culture to preserve wisdom and information.
Goals:

- The learner will read and listen to stories from the oral traditions of a variety of indigenous cultures.

- The learner will participate in whole group "compare and contrast" activities, identifying unique and similar elements in two or more stories and show his or her understanding using a graphic organizer.

- The learner will recognize and identify common themes across different cultures.

- The learner will respond to the stories through independent and small group discussion, journal writing, drawing, webbing or diagrams.

- The learner will engage in one or more creative extensions, such as creative writing of his or her own pourquoi tale, publishing a pourquoi tale in multimedia format, storytelling, or participating in shadow puppet theater.

STARTING UP: GROUP READ-ALOUDS AND ACTIVITIES

To launch the unit, start by reading selected tales aloud to the whole group. This gives students a "feel" for pourquoi tales and provides examples of the pourquoi genre. Follow up a cluster of two or three tales with discussions and compare-and-contrast activities. A reasonable time frame for this sequence would be three days. Read aloud two to four stories during the first two days; most stories take 15 to 25 minutes, and add 5 to 15 minutes to introduce and discuss the story. On the third day, plan 30 to 40 minutes to complete a Venn diagramming or charting activity. The tales in the following story clusters were chosen because they provide four distinct manifestations of the pourquoi genre:

- Tales explaining the origin of an animal trait. In Story Cluster A, four tales describe physical and behavioral characteristics of bats.

- Tales about obtaining something of crucial importance to human survival. In Story Cluster B, the three tales are about the acquisition of fire.

- Tales that ponder the beginnings of the world; of life; and of animals, plants, and humans. In Story Cluster C, five creation myths explain how the world came to be.

- Tales that muse over why things are the way they are. In Story Cluster 4, events point out the need for balance in nature.

Refer to the "Story Themes and Topics" chart in chapter 3 for additional tales to compare or substitute if the suggested titles are not available. The chart lists many other themes and topics that can be used with the same processes described here. The following clusters of stories are models for involving children in the literature; other clusters of tales also work well. Refer to the annotated bibliography in Chapter 4 for more complete information on any title.

Story Cluster A:
Tales Explaining an Animal Trait: Bats and Their Characteristics

Introduction to the Stories

Students would benefit from introductory remarks similar to this: Pourquoi tales explain how things came to be the way they are. "Pourquoi" is a French word meaning "why." These folktales explain "why" things are the way they are. These stories come from long ago, before books, before TV, before knowledge was written down or put into computers. People lived with nature, observed what was happening around them, wondered about it, and talked about it. Sometimes they put their wondering and their knowledge into stories. This group of stories is about how an animal got its characteristics. Lots of pourquoi stories explain how an animal got its colors or why it flies or crawls or what happened to its tail. The animal stories we're about to read are about bats.

■ Story 1: Bruchac, Joseph. *The Great Ball Game: A Muskogee Story.*
Introduction to the book: Long ago when this story started, Native Americans played different kinds of ball games, some like lacrosse or hockey, and some like soccer. Sometimes they would play these games as a way of settling a disagreement instead of having a war. This is a story of how the birds and the animals use a ball game to settle their dispute. A very special player on the team is the bat.

■ Story 2: Mollel, Tololwa M. *A Promise to the Sun: An African Story.*
Introduction to the book: There are many pourquoi stories about the need for rain. Just think what happens when there is a drought and all the water and plants dry up. In the old days when this story began, people couldn't go to the grocery store for food! If the plants and animals died, there was no food. In this story, the birds send the bat to search for rain. And the bat makes a promise.

Note: As stated in the introductory material of this guide, students need to learn that pourquoi tales are not simply "quaint" stories, given the lack of "science," to explain some aspect of nature. These tales actually are a manifestation of scientific wisdom despite the lack of technology at the time these tales were conceived. *A Promise to the Sun* provides an opportunity for such a discussion. After the reading, ask students to list the scientific information contained in this tale and to determine how this knowledge was gained. Here is a partial list of scientific knowledge in this story:

• The winds must blow the clouds together for rain to fall.

• The sun must bring steam up into the sky.

• The bat cannot build the right kind of nest, but the birds can.

• Rain renews the earth and makes the crops grow.

• The bat comes out at night and hides during the day.

Discuss with students that somehow the people learned not from books as we do but from observation of primary sources. Relate this to a science unit the students have participated in, such as growing plants.

■ Story 3: Caduto, Michael J., and Joseph Bruchac. "How the Bat Came to Be," in *Keepers of the Night: Native American Stories and Nocturnal Activities for Children.*
Introduction to the book: This book has the same talented Native American author as *The Great Ball Game*—Joseph Bruchac, an Abenaki storyteller. It comes from the Anishinabe people, who lived in the woodlands of the eastern United States.
Note: Again, this story provides an opportunity for students to recognize that native peoples learned from observation of the natural world and recorded this scientific knowledge in their stories. Ask students to list the scientific facts found in the story and to speculate on how the Anishinabe people came to understand their environment without the benefits of "modern science."

For instance, the story points out that bats are blind and can hear all around them while they fly at night. Ask, "If *you* watched a bat, could you know all that?"

■ Story 4: Hamilton, Virginia. "Still and Ugly Bat," in *When Birds Could Talk & Bats Could Sing: The Adventures of Bruh Sparrow, Sis Wren, and Their Friends.*
Introduction to the book: This is a collection of eight folktales about birds. These stories were told by African Americans during slavery times. A woman named Martha Young learned the stories from former slaves, and she wrote them down. Virginia Hamilton is a talented storyteller, and she writes these stories in a dialect style of African Americans in the South. They are funny and beautifully illustrated by Barry Moser. In this selection, Bat used to have multicolored feathers. She is very vain and thinks she is too special to have the same colors as the other birds. This story also teaches a lesson at the end; listen for it.

Compare and Contrast Activities for Bat Stories

To provide structure for the discussion following the reading of each book, prepare a *blank* chart (see table 2.1) to display in the classroom. It can be drawn on a long roll of paper or tagboard large enough for the whole class to see and filled in as each tale is read and discussed. Table 2.1 is filled in with some key points; students may come up with other ideas as well.

These initial discussions work well as a collaborative effort between the library media specialist and the classroom teacher. When students discuss the stories and contribute to a chart or Venn diagram, the teacher and media specialist make an effective team for questioning students and recording their ideas.

Table 2.1. Pourquoi Animal Tales: Bat Characteristics

Title/Reteller	Culture	Characteristic	Reason for the Characteristic	Other Explanations
The Great Ball Game; Bruchac	Native American Muskogee	Bat accepted as an animal, not as bird Bat comes flying at dusk	Bat wins the ball game for the animals' team against the birds To see if the animals need him to play ball	Why birds fly south for the winter
Promise to the Sun; Mollel	African	Bat hides from the sun in a cave and comes out only at night	She feels guilty that she promised the birds would build the sun a nest and they never did	Why the rain came to renew the forests
"How the Bat Came to Be;" Caduto and Bruchac	Native American Anishinabe	Black color No tail Flies Blind	Sun burns squirrel's fur Sun burns tail off Sun gives him wings Sun is too close	
"Still and Ugly Bat;" Hamilton	African American	Skin and bone Blind Flies at night Sleeps in attic	She sheds her feathers because she is vain & doesn't want to be like the other birds She cries her eyes out She is ashamed to be seen She hides to make her nest	"Stars do fall" lesson about too much pride

Story Cluster B:
Tales About Obtaining Something Important to Human Survival: Fire

Introduction to the Stories

Review the meaning of pourquoi tales as given in the introduction to Story Cluster A. Some pourquoi stories show how people wondered about other things than just the way an animal looks. They wondered and told stories about things that made a life-or-death difference. Just think about how important fire must have been to people long ago. What did people need fire for? No wonder they made up stories about fire; it was so important to their survival! Some stories begin, "Long ago, there was no fire . . ." as they wondered what life must have been like without fire.

■ Story 1: London, Jonathan. *Fire Race: A Karuk Coyote Tale About How Fire Came to the People.*
Introduction to the book: This story is from the Karuk Native Americans, who come from northern California. Keep your eye on Coyote, the great Native American trickster. Sometimes Coyote plays tricks just for fun, but this time, his tricks are for the benefit of the other animals.

■ Story 2: Crespo, George. *How Iwariwa the Cayman Learned to Share.*
Introduction to the book: The native peoples of the Amazon rain forest, the Yanomami, told this story. Some of their names are in their own language, and so is one of their important foods, sweet potatoes, called *hukomo*. (Note: the reader will benefit from the pronunciation guide on the last page of the book.) The main character, the cayman, is a reptile related to an alligator.

■ Story 3: Greene, Jacqueline Dembar. "How Manabozho Stole Fire," in *Manabozho's Gifts: Three Chippewa Tales.*
Introduction to the book: Manabozho is a powerful character in the folktales of the Chippewa Native Americans. The Chippewa are sometimes known as the Ojibwa and live in the northern woodlands and lakes regions of Minnesota and Wisconsin. Manabozho has powers beyond those of a human and can transform himself into other shapes. He often does this to help other people and animals.

As an optional fourth story with similar thematic elements, read aloud "Blue Jay and Swallow Take the Heat," in Virginia Hamilton's *When Birds Could Talk & Bats Could Sing: The Adventures of Bruh Sparrow, Sis Wren, and Their Friends.* This story could be substituted for one of the three stories included in the Venn diagram activity (see fig. 2.1), or simply as an additional variant to wrap up this portion of the unit. This tale also features a relay race to steal fire from the Firekeeper.

After comparing these stories and again at other "teachable moments" during the unit, the teacher can point out to students how remarkable it is that the same concerns, motifs, or plot elements appear in stories from completely different cultures and people who lived thousands of miles apart.

Compare and Contrast Activities for Fire Stories

This comparison activity is more complex than listing attributes of an animal and requires students to exercise recall skills and higher-level skills of analysis and comparison. These are thinking skills that carry over into other disciplines and situations.

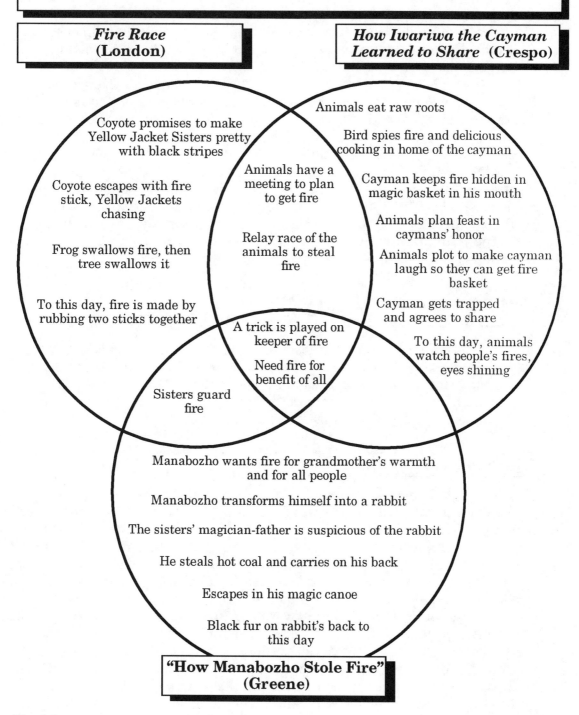

Unique and Overlapping Elements of "How Manabozho Stole Fire," *How Iwariwa the Cayman Learned to Share,* and *Fire Race*

**Fire Race
(London)**

**How Iwariwa the Cayman
Learned to Share** (Crespo)

Coyote promises to make
Yellow Jacket Sisters pretty
with black stripes

Coyote escapes with fire
stick, Yellow Jackets
chasing

Frog swallows fire, then
tree swallows it

To this day, fire is made by
rubbing two sticks together

Animals have a
meeting to plan
to get fire

Relay race of the
animals to steal
fire

Animals eat raw roots

Bird spies fire and delicious
cooking in home of the cayman

Cayman keeps fire hidden in
magic basket in his mouth

Animals plan feast in
caymans' honor

Animals plot to make cayman
laugh so they can get fire
basket

Cayman gets trapped
and agrees to share

To this day, animals
watch people's fires,
eyes shining

A trick is played on
keeper of fire

Need fire for
benefit of all

Sisters guard
fire

Manabozho wants fire for grandmother's warmth
and for all people

Manabozho transforms himself into a rabbit

The sisters' magician-father is suspicious of the rabbit

He steals hot coal and carries on his back

Escapes in his magic canoe

Black fur on rabbit's back to
this day

**"How Manabozho Stole Fire"
(Greene)**

Fig. 2.1.

This time, students will note similar motifs (persistent elements in a story) and thematic elements. The Venn diagram is a useful graphic organizer for this task because it allows for presentation of elements common to one, two, or all three stories. Prepare a large, blank, three-circle Venn diagram for this whole-classroom activity or start with a two-circle Venn and add a third circle for the third story. The Venn can be produced on large chart paper, an overhead transparency, or a computer screen. A computer with large-screen display capabilities is an effective way to produce Venn diagrams. Use a "draw" program (such as Adobe Superpaint, Color-It, or the "draw" portion of ClarisWorks).

Led by the teacher or media specialist, the class can begin in one of two ways. Students can just begin to contribute their ideas about features of the story that are the same or different and tell the teacher where that idea belongs on the diagram (in the overlapping part or by itself in the left, right, or bottom circle). Some teachers find it useful, the first time, to ask students to list basic elements of each story after each is read aloud and record these ideas on large lists posted in the classroom. Then, as the class looks at the lists, they circle elements common to two or three stories. These are transferred to the Venn diagram in the overlapping sections. Other story elements are placed in their appropriate circle of the diagram.

The Venn diagram in figure 2.1 is filled in with basic elements of each story. Once students are warmed up, they will probably think of more.

Story Cluster C:
Tales That Ponder the Beginnings of the World: Creation Myths

The following titles are suggested for the library media specialist's role, in addition to the times she spends collaborating with the teacher in the classroom on Story Cluster A and B. Because media specialists have devoted time to gaining a background in literature, they are well prepared to present origin stories, particularly creation myths, with a sense of respect and wonder.

Introduction to the Stories

To introduce these stories, acknowledge to the children that some of them present a very different way of viewing the world than many of us are used to. Long ago, when people pondered how the world came to be, these stories evolved as explanations. The stories have a mystical, sometimes magical, quality. Students may ask logic-oriented questions during a story, such as, "How could Raven be flying with a sack full of trees and wild animals?" The media specialist or teacher can simply acknowledge the question and indicate that sometimes we must just accept the magical elements of folktales.

Discuss with students that many Native American stories contain a concept of the universe that is different from modern-day conceptions—the idea that there are two parallel worlds, the sky world and the earth world. When we read these stories, it helps to picture the two worlds in our minds. Once in a great while, a character moves between the sky world and the earth world, as happens in three of these stories. Another concept we need to understand is the view of the world as "earth on turtle's back," or "turtle island." This is the idea that the earth was formed on and rests on the back of a turtle. Again, this is a different way of looking at the world. Developing cultural literacy involves learning about and appreciating such different views.

As long as these stories are related to students with the awe and wonder inherent to them, students will respond with openness and enjoyment. If the reader is not well acquainted or comfortable with these tales, they may be viewed as simply "different." Before reading these tales with students, the media specialist or teacher should be familiar with the stories and eager to share them with respect. A quiet, reverent tone when reading often helps students to listen quietly and responsively.

■ Story 1: Hamilton, Virginia. "The Woman Who Fell from the Sky," in *In the Beginning: Creation Stories from Around the World*.

Introduction to the story: Refer to the introduction to this cluster of stories to prepare students. In addition to the origin of the earth, this tale offers explanations for other aspects of life, including plant life. Some students may find it "gross" to think about plants growing up from Sky Woman's dead body. A proactive discussion will help at this point; ask students if they have ever heard the idea of Mother Nature or Mother Earth. We think of a mother as someone who takes care of us and feeds us. Some Native Americans (and others) have the idea that the earth is our mother, giving us food and other things we need to live. In this story, food comes from the first woman on earth.

Another discussion to have with students at the end of the book is the meaning of the two sons, one evil and one good. Who won the fight? Even though the evil one died, was he completely destroyed? Have you ever wondered why bad things happen to people? Why there is stealing and hurting? Probably Native Americans wondered this also, and this story helps explain the struggle between good and evil.

Bierhorst's *The Woman Who Fell from the Sky*, listed in Cluster 4, also fits well in this cluster of tales. Not only does it feature the woman falling from the sky and earth on Turtle's back but it also has the two sons. Each of the brothers has a distinct personality, one hard and one gentle. How do these personalities affect the creation of the world?

■ Story 2: Caduto, Michael J., and Joseph Bruchac. "The Earth on Turtle's Back," in *Keepers of the Earth*.

Introduction to the story: This story also contains the motifs of the woman falling from the sky and earth on Turtle's back. This version is different in that we learn more about what happens in the sky world before the woman falls. Points of discussion in this story include the importance of dreams. When a dream occurs in a Native American story, it is powerful and usually must be heeded. Students should make note of what the woman clutches in her hand as she falls to the world below; these seeds will be the start of plant life on earth. Compare this to the origin of plants in Hamilton's version of this tale.

■ Story 3: Shetterly, Susan. *Raven's Light*.

Introduction to the story: This story tells of the creation of earth in a watery world. The story is similar to the first two, but this time the creator/hero is Raven, the famous trickster from the Pacific Northwest. Although Raven plays tricks, he also acts for the benefit of the world. Many students may already be familiar with this story as it is told in *Raven* by Gerald McDermott. This is a more lengthy and detailed telling and includes the creation of the world prior to Raven's stealing the sun. Note the torn hole in the sky, through which Raven flies into the Sky World.

■ Story 4: Taylor, C. J. "From Darkness to Light," in *Bones in the Basket*.

Introduction to the story: This one-page story makes an interesting contrast to the first three. Many creation tales begin with the sky world; here is one in which the people come from the underworld. As in some sky stories, the people emerge through a hole into the earth world.

■ Story 5: Mayo, Margaret. Selections from *When the World Was Young: Creation and Pourquoi Tales*.

Introduction to the story: Additional stories from this collection make good read-alouds and provide further insight into creation myths. The first four stories in this cluster come from the Native American tradition; this anthology also provides accessible stories from other cultures. Background notes are useful for introducing and discussing each story. Recommended stories are "The Girl Who Did Some Baking," which explains why human beings have different colors of skin, and "Raven and the Pea-Pod Man."

Story Cluster D:
Tales About the Complex Issues of Life: The Need for Balance in Nature

Introduction to the Stories

We've seen that pourquoi stories can explain the way an animal looks or how people obtained something crucial to their survival, such as fire. There are still other pourquoi tales that ponder the ongoing complexities of daily life. They were wondering not just about why the turtle's back has a pattern on it or how the stars got into the sky. They were wondering about big issues: Why is life the way it is? Why are the days as long as they are? What if we didn't have enough sunlight or rain? What if the animals were so huge and ferocious that we couldn't be safe? What if everything were easy and we didn't have difficulty in our lives? Why do we have to work? These next four stories look at some of these ideas and help us think about achieving balance in our lives.

■ Story 1: Bishop, Gavin. *Māui and the Sun: A Maori Tale*.

Introduction to the book: Do you remember when we read the tales about how the people and animals got fire? People thought about fire and how much they needed it and how life might be difficult or even impossible without it. The same is true of the sun. There are many, many stories about how the sun was obtained or how the sun was stolen and how someone got it back. People recognized the life-giving power of the sun.

This story features Māui, a trickster character of the Maori people of the Polynesian islands. The author's ancestors came from New Zealand, where this story was told. Māui's problem is that the sun moves across the sky too quickly; people don't have enough daylight to get things done. Māui decides to do something about it, and he is very determined.

■ Story 2: Oliviero, Jamie. *The Fish Skin.*

Introduction to the book: The Cree people of central Canada tell this story. It is another story about the importance of the sun. The people in the story are tired of rainy, cloudy weather. But what if it were sunny all the time? See what happens when the weather gets out of balance.

Note: At this point, a quick two-circle Venn diagram activity would facilitate discussion of the first two titles. See the compare-and-contrast activities for this cluster (fig. 2.2, page 16). Keep this comparison brief in order to move on to two more stories and the main charting activity.

■ Story 3: Bierhorst, John. *The Woman Who Fell from the Sky: The Iroquois Story of Creation.*

Introduction to the book: There are many Native American stories about the beginnings of the earth world. The stories start with a woman living in the sky world who falls through a hole in the sky. The earth world is below, but it is all water. Animals help her, and from this point, the earth develops. In this Iroquois version, the woman has two sons with very different personalities. Listen for the ways these different personalities affect the world.

■ Story 4: Howard, Norman. "How Glooskap Made Human Beings." *How Glooskap Outwits the Ice Giants and Other Tales of the Maritime Indians.*

Introduction to the book: Glooskap is a hero of stories of the Native Americans who lived in what is now New England and eastern Canada. As their first human being, he has special powers to create. He is a giant, making the animals. When he decides to make human beings, he realizes there are some problems to solve.

■ Story 5: Duncan, Lois. *The Magic of Spider Woman.*

Introduction to the book: This Navajo tale recounts how Spider Woman taught the art of weaving to the people so that they could stay warm. A more complex issue of this story is balance. When Spider Woman teaches Wandering Girl/Weaving Woman how to weave, she warns her to walk the Middle Way. She must keep balance in her life, not getting over involved in one thing to the exclusion of others. This lesson in balance is in evidence to this day in the tradition of Navajo weaving.

■ Story 6: Haley, Gail E. *Two Bad Boys: A Very Old Cherokee Tale.*

Introduction to the book: Have you ever gotten talked into doing something you shouldn't? In this Cherokee tale, one boy in this story lures another into some troublesome situations. At the start, life is easy and there is no work until a newcomer, the boy's "wild brother," influences the boy to participate in forbidden spying and meddling. The boys' behavior permanently affects the balance of life for people.

Compare and Contrast Activities for Stories on Balance in Life

There are two comparison activities for this cluster of books. The first two stories, *Māui and the Sun* and *The Fish Skin*, may be compared on a two-circle Venn diagram (see fig. 2.2). The main activity is a chart outlining the problem, change, and outcome of the "balance" issue in all six stories (see table 2.2). Again, prepare a classroom-sized Venn diagram or chart so that students can see the products of their thinking. Direct questions to get students to think about the issues of balance: What is the problem? What is out of balance in these stories? What do the characters do to affect the balance of life?

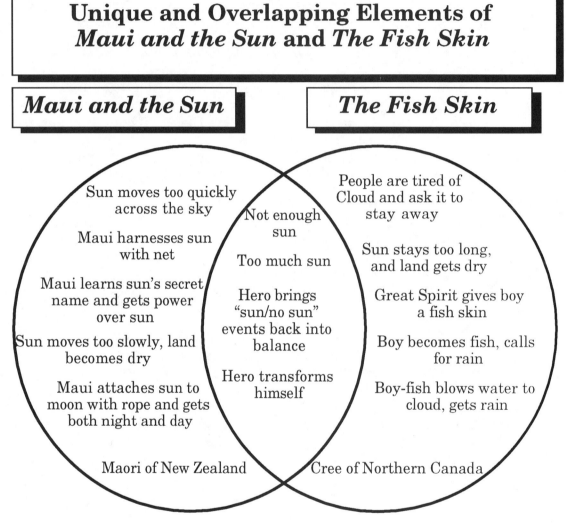

Unique and Overlapping Elements of *Maui and the Sun* and *The Fish Skin*

Maui and the Sun

The Fish Skin

Sun moves too quickly across the sky

Maui harnesses sun with net

Maui learns sun's secret name and gets power over sun

Sun moves too slowly, land becomes dry

Maui attaches sun to moon with rope and gets both night and day

Maori of New Zealand

Not enough sun

Too much sun

Hero brings "sun/no sun" events back into balance

Hero transforms himself

People are tired of Cloud and ask it to stay away

Sun stays too long, and land gets dry

Great Spirit gives boy a fish skin

Boy becomes fish, calls for rain

Boy-fish blows water to cloud, gets rain

Cree of Northern Canada

Fig. 2.2.

Table 2.2. Pourquoi Tales on Balance in Life

Title/Author/ Culture	How does it start? What is out of balance?	What is changed?	This story explains
Māui and the Sun Gavin Bishop Maori (New Zealand)	The sun moves too quickly across the sky	Māui catches the sun in a net and attaches it to the moon Day and night are in balance	Why day and night are of same length
The Fish Skin Jamie Oliviero Native American (Cree of Canada)	Too much cloud; people ask cloud to stay away Too much sun, no rain, drought	Boy in the fish skin creates rain to renew the earth Rain and cloud come	Why we have and need clouds and rain
The Woman Who Fell from the Sky John Bierhorst Native American/ Iroquois	Two-way rivers Fish created Monsters created Snow couldn't move	One-way rivers Small bones added Monsters sent underground Spring is created	Why there are both easy and difficult things in nature
How Glooskap Out-wits the Ice Giants Howard Norman Native American/ Northeast	The animals are giant-sized and would overpower human beings	Glooskap shrinks animals' sizes so he can create humans who will survive	Why animals are the size they are (so they are in proportion to humans)
The Magic of Spider Woman Lois Duncan Native American/ Navajo	Weaving Woman weaves too long and becomes too proud	She pulls a strand loose, making the weaving imperfect	Why people must keep balance in activities and not be proud Why Navajo blankets have a spirit pathway
Two Bad Boys Gail E. Haley Native American/ Cherokee	There is no hard work; food is easy to get Wild Boy meddles with secrets	The animals are let out to the world The vegetable storehouse is raided	Why people must work (hunt, plant, harvest) for their food

INDEPENDENT READING: TITLES FOR READING GROUPS WITH DISCUSSION QUESTIONS AND ACTIVITIES

Schools that support the whole language approach to reading instruction often purchase books in multiple copies for thematic units. Sets of five to ten copies of each title provide the opportunity for students to read in small groups. An assortment of titles, such as those in the following list, offer students a range of reading levels and also some measure of choice in what they read. The titles in the list span the reading levels typically found in a class of third and fourth graders. Refer to the annotated bibliography in Chapter 4 for complete information on each title.

Bruchac, Joseph. *The Boy Who Lived with the Bears and Other Iroquois Stories.*

Van Laan, Nancy. *In a Circle Long Ago: A Treasury of Native Lore from North America.*

Rosen, Michael. *How Giraffe Got Such a Long Neck . . . and Why Rhino Is So Grumpy.*

Martin, Francesca. *The Honey Hunters: A Traditional African Tale.*

Aardema, Verna. *How the Ostrich Got Its Long Neck.*

Students read and discuss in small groups, and the groups take turns meeting with the teacher. Plan one or two weeks for students' independent reading, about one hour per day. While reading independently, students typically are expected to respond to the stories by writing in their journals. Questions are provided for each book; these questions can be used in two ways. While working independently, students can use the questions for their journal responses. The questions may also be used as a guide for small-group discussions. Titles are listed from higher to lower reading levels typically encountered in a class of third and fourth graders.

■ Bruchac, Joseph. *The Boy Who Lived with the Bears and Other Iroquois Stories.*

Start by reading the third story in this book, "How the Birds Got Their Feathers."

1. In Native American folktales, a dream is considered to be very important. The characters take it seriously and try to follow its message. What is the message in the dream the birds had? What do the birds decide?
   Or—Draw a picture of the meeting the birds had and put "word balloons" over their heads to show what they talked about.

2. What are Buzzard's two jobs?

3. As his reward, Buzzard gets to choose the first suit of feathers. He starts trying them on. What does he think of them? What does he want?

4. Buzzard must wear the last suit of feathers. What does it look like?
   Or—Draw a picture of how Buzzard looks. *Or*—Find a picture of Buzzard in a book or CD-ROM source to see for yourself. *Or*—Draw a picture of what your suit of feathers would look like if *you* were Buzzard.

5. This pourquoi tale explains how Buzzard got his feathers. What other characteristics of buzzards are explained in this story?

Next, read "Turtle Makes War on Man."

1. Why does Turtle want to make war on humans?

2. When Turtle sets off to make war, the first two animals he meets want to join him. Who are they, and why does Turtle tell them they can't come along?

3. Turtle meets two more animals, and he lets them come along in his canoe. When they come to the village of the people, they get out and hide. Each animal meets a human, and something happens to make that animal look a certain way to this very day. What are these animal characteristics and how did they come about? Use a chart for your answers. (Provide the student with a copy of table 2.3.)

4. When Man catches Turtle and threatens to put him in the fire, Turtle does some thinking. How does he get the man to put him in the river instead? This is a trick found in many stories. Do you know another story in which this same trick is used?

Table 2.3. Pourquoi Tale Elements Found in "Turtle Makes War on Man" in *The Boy Who Lived with the Bears* by Joseph Bruchac

"Turtle Makes War on Man"
from *The Boy Who Lived With the Bears* by Joseph Bruchac

Animal	Characteristic	Reason
Skunk		
Rattlesnake		
Turtle		

Next, read "Chipmunk and Bear."

1. Chipmunk hears Bear boasting that he can do anything. Chipmunk challenges Bear that there's something he can't do. What is it?

2. What marks and behavior does Chipmunk have as a result of insulting Bear? What are these marks from?
    Or—Draw a picture of Chipmunk and where he hides.

Next, read "Rabbit's Snow Dance."

1. How did Rabbit look long ago that is different from the way he looks today?

2. How does Rabbit get caught in the top of a tree?

3. When Rabbit falls, four things happen to his body that change forever the way he looks. What are they?
    Or—Draw a picture of the four things that happened to Rabbit, plus the little "rabbit-tail trees."

4. What are the little "rabbit-tail trees" that we see in the forest to this day to remind us of Rabbit's snow story?

Last, read the first two stories in the book: "Rabbit and Fox" and "The Boy Who Lived with the Bears"

1. Do you think either of these stories is a pourquoi story? Why or why not?

2. Do you think either of them teaches us a lesson? What?

■ Van Laan, Nancy. *In a Circle Long Ago: A Treasury of Native Lore from North America.* A collection of twenty-five stories and poems organized into seven regions of North America.
    Note: Response questions are provided for five of the stories in the book. For the remainder of the stories, students can summarize any story by answering the general question, "What would you share with the class about this story?"

Selection: "The Long Winter"

1. The bears steal the warm summer heat and take it to the world above. Describe, with words or a picture, how the animals find the warmth of summer.

2. The animals find where the bears live. What is in the four bags?

3. The animals make a plan to steal the bag of heat. For this plan, why does Lynx change himself into a deer? And why does Mouse gnaw some of the wood out of the canoe paddle?

4. When the animals get back to earth with the heat, the world starts to warm up. What happens to cause danger to the animals?

5. From that time on, how have the seasons been on earth?

Selection: "Raven, the River Maker"

1. What color did Raven used to be? How could he see Wolf without Wolf seeing him?

2. Raven drinks up all of Wolf's fresh water. How does this make problems for Raven?
    Or—Draw a picture of what happens to Raven after he drinks all Wolf's water.

3. What causes Raven's feathers to turn black?

4. Raven often does things to help the rest of the world. When he escapes from Wolf, what happens to help the animals all over the earth? Do you know any other stories in which Raven helps others?

Selection: "How Beaver Stole Fire"

1. When Beaver grabs the hot coal and runs, the pine trees chase him. When he runs, the Grande Ronde River follows him. How does Beaver change the path of the river so that its path is still that way today?

2. The great cedar tree does not want animals and other trees to know about fire. Is this just selfish? Why is the great cedar tree concerned?

3. After Beaver gives fire to the other trees, these trees can now become "givers of fire." How? Compare this to the end of *Fire Race* by Jonathan London. How is it the same?
   Or—Draw the way that trees can become fire givers.

Selection: "How Possum Got His Skinny Tail"

1. How does Possum talk and act when he thinks of his tail? How do the other animals feel when he acts this way?
   Or—Draw a picture of Possum showing his tail. Draw the other animals who hear him.

2. What happens when Possum takes off the snakeskin with the potion and swings his tail in front of the council meeting? How does Possum feel? How do the other animals react?
   Or—Draw the council meeting with Possum showing his tail and the animals around him talking. Add word balloons showing possum's feelings and the animals' comments.

3. What two characteristics does Possum have as a result of what happened in the story?
   Or—Draw the two behaviors that Possum has to this day.

Selection: "Rabbit and the Willow"

1. Rabbit used to look much different than he does now. How does he look at the start of the story?

2. Rabbit goes to sleep in the snow, but he wakes up high in the branches of a willow tree. How does this happen?

3. Three things happen to Rabbit when he falls out of the tree, and he looks like that to this day. What are these three things? Write or draw your answer.

4. Think of the pussy willow tree in the spring. The story says the little puffs of gray fur come from what?

5. Talk to a student who read "Rabbit's Snow Dance" from *The Boy Who Lived with the Bears* by Joseph Bruchac. Tell each other your story about Rabbit, and identify the parts that are the same.

■ Rosen, Michael. *How Giraffe Got Such a Long Neck . . . and Why Rhino Is So Grumpy.*

1. The story says that long ago, Giraffe looked different than she does today. What did she look like?
   Or—Draw a picture of what Giraffe used to look like long ago.

2. When the land is hot and dry, Giraffe and Rhino meet and talk. They see one kind of food that they wish they could eat. What is it, and why can't they have it?
    Or—Draw a picture of what they want and why they can't have it.

3. Giraffe and Rhino go off to get some help. Whom do they ask?

4. Man tells Giraffe and Rhino he needs a day to prepare the magic herb. What is a magic herb? Ask for help if you need it with this question.

5. The next day Giraffe comes back to Man's hut. What happens to Rhino?

6. What does Giraffe do with the magic herb? What happens to Giraffe?
    Or—Draw a picture of what happens to Giraffe.

7. Why is Rhino grumpy to this very day?

■ Martin, Francesca. *The Honey Hunters: A Traditional African Tale.*
A honey guide is a real bird that finds honey and calls out to other animals and humans for help getting it out of the tree. It lives in Africa. You can learn more about the honey guide in the nonfiction book *If You Should Hear a Honey Guide* by April Pulley Sayre.

1. A boy hears the honey guide call. What does the boy do?

2. As the boy and the bird move through the bush, they meet other animals. What happens with these animals?
    Or—Draw a picture of the boy and the animals as they follow the honey guide.

3. When they find the honey, the boy gives out a piece of honeycomb to each pair of animals. What happens then?
    Or—Draw a pair of animals as they must share a piece of honeycomb.

4. The elephant tells the boy, "The damage is done." What does he mean by that?

5. This pourquoi tale says that, from now on, certain animals will behave in what way? Why?

■ Aardema, Verna. *How the Ostrich Got Its Long Neck.*

1. Long ago, the ostrich had a short neck. How did this make life hard for him?
    Or—Draw some of the problems the ostrich had because of his short neck.

2. Ostrich doesn't want to look at Crocodile's toothache. Why does she change her mind and try to help him?

3. If you were Ostrich with your head stuck inside Crocodile's mouth, what would you be thinking?
    Or—Draw a picture of what you would be thinking if you were Ostrich with your head stuck inside Crocodile's mouth. Draw a word balloon as part of your picture.

3. After Crocodile clamps down on Ostrich's head, Ostrich pulls to get free. How does he finally get free from crocodile?

4. To this day, ostriches have long necks. What is the other way ostriches were changed by the events in this story?

5. Compare this story to *How Giraffe Got Such a Long Neck* by Michael Rosen. How are the two stories the same? How are they different?

COOPERATIVE GROUPS: CLUSTERS OF STORIES FOR COMPARISON ACTIVITIES

Now that students have been through 1) whole-group read-alouds and modeling of compare-and-contrast activities and 2) independent reading in literature groups with a book at their reading level, they are ready for a new challenge and a different configuration. The main goal for this portion of the unit is for small, cooperative groups of students to read a cluster of stories (two to five titles) and then engage in the same compare-and-contrast activities that were modeled at the start of the unit. The difference is that students will now be conducting some fairly sophisticated Venn diagramming and charting on their own. In addition, the groups are different. In the independent reading groups, students were generally reading a book with other students at the same reading level. Now the group changes; students with diverse reading levels and book experiences are in a cooperative group. They have a cluster of different titles, and they take turns reading them or reading them to each other. Then they engage in discussion and fill out a graphic organizer (Venn diagram or chart) that shows the product of their thinking. They practice higher thinking skills more independently than in a whole-group, teacher-led class. Therefore, students take greater ownership for the thinking skills involved and demonstrate their ability to identify common and differing elements of a story. They also demonstrate their ability to work cooperatively, discussing and producing a visual representation of their thinking. Plan one or two weeks for this activity, about an hour per day.

The media specialist or teacher groups the books by a common topic or theme. The books should be arranged and prepackaged (in boxes or plastic tubs, or rubber-banded together) in their clusters according to theme or topic. A label should be taped to the front cover of each book. The label identifies the topic or theme for that cluster of books along with all the titles of the books in that cluster. Fig. 2.3 shows prepared labels that can be duplicated and affixed to the clusters of books. If the classroom does not have these titles, the teacher will need to produce labels reflecting the titles available for each cluster. In some cases, the story is found in a collection of several stories; a stick-on bookmark will save time locating the correct story.

Each cluster of books includes a blank chart or Venn diagram for the small group of students to record its ideas. The decision on whether to use a Venn or chart is primarily made by the teacher (notice that this information is also written on the labels) based on which would work better. However, if students have their own ideas, they should give them a try. Drawing pictures is also an option for students who are especially visually oriented, and the teacher should arrange special instructions for those students.

Provided at the end of this section are blank Venn diagrams and a chart to duplicate for cooperative student groups (figs. 2.4–2.6 and table 2.4). Also provided are samples of these graphic organizers that were filled out by third and fourth graders working in small cooperative groups (fig. 2.7).

(Text continues on page 32.)

THE SEASONS:

1. "The Long Winter," in *In a Circle Long Ago* by Nancy Van Laan
2. *Peboan and Seegwun* by Charles Larry
3. *When Bear Stole the Chinook* by Harriet Peck Taylor
4. "How Averiri Made the Night and the Seasons," in *Moon Was Tired of Walking on Air* by Natalia M. Belting
5. "Spring Defeats Winter," in *Keepers of the Earth* by Michael J. Caduto and Joseph Bruchac

USE A CHART TO SHOW YOUR COMPARISON.

FOOD:

1. *Why the Sky Is Far Away* by Mary-Joan Gerson
2. *How the Ox Star Fell from Heaven* by Lily Toy Hong
3. "Star Girl Brings Yucca from the Sky," in *When Jaguars Ate the Moon* by María C. Brusca and Tona Wilson

USE A 3-CIRCLE VENN DIAGRAM TO SHOW YOUR COMPARISON.

BIRDS:

1. *How the Guinea Fowl Got Her Spots* by Barbara Knutson
2. *Feathers Like a Rainbow* by Flora
3. *Pheasant and Kingfisher* by Catherine Berndt
4. *How the Birds Changed Their Feathers* by Joanna Troughton
5. "Cardinal and Bruh Deer," in *When Birds Could Talk and Bats Could Sing* by Virginia Hamilton

USE A CHART TO SHOW YOUR COMPARISON.

SUN:

1. "Greeting the Sun," in *Four Ancestors* by Joseph Bruchac
2. *The Day Sun Was Stolen* by Jamie Oliviero
3. "How Grandmother Spider Stole the Sun," in *Keepers of the Earth* by Michael J. Caduto and Joseph Bruchac

USE A 3-CIRCLE VENN DIAGRAM TO SHOW YOUR COMPARISON.

THUNDER AND LIGHTNING:

1. *The Story of Lightning and Thunder* by Ashley Bryan
2. *How Thunder and Lightning Came to Be* by Beatrice Orcutt Harrell
3. *Stolen Thunder* by Shirley Climo

USE A CHART TO SHOW YOUR COMPARISON.

FLOOD:

1. *The Tree That Rains* by Emery Bernhard
2. "Coyote Creates a New World," in *Coyote Goes Walking* by Tom Pohrt
3. *Llama and the Great Flood* by Ellen Alexander

USE A 3-CIRCLE VENN DIAGRAM TO SHOW YOUR COMPARISON.

STARS:

1. *The Star Maiden* by Barbara Juster Esbensen
2. *How the Stars Fell into the Sky* by Jerrie Oughton
3. *The Story of the Milky Way* by Joseph Bruchac
4. *Coyote Places the Stars* by Harriet Peck Taylor
5. *Her Seven Brothers* by Paul Goble

USE A CHART TO SHOW YOUR COMPARISON.

SUN AND MOON:

1. "The Traveling Sky Baskets," in *Moon Was Tired of Walking on Air* by Natalia M. Belting
2. "Why the Sun Has a Headdress and Moon Has None," in *Moon Was Tired of Walking on Air* by Natalia M. Belting
3. "Why the Sun and the Moon Live in the Sky," in *How Many Spots Does a Leopard Have?* by Julius Lester

USE A CHART TO SHOW YOUR COMPARISON.

Fig. 2.3. Labels.

ILLNESS AND HEALING: 1. *Ladder to the Sky* by Barbara Juster Esbensen 2. *The Rabbit's Escape* by Suzanne Crowder Han USE A 2-CIRCLE VENN DIAGRAM TO SHOW YOUR COMPARISON.	**MUSIC:** 1. *How Music Came to the World* by Hal Ober 2. *The Eagle's Song* by Kristina Rodanas 3. *Musicians of the Sun* by Gerald McDermott USE A 2-CIRCLE VENN DIAGRAM TO SHOW YOUR COMPARISON.
POSSUM'S TAIL: 1. "Why Possum's Tail Is Bare," in *How Rabbit Tricked Otter* by Gayle Ross 2. "How Possum Lost His Tail," in *How Chipmunk Got Tiny Feet* by Gerald Hausman USE A 2-CIRCLE VENN DIAGRAM TO SHOW YOUR COMPARISON.	**SEA CREATURES:** 1. *The Rainbow Bridge* by Audrey Wood 2. *How the Sea Began* by George Crespo USE A CHART TO SHOW YOUR COMPARISON.
BUFFALOES: 1. *Animal Lore and Legend: Buffalo* by Tiffany Midge 2. *The Return of the Buffaloes* by Paul Goble USE A CHART TO SHOW YOUR COMPARISON.	**OWLS:** 1. *Animal Lore & Legend: Owl* by Vee Browne 2. "Owl Feathers," in *The Acorn Tree* by Anne Rockwell USE A 2-CIRCLE VENN DIAGRAM TO SHOW YOUR COMPARISON.
HUMAN BEINGS: 1. *People of Corn* by Mary-Joan Gerson 2. *The Origin of Life on Earth* by David A. Anderson 3. *Lord of the Animals* by Fiona French USE A 3-CIRCLE VENN DIAGRAM TO SHOW YOUR COMPARISON.	**TURTLE'S BACK:** 1. *How Turtle's Back Was Cracked* by Gayle Ross 2. "Tortoise and Crane," in *Crow and Fox* by Jan Thornhill 3. "How Turtle Flew South for the Winter," in *Native American Stories* by Joseph Bruchac USE A 3-CIRCLE VENN DIAGRAM TO SHOW YOUR COMPARISON.
MORNING STAR: 1. *How Night Came from the Sea* by Mary-Joan Gerson 2. *The Orphan Boy* by Tololwa M. Mollel 3. "Lighting the Way," in *Tales Alive!* by Susan Milord USE A CHART TO SHOW YOUR COMPARISON.	**WEAVING:** 1. *The Magic Weaver of Rugs* by Jerrie Oughton 2. *The Magic of Spider Woman* by Lois Duncan USE A 2-CIRCLE VENN DIAGRAM TO SHOW YOUR COMPARISON.

MOUNTAINS AND ISLANDS:

1. *The Golden Flower* by Nina Jaffe
2. *How the Sea Began* by George Crespo
3. *Māui Goes Fishing* by Julie Stewart Williams
4. "Loo-Wit, the Fire-Keeper" by Michael J. Caduto and Joseph Bruchac
5. *The Sleeping Lady* by Ann Dixon

USE A CHART TO SHOW YOUR COMPARISON.

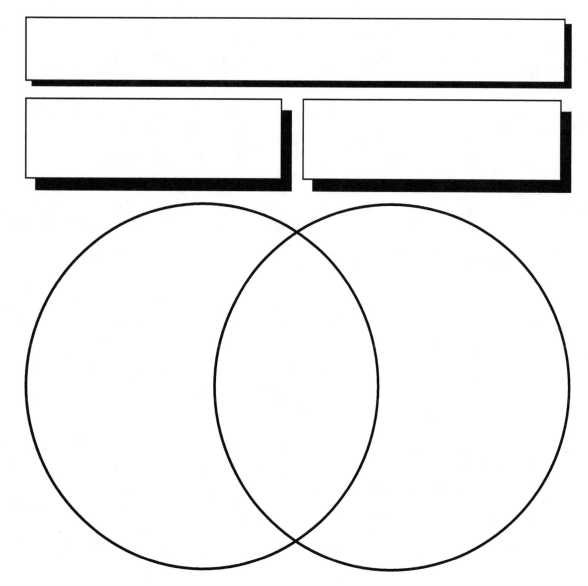

Fig. 2.4.

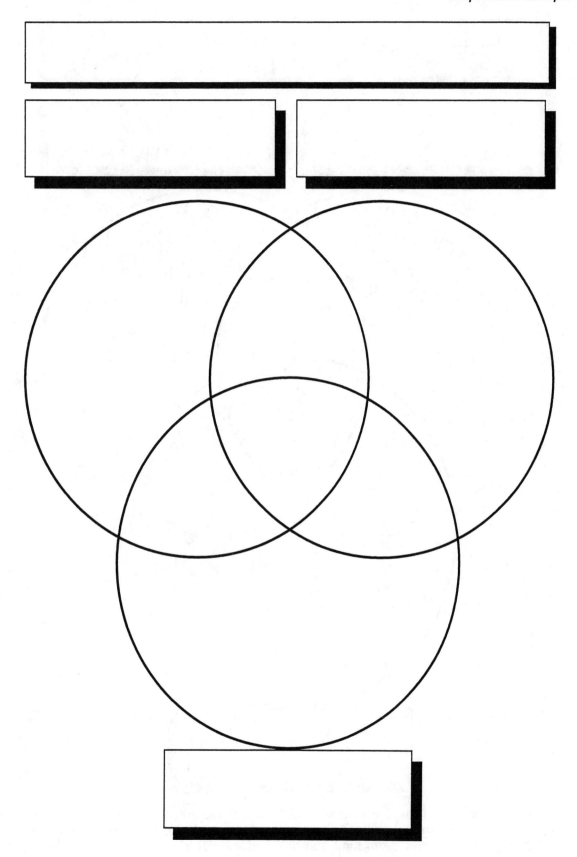

Fig. 2.5.
From *Folktale Themes and Activities for Children.* © 1998 Anne Marie Kraus. Libraries Unlimited. (800) 237-6124.

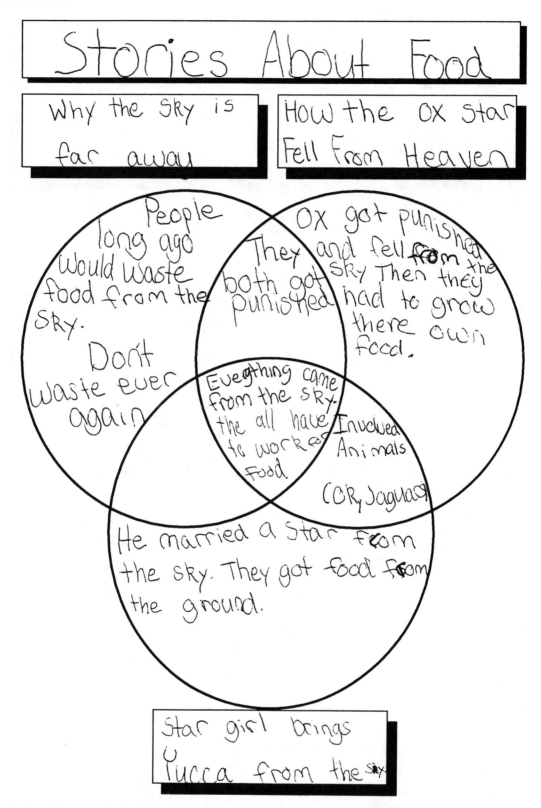

Stories About Food

Why the sky is far away

How the Ox Star Fell From Heaven

People long ago would waste food from the sky. Don't waste ever again

They both got punished

Ox got punished and fell from the sky Then they had to grow there own food.

Eveything came from the sky. the all have to work for Food

Inucued Animals (O Ry Jaguace)

He married a star from the sky. They got food from the ground.

Star girl brings Yucca from the sky

Fig. 2.6. Students working independently in small cooperative groups produced these diagrams demonstrating their skills in comparing and contrasting tales with similar themes. These third and fourth graders compared tales about food, the sun, and stars on their own after having this skill modeled by the teacher in a whole-class setting.

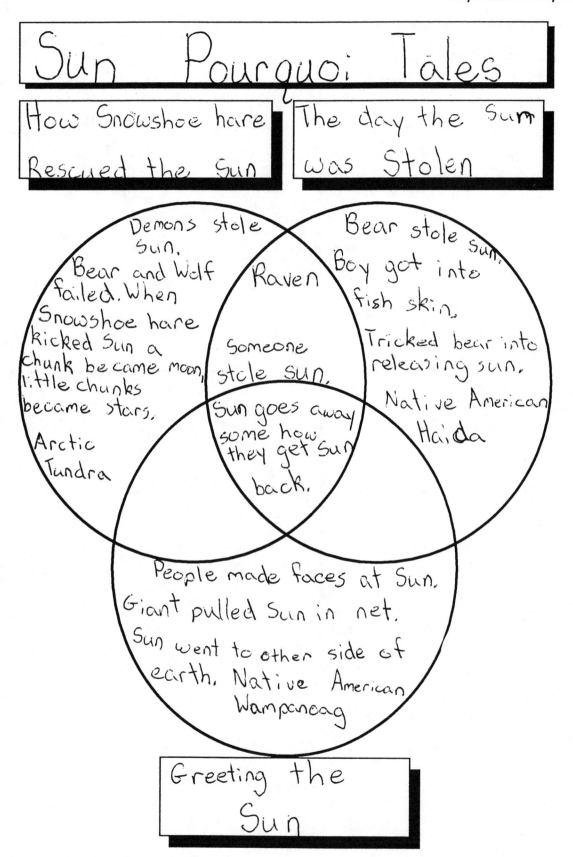

Sun Pourquoi Tales

How Snowshoe hare Rescued the Sun

The day the Sun was Stolen

Demons stole Sun. Bear and Wolf failed. When Snowshoe hare kicked Sun a chunk became moon, little chunks became stars.

Arctic Tundra

Raven

Someone stole sun.

Sun goes away some how they get Sun back.

Bear stole sun. Boy got into fish skin. Tricked bear into releasing sun.

Native American Haida

People made faces at Sun. Giant pulled Sun in net. Sun went to other side of earth. Native American Wampanoag

Greeting the Sun

Fig. 2.6. Continued.

From *Folktale Themes and Activities for Children.* © 1998 Anne Marie Kraus. Libraries Unlimited. (800) 237-6124.

Table 2.4. Pourquoi Tales Comparison Chart

Theme or Topic: _____

Title	Culture	Pourquoi Explanation: How or Why Things Came to Be

Theme or Topic: Stars

Title	Culture	Pourquoi Explanation: How or Why Things Came to Be
The Milky Way	Cherokee	How the stars got into the Milkyway. Big dog cornmeal
How the Stars fell into the Sky	Navajo	How coyote threw stars into the sky. Why we have confusion.
Her Seven Brothers	Cheyenne	The seven brothers and the girl become the big dipper.
Star Maiden	Ojibway	How water lillies came to be. Stars become water lillies.
Coyote places the Stars	Wasco Indian lengend	Why coyote howls at the moon. Why we see shapes in the sky

Fig. 2.7.

From *Folktale Themes and Activities for Children.* © 1998 Anne Marie Kraus. Libraries Unlimited. (800) 237-6124.

CREATIVE EXTENSIONS: WRITING, MULTIMEDIA PROJECTS, SHADOW PUPPETS, STORYTELLING

Creative Writing

Students are eager to come up with their own ideas for pourquoi tales. Classroom anthologies of student-written pourquoi tales are very successful and make a meaningful culminating project and keepsake for each student. Some classes engage in their writing projects while simultaneously producing a picture in art class that can be photocopied and integrated into their anthology. These original stories can also lead to multimedia presentations, shadow puppet theater, or storytelling.

A few suggestions and some brainstorming should get the students launched. Ask them to think about any aspect of life that arouses their curiosity and imagine what might happen if that thing were different. Was it different in the past? To further prime the pump of ideas, students may be given options such as the following:

- Animals
  Color (Why the _____ is _____ .)
  Behavior (Why the hyena laughs.)
  Characteristic (Why the snake has fangs.)

- Plants
  Benefit (Why the oak tree gives shade.)
  Characteristic (Why the cactus has prickers.)
  Interdependence (Why the hummingbird sips nectar from the flowers.)

- Landmarks and earth formations
  Rivers, lakes (Why the _____ River comes through our town.)
  Mountains, hills, valleys (How the valley was scooped out.)
  Deserts (Why the desert is so hot.)

- Modern-day objects
  Classroom objects (How the desk, chair, computer, or pencil came to be.)
  Structures (Why we have bridges, towers, tunnels.)
  Roads (How the route of Highway _____ was changed forever.)

- Modern-day activities
  Games (Why we play basketball.)
  Music (How the first song was sung.)
  Parties (How the party came to be.)

- Everyday life
  Common behavior (Why people sit in chairs.)
  Goal behavior (How I got to be brave.)
  Observing life (Why people drive around in cars so much.)

- Total fantasy; the world as we might wish it to be

  School (Why everyone knows how to spell everything.)

  Home (How brothers and sisters learned to get along.)

  Community (Why we don't need money anymore.)

A crucial element in writing a pourquoi tale is *cause-and-effect*. Have a discussion with students about this so that they realize its importance to the success of the story. Ask them to think about the pourquoi folktales they have read together. Why do bats hide in caves? Why do the animals and people have fire to cook their food? Why do we have equal amounts of daylight and night? The answer to each question can become a story.

Once students have an idea for a story—for example, why roosters crow—they must think backwards. That is, students are starting with the end of the story (the way things are now), then going back in time to the way things used to be, and then filling in the middle. This middle section is the main part of the story. To help students get organized and to get the main events mapped, use the story-organizer sheet provided (see fig. 2.8). After working out their ideas in rough-draft form on the organizer sheet, students can proceed to write the story in final form in chronological order.

Another component to the writing of an original tale is creating a title. Encourage descriptive titles that hint at the events of the story. The most common would be "How the _____" or "Why the _____ has a _____." Other titles work also, and creativity is the key. *Fire Race*, for example, hints at the theme of fire and a key activity in the plot. Brainstorm ideas such as "The Fang Game" or "The Rock Contest."

Students may also be helped by a discussion of familiar phrases used in the telling of these tales. Go back over tales they are familiar with. Come up with a short list of phrases ("Once upon a time" is an example everyone will know, but go beyond this). Here are some ideas for starting a story:

- "Long ago, in the time when the animals and the people could talk the same language. . . ."

- "Long ago, when the world was new. . . ."

- "Time was, the _____ didn't used to be _____." (For example, "The possum had a full, bushy tail, not the skinny tail he has now.")

- "It used to be that the _____ was _____."

- "Long ago, the _____ wasn't _____ the way it is now."

and for ending a story.

- "And that is why, to this very day. . . ."

- "If you look, you will see that the _____ still _____ today."

Story Organizer

My story idea - The way things are now:
The way things used to be:
How it happened, the story of how it changed. (Note: draw a story web if you like.)

Fig. 2.8. Original Pourquoi Tale Writing: Story Organizer.

Multimedia Projects

Schools are trying to find meaningful ways to integrate technology into the curriculum. It may seem a stretch at first to use computers with a study of traditional folktales, but multimedia computer programs can be effective for publishing and presenting student projects. Students can use programs that incorporate drawing, sound, and slide show capabilities to produce writing or storytelling projects. One such program is The New Kid Pix. Students may elect to produce their own original pourquoi tales or retell traditional tales, in multimedia format.

The nuts-and-bolts teaching and learning of a particular multimedia application is not covered in this guide. Access to computers and any one of many multimedia programs varies widely, and the technology changes quickly. Collaboration between the school's media specialist and the teacher is key to success in this endeavor. The media specialist knows the software, the hardware, the students, and the literature. The media specialist can provide instruction and help to individual students as they plan and produce their pourquoi tales.

Students must first have their stories planned and written in some form. They could create an original pourquoi tale or retell a traditional one. The basic idea and a story narration should be established.

The first task in a multimedia project is to make a storyboard. The storyboard, planned on paper first, shows the sequence of graphics and text of the slide show. The student must show each graphic (a small sketch) along with the text or recorded speech that will accompany each picture. The number of slides must be determined. The length and detail of a story affects the number of slides. The model storyboard shown in fig. 2.9 suggests six slides for a beginning student and could be modified as needed.

There are two ways to handle the text of the story line: Either write out the entire story, typing part of the text on each slide, or simply read it aloud and record parts of the story on the slides. The latter option is much more manageable and makes more use of the multimedia aspects of the technology. Furthermore, the general guidelines for multimedia production state that the written text should be brief. Clearly recording the student's voice through the computer's microphone is much more effective for presenting a story in this format and has the added benefit of requiring the student to focus on read-aloud skills.

The general suggested storyboard sequence is as follows:

Slide 1. Title, author

Slide 2. Story introduction—"Long ago, the _____ used to be _____ . . ."

Slide 3. Plot—How it came to be

Slide 4. Plot—How it came to be, continued

Slide 5. Conclusion, ending—"That is why, to this very day, . . ."

Slide 6. Credits, copyright date, place

After students complete their plan on the storyboard, they need to draw the illustrations for each slide, record their voices telling the portion of the story for each slide, bring the pictures into the slide show portion of the program, and run the show!

(Text continues on page 39.)

Slide Show Storyboard

Picture: ## Text:

Slide #1: Title Screen

_____

(Title)

_____

_____

_____

_____

(Author)

_____

_____

_____

Slide #2: Story Introduction

_____

_____

_____

_____

_____

_____

_____

_____

_____

_____

Fig. 2.9.

From _Folktale Themes and Activities for Children._ © 1998 Anne Marie Kraus. Libraries Unlimited. (800) 237-6124.

Slide Show Storyboard

Picture: Text:

Slide #3: Plot—How it came to be

Fig. 2.9. Continued.

From *Folktale Themes and Activities for Children.* © 1998 Anne Marie Kraus. Libraries Unlimited. (800) 237-6124.

Slide #4: Plot—How it came to be, continued

Slide Show Storyboard

Picture: Text:

Slide #5: Ending

Slide #6: Credits

ⓒ **Date, School**

City, State

Fig. 2.9. Continued.

Shadow Puppet Theater

Shadow puppet theater is a low-cost, easy-to-produce art form particularly adaptable for pourquoi tales. Students who might not otherwise be comfortable in a performance situation can experience confident storytelling or dramatic action by working with simple silhouette puppets. Following are directions for constructing simple puppets and a shadow puppet stage. In addition, books are suggested for stories that are easily adaptable for shadow puppet plays. Finally, this book provides silhouette figures based on those in Paul Goble's book *Her Seven Brothers*, which students may use to reenact the story as a shadow puppet play.

Directions and suggestions given here are for very simple, accessible, entry-level shadow puppet theater experiences, which are very successful with children. For more complex and elaborate shadow puppet production, consult books such as:

Lynch-Watson, Janet. *The Shadow Puppet Book.* New York: Sterling, 1980.

Sierra, Judy. *Fantastic Theater: Puppets and Plays for Young Performers and Young Audiences.* New York: H. W. Wilson, 1991.

Wisniewski, David, and Donna Wisniewski. *Worlds of Shadow: Teaching with Shadow Puppetry.* Englewood, CO: Teacher Ideas Press, 1997. Includes techniques that work for different age levels.

A Simple Shadow Screen Stage

Construct a simple stage using a large corrugated cardboard box. The library may have a computer or TV box. Using a razor knife, cut the box in half vertically; you can get two stages out of one box. Then cut a rectangular hole (for the screen "stage") in the large side. The size will depend on the box, but the hole can range from approximately 16 to 24 inches wide by 16 to 20 inches tall. Leave a margin on all sides and a 3 to 6 inch border along the bottom edge. Set the stage on a table, placed in a way that allows three to five children to stand behind it to move the puppets. If the stage is unstable, place some heavy books inside to anchor the bottom flap. The two sides can remain at right angles to the front or they can be angled outward to provide more room for puppeteers in the back. If the top flaps fall inward, tape them at the corners. The exterior of the stage (the part facing the audience) may be painted with a flat black paint or any other color depending on time and supplies.

The hole then must be covered with a screen material. Large white paper (the kind that comes on a roll) works fine. More permanent shadow screens may be constructed with fabric stretched over a wooden frame, but white paper produces the desired effect quickly and inexpensively. Use masking tape to fasten the paper over the hole from the inside, making sure to stretch it as flat and taut as possible.

If desired, a scene can be drawn or painted on the paper screen before taping the paper in place on the box. This "scenery" is usually specific to one particular play and may be changed if a different play is performed on the same stage.

A Source of Light

The light source can be a simple lamp (minus the lampshade) with a bulb of 75–100 watts. If the lamp is placed behind the puppeteers, the audience may see dim shadows from the arms and rods backstage, but this is not an extremely distracting feature. A light placed at the top or bottom of the screen, closer to the screen than the puppeteers, gives the best effect. Try to angle the light up or down toward the screen. A light with a clamp and gooseneck offers more opportunities for experimentation with placement, and is inexpensive. But if time and resources are short, a secondhand living room lamp placed on a table behind the stage, close to the screen, does the job adequately. When putting on the play, darken the room so that the backlighting of the stage is more effective.

Create the Puppets

Silhouette puppets are the easiest to make. Children can draw their characters on construction paper and cut them out. Slightly heavier paper or cardstock may be used. Black is effective; colored construction paper may show a hint of color but still conveys the silhouette look. Obtain color effects with more elaborate puppets by cutting out parts of the puppet and putting in colored tissue paper or colored plastic material.

In general, keep puppets simple and one-piece, but an occasional moving part is effective. Give the puppets moving parts by using brass fasteners. For example, a crocodile's mouth can have a brass-fastener hinge on its upper jaw. Children get creative with this quickly. Keep in mind that every moving part will need its own stick.

Each puppet needs a stick, or rod, to hold onto from the rear. Thin doweling cut to 8 to 10 inch lengths works well. Bamboo skewers, found where Asian foods are sold, are less expensive and the right length, but children should be careful with the points. The rod can be fastened to the puppet a number of ways. The easiest method is to attach the rod with a hinge made of masking tape. Using a one inch piece of masking tape, press one end around the rod and press the other end onto the paper puppet. Allow the puppet to flap and wiggle just a little. This hinged method allows the operator to gently press the puppet to the paper screen from a variety of angles.

Pick a Story and Adapt It

The story or play can be as elaborate as time and creativity allow, but a simple first effort is often best. Take an already published tale and analyze it for characters, movement, and plot. A simple story can be read aloud by one or more readers while the puppeteers (two to five children) move their puppets accordingly. In this effective approach, the puppeteers display their recall of the story while the readers exercise their read-aloud skills. Some longer stories can be adapted to shorten the narrative and keep the action going. Text may also be rewritten as a play with dialog in addition to narration.

Some adaptable stories are listed on the following page along with characters and suggestions.

■ Caduto, Michael J., and Joseph Bruchac. "How Turtle Flew South for the Winter," in *Keepers of the Earth*.

    Children make puppets for
        2 birds
        1 stick
        turtle
    With adult help, make turtle's shell with cut-out shell design using a razor-knife. Use text as is from the book.

■ Aardema, Verna. *How the Ostrich Got Its Long Neck*.

    Children make puppets for
        Short-necked ostrich
        Long-necked ostrich; brass fastener joint at neck for bending and standing up
        Crocodile; brass fastener joint in jaw to open and close the mouth
        Kudu
        Baboon with her baby on her back

        Fish eagle
        Tall tree (or draw tree on the screen at the side)
    Use text as is from the book.

■ Temple, Frances. *Tiger Soup*.

    Children make puppets for
        Tiger
        Anansi the Spider
        Pot of soup
        Group of monkeys
        Tree (or draw tree on the screen at the side)
    Use text as is from the book.

■ Reneaux, J. J. *Why Alligator Hates Dog*.

    Children make puppets for
        Alligator with hinged jaw
        Dog
        Rabbit
        Porch (or draw porch on the screen at the side)
    Use text as is from the book.

Ready-to-Use Shadow Puppet Silhouette Figures

    Produce a shadow play of *Her Seven Brothers* by Paul Goble, using the silhouette drawings provided (see fig. 2.10). Because the plot is somewhat longer and more detailed than the stories listed previously, this tale is a good one for older children or adults to perform. Tell the story or use the book to read it. To retell the story as a play, it may be helpful to condense some of the narrative and maximize the dialog. For the conclusion of the story, when the brothers and the girl climb into the sky to become the Big Dipper, cut a piece of poster board large enough to fill the screen width, for the sky. Then draw the star pattern of the Big Dipper and cut out the stars with a razor knife (adults do this task). In addition to the seven stars, cut a small eighth star for the little brother, as shown in the book. Hold the Big Dipper design against the screen for a dramatic ending.

(Text continues on page 49.)

Fig. 2.10. Shadow puppet figures for *Her Seven Brothers* by Paul Goble. Figures may be enlarged to fit proportionally with the shadow screen. Silhouette figures drawn by Andrea McGann Keech. Based on the drawings of Paul Goble from *Her Seven Brothers*. Copyright © 1988 Paul Goble. Used by permission of Simon & Schuster Books for Young Readers, an imprint of Simon & Schuster Children's Publishing Division.

Fig. 2.10. Continued.

Fig. 2.10. Continued.

Fig. 2.10. Continued.

From *Folktale Themes and Activities for Children.* © Anne Marie 1998 Kraus. Libraries Unlimited. (800) 237-6124.

Fig. 2.10. Continued.

From *Folktale Themes and Activities for Children.* © 1998 Anne Marie Kraus. Libraries Unlimited. (800) 237-6124.

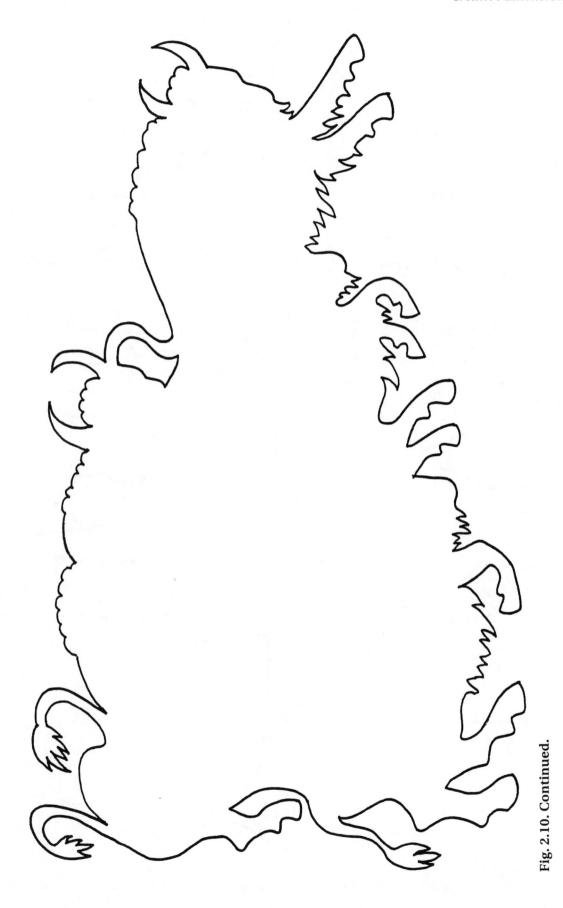

Fig. 2.10. Continued.

Fig. 2.10. Continued.

From *Folktale Themes and Activities for Children.* © 1998 Anne Marie Kraus. Libraries Unlimited. (800) 237-6124.

Storytelling

Because pourquoi tales come from the oral tradition, it is worthwhile trying to incorporate some storytelling into the children's experience. The storytelling idea described here is an easy way to involve an entire class in telling a story and incorporates the concept of the pourquoi elements very well.

This method of group storytelling is used by Jo Anne Ollerenshaw Lewis, storyteller and science educator. She gathers the class around her and tells the story "How Grandmother Spider Stole the Sun" (story available in *Keepers of the Earth* by Caduto and Bruchac). She tells it once and then asks the children to tell it again as a group with their own individual ideas. She has a short planning session with the group, in which every child offers a contribution of a "pourquoi" element. The child must name the animal and the consequence (for example, Dog and how it has black paws). Then she tells the story again, calling on each child to say his or her part during the story.

In this story, the world is new and there is no light. The animals meet and decide to find something they have heard of, called the sun, which is on the other side of the earth. One by one, the animals try to bring back Sun. Each time, the animal fails and gets a reminder of the effort in the form of a permanent marking. This is where the children contribute to the story. For example, a child might say, "Raccoon tried to bring back Sun on his head, but it slipped down and burned his eyes. Ever since that time, Raccoon has had two black burn marks around his eyes." Another child might say, "Deer tried to bring back Sun, but it burned her nose. Ever since that time, Deer has had a black nose." Children readily take part in telling the story, and they experience the folk process by changing the story a little with their creativity.

This group storytelling technique would work well with other stories that contain multiple pourquoi explanations. One such story is "Leelee Goro," from *Misoso* by Verna Aardema. In this story, the animals take turns trying to fight Leelee Goro in order to obtain fire. Each time, Leelee Goro tosses the animal high into the sky, and when the animal falls back to earth, it gets a mark that lasts to this day. Children could contribute new animals with new "pourquoi" consequences. Another tale for employing this technique is *How the Loon Lost Her Voice* by Anne Cameron. The animals take turns trying to get under, through, or around the great wall of ice. Each animal in turn receives a mark or behavior that continues to this day.

Other ideas and advice for storytelling can be found in *Tell Me a Tale: A Book About Storytelling* by Joseph Bruchac. His how-to strategies include techniques of listening, observing, remembering, and sharing. In addition, he provides some short stories for telling and activities.

SOCIAL STUDIES TIE-IN: REGIONS OF THE UNITED STATES

Pourquoi tales can contribute to student understandings as they study the regions of the United States. To expand their gathering of facts about a state or region, students can use pourquoi tales to get a "feel" for the place in terms of both culture and nature—animals, habitats, geology. Most regional tales are Native American; a few additional tales from other traditions are also included. Sometimes, identifying the regional aspect of a tale can be problematic because Native American tribes migrated through the centuries and, more notably, were relocated by the U.S. government. For example, in the 1830s, the Cherokee were forced to walk from their home in the Great Smoky Mountains to Oklahoma on the 1,200-mile Trail of Tears. Teachers and students should keep in mind that some tales would have been relocated along with their tellers.

Following the list of pourquoi tales representing regions, there is a selective list of nonfiction books on some Native American cultures; these help tie the tales to the people and region. There are several nonfiction series on Native American groups; the listed books are recommended because they show not only the early traditions of these peoples but also Native Americans in everyday contemporary life. Many students are surprised to learn that Native Americans are modern people, too, trying to balance old traditions with modern life.

Pourquoi Tales by Region: A Selective List

Note: Refer to the Annotated Bibliography for complete information on the books.

Several Regions Collected in One Book

Bruchac, Joseph. *Between Earth & Sky: Legends of Native American Sacred Places*. A stunning collection of short, reverent tales about well-known geographical formations, including Niagara Falls, El Capitan (rock formation in Arizona), Great Smoky Mountains, the Painted Desert, the Rocky Mountains, Mesa Verde, the Grand Canyon.

———. *Four Ancestors: Stories, Songs, and Poems from Native North America*. A collection of thirty-one songs and poems grouped into four sections: Fire, Earth, Water, and Air. Background notes help identify regions and cultures.

Van Laan, Nancy. *In a Circle Long Ago: A Treasury of Native Lore from North America*. A collection of 25 stories and poems organized into seven regions of North America. The book includes a simple map to identify the regions. Some specific sites are identified in these tales, including the Grande Ronde River in Idaho in "How Beaver Stole Fire."

Northeast

Bruchac, Joseph. *The Boy Who Lived with the Bears and Other Iroquois Stories*. A collection of six stories featuring animals, woodland habitats, and weather of the Iroquois people of New York state.

Gates, Frieda. *Owl Eyes*. This Kanienkehaka (Mohawk) story traces the origin of the owl's features. This story features animals and habitats of Upper New York State.

Norman, Howard. *How Glooskap Outwits the Ice Giants and Other Tales of the Maritime Indians*. A collection of stories from the coastal areas of Maine and northward. Glooskap, a giant hero-creator, walks and works among the animals, in the woodlands and along the ocean shore.

Taylor, C. J. "The Birth of Niagara Falls," in *How We Saw the World*. An Algonquin story of five sisters who come to play and dive on the rocks near the sea.

———. "Creation," in *Bones in the Basket*. This Mohawk tale traces the origin of the earth and its plant life.

Southeast

Bruchac, Joseph. *The Great Ball Game: A Muskogee Story.* The Muskogee, also known as Creek Indians, are from the area now known as Georgia. Birds, a bat, and a tradition of settling disputes by means of a ball game are featured in this entertaining tale.

Haley, Gail E. *Two Bad Boys: A Very Old Cherokee Tale.* The animals and woodlands of North Carolina are featured in this "very old" tale.

Harrell, Beatrice Orcutt. *How Thunder and Lightning Came to Be: A Choctaw Legend.* Told by Native Americans from Mississippi, this tale is full of humor.

Reneaux, J. J. *Why Alligator Hates Dog: A Cajun Folktale.* A Cajun story set in the bayou country. Cajun pronunciations of four words enhance the flavor of this telling.

Ross, Gayle. *How Turtle's Back Was Cracked, How Rabbit Tricked Otter,* and *The Story of the Milky Way* (told with Joseph Bruchac). All three books contain Cherokee tales told by an experienced Cherokee storyteller. It is notable that many of these stories are humorous; even though the Cherokee people suffered so miserably at the hands of the government, they continued the storytelling traditions of good-natured humor.

Middle West

Esbensen, Barbara Juster. *The Star Maiden: An Ojibway Tale.* The origin of water lilies in the northern lake country of Minnesota, Michigan, and Wisconsin.

Goble, Paul. *Crow Chief: A Plains Indian Story.* A Dakota tale set in the Great Plains. The story focuses on the buffalo hunt.

———. *The Gift of the Sacred Dog.* Also focusing on the buffalo hunt, this tale of the Great Plains recounts how the Great Spirit makes a gift of the first horses to the people.

———. *Remaking the Earth: A Creation Story from the Great Plains of North America.* A myth that recounts the origins of many earth phenomena, including the buffalo and the Thunderbirds (from which thunder come).

———. *The Return of the Buffaloes: A Plains Indian Story About Famine and Renewal of the Earth.* The origins of the wind found in Wind Cave in the Black Hills of South Dakota are recounted in this Lakota tale. Again, the buffalo figure prominently.

Greene, Jacqueline Dembar. *Manabozho's Gifts: Three Chippewa Tales.* Three tales about Manabozho, hero of tales of the Chippewa (Ojibwa) people of Minnesota, Wisconsin, and Michigan. The second tale describes Manabozho's arduous vision quest for food for his people. He is rewarded with the discovery of wild rice harvesting, still an important activity in the northern lake country.

Larry, Charles. *Peboan and Seegwun.* The two characters named in the title are the originators of winter and spring. The author's notes not only give the source of the story but also fill in valuable information about the Anishinabe people of Michigan, Wisconsin, and Minnesota, called Ojibwa by others.

Taylor, C. J. "The Snake That Guards the River," in *The Monster from the Swamp: Native Legends of Monsters, Demons and Other Creatures*. A man is transformed into a water snake after eating some giant eggs. He finds his home in the Mississippi River. This tale explains why the Cheyenne people make an offering to the snakeman before crossing the Mississippi River.

Van Laan, Nancy. *Shingebiss: An Ojibwe Legend*. A story of the merganser duck who survives the brutal winter of the northern Great Lakes region by diving for fish under the ice.

Wood, Douglas. *The Windigo's Return: A North Woods Story*. The origins of mosquitoes among the Ojibwa (Anishinabe) people of the north woods are recounted in this intriguing, slightly scary story.

Southwest

Anderson, Peter. *A Grand Canyon Journey: Tracing Time in Stone*. A nonfiction walking tour of the Grand Canyon, including two creation myths about how the Canyon came to be.

Duncan, Lois. *The Magic of Spider Woman*. A Navajo tale that teaches about Navajo weaving and also the cultural importance of walking the Middle Way, not giving into excesses.

Jackson, Ellen. *The Precious Gift: A Navajo Creation Myth*. An origin tale of how the people came to this world. One striking theme is the preciousness of water in this arid land.

McDermott, Gerald. *Coyote: A Trickster Tale from the American Southwest*. Trickster Coyote finds himself tricked by the birds in this tale set in the dry, mesa landscape of the Southwest.

Oughton, Jerrie. *The Magic Weaver of Rugs: A Tale of the Navajo*. A story of how Spider Woman taught weaving to the people. It is set in the rocky mesa landscape of the Southwest.

Taylor, Harriet Peck. *Coyote and the Laughing Butterflies*. A tale of the Tewa people, a part of the Pueblo culture of the Southwest. Coyote is tricked in this tale set in the mesa country.

Rocky Mountains

Caduto, Michael J., and Joseph Bruchac. "How Coyote Was the Moon," in *Keepers of the Earth*. The Kalispel people of Idaho tell this story of Coyote, who became the moon but couldn't keep his mouth shut.

Goble, Paul. *Her Seven Brothers*. This tale describes the origin of the stars that form the Big Dipper. Coming from the Cheyenne people of Colorado, it features the art of quill decoration of deerskin clothing.

Rodanas, Kristina. *Dance of the Sacred Circle: A Native American Tale*. This legend tells how the first horses came to the Native Americans of the plains. It comes from the Blackfoot people of Montana and other high plains environs.

Van Laan, Nancy. "How Beaver Stole Fire," in *In a Circle Long Ago: A Treasury of Native Lore from North America*. This selection, from a collection of 25 tales, explains the reason for the winding route taken by the Grande Ronde River in Idaho.

Pacific Coast

Caduto, Michael J., and Joseph Bruchac. "How Thunder and Earthquake Made Ocean," in *Keepers of the Earth*. The Yurok people of California tell this story, which contains many unique phenomena of the region: earthquakes, ocean, salmon, and shells.

———. "Loo-Wit, the Fire-Keeper," in *Keepers of the Earth*. Told by the Nisqually people of the Pacific Northwest, this dramatic tale explains the origins of Mt. St. Helens with a sobering warning that came true when it erupted. Other sites in the story include Mt. Adams, Mt. Hood, the Willamette River, and the Dalles.

Dixon, Ann. *The Sleeping Lady*. Set near Cook Inlet, Alaska, this sad tale explains the origin of the mountain still known as the Sleeping Lady, Mt. Susitna.

Dwyer, Mindy. *Coyote in Love*. A Coquelle Native American story of how Coyote's tears, and his fall from the sky, create Crater Lake in Oregon.

London, Jonathan. *Fire Race: A Karuk Coyote Tale About How Fire Came to the People*. The Karuk people of Northern California tell this tale of cooperation in the wooded mountain country.

Luenn, Nancy. *The Miser on the Mountain: A Nisqually Legend of Mount Rainier*. A greedy man is obsessed with material wealth until he grapples with the powerful forces of nature atop Mount Rainier.

Oliviero, Jamie. *The Day Sun Was Stolen*. This Haida legend features animals of the Northwest coast. The illustrations, by a native artist, give an authentic feel for Haida art style.

Robbins, Ruth. *How the First Rainbow Was Made: An American Indian Tale*. The winter rains on Mt. Shasta are so strong that the people cannot get food. They ask Coyote to help them approach Old-Man-Above for help.

Rodanas, Kristina. *The Eagle's Song: A Tale from the Pacific Northwest*. This tale explains the origin of social celebrations, music, and sharing among the people. The cultural value of social gatherings is an important aspect of the tribes of the Northwest.

San Souci, Robert D. *Two Bear Cubs: A Miwok Legend from California's Yosemite Valley*. The wildlife and landscape of Yosemite are brought to life in this story of the harrowing adventure of two grizzly bear cubs and a rock that becomes the famous El Capitan.

Shetterly, Susan Hand. *Raven's Light: A Myth from the People of the Northwest Coast*. Using the sources of the Tlingit, Kwakiutl, Haida, and Tsimshian peoples of the Pacific Northwest, this tale features Raven as creator of the world and bringer of its animals and plants.

Simms, Laura. *Moon and Otter and Frog.* The Modoc people of Northern California and Southern Oregon tell this tale. It features water animals of this region, especially the otter.

Smith, Don Lelooska. *Echoes of the Elders: The Stories and Paintings of Chief Lelooska.* Five stories featuring the animals and environs of the Pacific Northwest, accompanied by the art of the Kwakiutl people.

Varez, Dietrich. *Pele: The Fire Goddess.* The adventures of Pele, keeper of the fires of the volcanoes of Hawaii.

Williams, Julie Stewart. *Māui Goes Fishing.* The story of trickster Māui, who fishes the islands of Hawaii out of the ocean.

Wood, Audrey. *The Rainbow Bridge: Inspired by a Chumash Tale.* This creation myth takes place on an island off the California coast. It explains the origins of dolphins.

Nonfiction Resources on Native Americans: A Selective List

Reference Books

Ciment, James, and Ronald La France. *Scholastic Encyclopedia of the North American Indian.* New York: Scholastic Reference, 1996.

Griffin-Pierce, Trudy. *The Encyclopedia of Native America.* New York: Viking, 1995.

Waldman, Carl. *Encyclopedia of Native American Tribes.* Illustrated by Molly Braun. New York: Facts on File, 1988.

Wolfson, Evelyn. *From Abenaki to Zuni: A Dictionary of Native American Tribes.* Illustrated by William Sauts Bock. New York: Walker, 1988.

Maps

A Map of American Indian Nations. Phoenix, AZ: Russell, 1993.

The Map of American Indian History. Phoenix, AZ: Russell, n.d.

Nonfiction Books

Asikinack, Bill, and Kate Scarborough. *Exploration into North America.* Parsippany, NJ: New Discovery Books, 1996. This book provides a historical perspective of Native Americans with an eye toward revealing the invasion by European explorers, subsequent colonization of native lands by white settlers, and treaties.

Braine, Susan. *Drumbeat Heartbeat: A Celebration of the Powwow.* We Are Still Here Series. Photographs by the author. Minneapolis, MN: Lerner, 1995. An overview of modern powwow celebrations, including details on the different styles of dancing.

Crum, Robert. *Eagle Drum: On the Powwow Trail with a Young Grass Dancer.* Photographs by the author. New York: Four Winds Press, 1994. The narrative follows a contemporary nine-year-old boy of the Pend Oreille (Kalispel) tribe on the Flathead Reservation in Montana as he prepares and travels to powwows. He is a grass dancer, a special kind of dance that showcases a costume hung with strands of wool.

Hoyt-Goldsmith, Diane. *Arctic Hunter.* Photographs by Lawrence Migdale. New York: Holiday House, 1992. An Inupiat boy named Reggie describes his life in Alaska north of the Arctic Circle. He lives a modern life with grocery stores and pizza but also helps his family keep old traditions alive. They make summer camp to hunt and fish in the old ways, providing themselves with food for winter.

———. *Cherokee Summer.* Photographs by Lawrence Migdale. New York: Holiday House, 1993. A ten-year-old girl named Bridget describes her life and family in Oklahoma. Sections of the book feature contemporary life among the Cherokee people; others fill in a brief history of the Cherokee. Photographs show modern-day practices of old traditions.

———. *Potlatch: A Tsimshian Celebration.* Illustrated by Lawrence Migdale. New York: Holiday House, 1997. Tsimshian people in Metlakatla, Alaska, prepare for and celebrate a contemporary potlatch festival.

———. *Pueblo Storyteller.* Photographs by Lawrence Migdale. New York: Holiday House, 1991. Everyday life in a Cochiti Pueblo family in New Mexico as related by April. She tells how her grandfather and grandmother work to produce "storyteller" clay art figures. The book ends with a two-page pourquoi story, "How the People Came to Earth: A Pueblo Legend."

———. *Totem Pole.* Photographs by Lawrence Migdale. New York: Holiday House, 1990. A Tsimshian boy named David watches and learns as his father carves a totem pole. Other traditions of the Northwest coast are described.

Hunter, Sally M. *Four Seasons of Corn: A Winnebago Tradition.* We Are Still Here Series. Minneapolis, MN: Lerner, 1997. A 12-year-old boy learns about growing traditional many-colored corn. He periodically leaves his St. Paul home to spend time with his grandfather during the cultivating moon, the corn tasseling moon, and so on.

King, Sandra. *Shannon: An Ojibway Dancer.* We Are Still Here Series. Photographs by Catherine Whipple. Minneapolis, MN: Lerner, 1993. A 13-year-old Minneapolis girl prepares and dances at a powwow, learning about her traditions from her grandmother.

Peters, Russell M. *Clambake: A Wampanoag Tradition.* We Are Still Here Series. Photographs by John Madama. Minneapolis, MN: Lerner, 1992. A 12-year old boy of the Wampanoag people of Massachusetts learns a traditional practice from his grandfather: a special preparation of a clambake.

Regguinti, Gordon. *The Sacred Harvest: Ojibway Wild Rice Gathering.* We Are Still Here Series. Photographs by Dale Kakkak. Minneapolis, MN: Lerner, 1992. Eleven-year-old Glen Jackson Jr. participates in his first wild rice gathering with his father in northern Minnesota.

Reynolds, Jan. *Frozen Land: Vanishing Cultures.* San Diego: Harcourt Brace, 1993. An Inuit family goes about its daily life in the Northwest Territories of Canada. Although the Inuit keep some traditional lifeways such as igloo building and ice fishing, twentieth-century influences have caused them to lose resources and make adjustments.

Roessel, Monty. *Kinaaldá: A Navajo Girl Grows Up.* We Are Still Here Series. Photographs by the author. Minneapolis, MN: Lerner, 1993. A contemporary 13-year-old girl works, prepares, and takes part in her Kinaaldá, the coming-of-age ceremony for Navajo girls.

———. *Songs from the Loom: A Navajo Girl Learns to Weave.* We Are Still Here Series. Photographs by the author. Minneapolis, MN: Lerner, 1995. Jaclyn lives in Arizona and asks her Navajo grandmother to teach her how to weave Navajo rugs. Grandmother teaches her the whole process, not only the care and shearing of sheep, the dying and weaving, but also the cultural stories and traditions that are such an important part of Navajo life.

Swentzell, Rina. *Children of Clay: A Family of Pueblo Potters.* We Are Still Here Series. Photographs by Bill Steen. Minneapolis, MN: Lerner, 1992. A Tewa family belonging to the Santa Clara Pueblo in New Mexico shows its modern-day practice of traditional clay art.

Wittstock, Laura Waterman. *Ininatig's Gift of Sugar: Traditional Native Sugar Making.* We Are Still Here Series. Photographs by Dale Kakkak. Minneapolis, MN: Lerner, 1993. In Minnesota, an Anishinabe man shows students how to tap and extract maple sugar.

Yamane, Linda. *Weaving a California Tradition: A Native American Basketmaker.* We Are Still Here Series. Illustrated by Dugan Aguilar. Minneapolis, MN: Lerner, 1996. The author, herself a basketweaver and member of the California Rumisen Ohlone people, describes how 11-year-old Carly Tex learns basket-weaving techniques from her family. She gathers plants, prepares them, and learns weaving patterns.

SCIENCE TIE-IN: POURQUOI TALES AS A CATALYST FOR STUDENT INQUIRY AND RESEARCH

The Science Connection

Pourquoi tales focus on subjects such as animal characteristics, animal behavior, weather, stars, plants, geological formations. The content and wonder of these stories provide natural connections to science, and the school science curriculum. Using these tales to their best advantage is worth careful consideration. Science education is undergoing a transformation, as evidenced by new national standards and the advent of the "constructivist" approach to learning. The integration of pourquoi tales is harmonious with these new trends and can add to the joy of learning in classrooms that embrace these student-centered approaches.

When students hear a folktale explaining the origins of some natural phenomenon, more often than not someone asks the question, "Is that *true*?" There are many possible responses. This matter is discussed earlier in terms of cultural context and evidence of much scientific knowledge being encoded in the story. In the context of students' science learning, perhaps the best response is another question, "What do you think?" This alone can spark a lively debate and lead to further questions, "What do you already know about it?" and "How can we find out more?" Then the story becomes a catalyst for discourse, which is at the heart of the new constructivist approach to learning science.

The use of language is central to science learning; it is important as a starting point before students even begin to investigate a concept. At this early stage, students bring their own experiences, conceptions or misconceptions, and cultural backgrounds to the science classroom. Before they begin a learning task, they need to articulate their present understandings. A folktale, rich in language and readily appealing, provides fertile ground for articulation of ideas. In his book *Talking Science: Language, Learning, and Values*, Jay Lemke states that mastering a concept requires the learner to use language systems effectively, in other words, to "talk science" (Lemke 1990, 95). Furthermore, "concepts and meanings do not exist in the abstract. . . . Rather, they are constructed by our speaking or picturing, constructed through our use of words or other signs" (98). Reading and discussing a pourquoi tale at the outset of a scientific investigation can "prime the pump" for the linguistic interchange. Students can move on from the story to articulate their own conceptions. Then the stage is set for investigations that include hands-on activities and research. Lemke believes that "scientific theories and 'conceptual systems' are mainly taught through language, supplemented by diagrams and mathematics, and by practical hands-on experience" (99).

The constructivist approach focuses on what the students bring to their learning and on how they construct meaning for themselves. Bonnie L. Shapiro, in her book *What Children Bring to Light: A Constructivist Perspective on Children's Learning in Science*, describes the work of George Kelly, who "considered each person to be an 'intuitive scientist,' formulating hypotheses about the world, collecting data that confirm or disconfirm these hypotheses, and then altering his or her conception of the world to include this new information" (Shapiro 1994, xv). Again, Shapiro reaffirms the role of language in this process: "Language is not only a *medium* for conveying new ideas, it is also a *means* whereby new meanings are constructed. . . . Words . . . contain the two dimensions of *reflection* and *action*. To use a new word is to transform one's world" (33). Learners use language as a way to build bridges from their present conceptions (or misconceptions) to new and unfamiliar ideas. For this kind of personal transformation to take place, Shapiro points out that the classroom environment must convey an atmosphere of trust (37). One way to build trust, to build a sense of community, is by telling stories. A story can bring relaxation and focus to a group. A story can set the stage for the linguistic discourse that is central to constructivist learning.

Children's understandings in science unfold in developmental stages. This lends even more credence to the constructivist approach. Students don't grasp concepts such as the geological formation of mountains or the size and temperature of the sun just by being told about them, and they may be at different points on a continuum of understanding. Folktales provide a common language as a starting point and bridge the disparities among children with different levels of understanding. Children hold many misconceptions of scientific concepts, and they need to revisit ideas in a process-based approach. Jean Piaget documented children's incomplete conceptions about the origins of mountains, trees, the sun, water, and the moon (Piaget 1960). An overview of research on students' science misconceptions is summarized in *Benchmarks for Science Literacy* (American Association for the Advancement of Science 1993). Adults need awareness of these misconceptions as a developmental reality. The use of folk literature is a way to re-visit scientific concepts and keep the gears of this process turning.

Pourquoi tales contain concepts and topics that are central to science learning. But this is not the only reason they make good jumping-off points for science teaching units. They come from a time when humans were much closer to nature than they are now, when the lives of people were deeply connected to the rhythms of the land, the seasons, the stars, the animals and plants. Science and life and stories and language and survival flowed as one. Science educator and professional storyteller Jo Anne Ollerenshaw Lewis interweaves these ideas in her teaching and in her writing. Her current research, now in press, bears out the validity and the benefits of using folk literature as a basis for discourse and constructivist learning in the science classroom (Lewis 1997). (For further information on Lewis's work linking science education to storytelling, consult the Lewis entries in the reference section of this chapter.)

And so what of the question, "Is that story true?" In the spirit of discourse and trust that a classroom community of learners has built, the class can return to the tale after having done investigations, hands-on activities, and book research. Just as the students' own constructivist views have been valued, now they can value the view presented by the tale. They can look at the culture that created the tale and recognize both the truth in the tale and the constructivist reality for that culture in that time. The story still holds meaning. And to dispel any doubts about Native Americans as scientists, refer to the book *American Indian Science* by Fern G. Brown, described in the next section.

Native Americans and Science

While Native Americans demonstrated their knowledge of science in their tales, it should be noted that they had a firm grasp of the hard sciences. *American Indian Science: A New Look at Old Cultures,* by Fern G. Brown (New York: Henry Holt, 1997) examines Native Americans' contributions to scientific practices. Written for fifth grade and up, this 78-page book contains chapters on agriculture, medicine, architecture, math and astronomy, and tools and technology. Native peoples' knowledge of drugs, healing, and astronomy are particularly impressive. Ancient and modern use of herbs, drugs, and medical treatments are discussed. Indians of the Amazon River regions developed technologies for extracting and processing rubber, a resource ignored by Europeans for 300 years after Columbus. Ancient architectural practices incorporated techniques now adopted by modern builders. Some contemporary Native American scientists are highlighted. Additional resources are provided, including websites and addresses of agencies and museums. The conclusion provides this historical perspective:

> We are just now beginning to realize that the Indian peoples had a rich, spiritual life, a diversified culture, and a body of wisdom that we know little about. . . . Non-Indians had a certain Eurocentric way of viewing

the Indian civilizations that they have passed on to their descendants. It was the view that Euro-American values, religions, and achievements were much more advanced than the Indians' values. . . . In truth, New World cultures had superior know-how in farming and technology, and they were ahead of the Old World in their knowledge of pharmacology. Indian calendars were far more sophisticated than that of the Europeans, and the Indians of Mexico had a math system superior to the numerical systems then used by the Spaniards.

Poised at the beginning of a new century, we are becoming more aware of the fragility of our ecosystem. . . . Today, our system of Western science is beginning to look to Indian science, with its holistic approach to life, for survival ideas. (Brown 1997, 65–66)

Pourquoi Tales, Nonfiction Research, and the National Science Education Standards

National Science Education Standards (National Research Council 1996) was published to help bring about a transformation in science education. Developed by a number of groups, this visionary work includes standards for teaching, content, assessment, and other areas. Folk literature can be integrated into the application of some of the teaching and content standards. Following are applicable teaching and content standards accompanied by a rationale for using pourquoi tales in teaching science. Further, see tables 2.5–2.10 for suggested literature relating to some of the content standards.

Teaching Standard A

"Teachers of science plan an inquiry-based science program" that includes the nurturing of "a community of science learners" working "across disciplines" (National Research Council, 30). The simple sharing of a story is a time-honored method of nurturing a sense of community within a group. The inclusion of literature in the science classroom is a multidisciplinary approach. Introducing a unit with a folktale can provide the catalyst for the spirit of inquiry.

Teaching Standard B

"Teachers guide and facilitate learning. In doing this, teachers

- Focus and support inquiries while interacting with students.
- Orchestrate discourse among students about scientific ideas.
- Recognize and respond to student diversity." (National Research Council, 32)

A folktale brings focus to the group and provides a vehicle for discourse. Folktales reveal cultural diversity and can be chosen to reflect the cultural backgrounds of the students. Discussions can serve to recognize student diversity by accepting different students' interpretations of the stories and of scientific phenomena.

Content Standard A: Science As Inquiry

Students need to acquire the abilities to "ask a question about objects, organisms, and events in the environment" and "communicate investigations and explanations" (National Research Council, 122). They must understand that "scientific investigations involve . . . comparing the answer with what scientists already know about the world" (123).

A pourquoi tale can spur the initial questioning process. A pourquoi tale is itself an "explanation" for an organism or object. Students can offer their own explanations for phenomena both before and after their inquiry process. The standards state the importance of comparing students' answers to what is already known by scientists. This is an optimal opportunity for research in nonfiction sources.

Content Standards C, D, and F

Many of the pourquoi tales covered in this book apply directly to individual content standards established by the National Research Council. Some of the pourquoi titles in the chart in chapter 3 are listed here as they relate to these standards. Pairing one or more of the pourquoi tales with selections from the list of nonfiction sources makes for an effective research study unit. See tables 2.5–2.10 for ideas.

Content Standard G: History and Nature of Science

Science as a human endeavor: "Science and technology have been practiced by people for a long time." (141) The use of folktales is a manifestation of this principle. A pourquoi tale embodies and communicates scientific information about the world. The tale shows how people observed phenomena and tried to make sense of their world. Pourquoi tales come out of the past; even in these old times, people were natural scientists, observing, encoding, and passing on their constructed view of science.

(Text continues on page 68.)

Table 2.5. The Characteristics of Organisms (127)
Suggested Titles for Content Standard C: Life Science, the Characteristics of Organisms

Pourquoi Tales	Nonfiction sources for students' inquiry-based research
Birds Bruchac, Joseph. "How the Birds Got Their Feathers," in *The Boy Who Lived with the Bears*. Knutson, Barbara. *How the Guinea Fowl Got Her Spots*. Hamilton, Virginia. "Hummingbird and Little Breeze," in *When Birds Could Talk & Bats Could Sing*. Brusca, María Cristina, and Tona Wilson. "Why the Quetzal Is the Most Beautiful Bird," in *When Jaguars Ate the Moon*. Gates, Frieda. *Owl Eyes*. Ehlert, Lois. *Cuckoo*. Goble, Paul. *Crow Chief*.	***Birds*** Patent, Dorothy Hinshaw. *Feathers*. Illustrated by William Muñoz. New York: Cobblehill Books, 1992. Biel, Timothy Levi. *Hummingbirds*. Zoobooks. Mankato, MN: Creative Education, 1991. Patent, Dorothy Hinshaw. *Quetzal: Sacred Bird of the Cloud Forest*. Illustrated by Neil Waldman. New York: Morrow Junior Books, 1996. Sattler, Helen Roney. *The Book of North American Owls*. Illustrated by Jean Day Zallinger. New York: Clarion Books, 1995. Harrison, Colin, and Alan Greensmith. *Birds of the World*. Eyewitness Handbooks. New York: Dorling Kindersley, 1993. Markle, Sandra. *Outside and Inside Birds*. New York: Bradbury Press, 1994. Bishop, Nic. *The Secrets of Animal Flight*. Boston: Houghton Mifflin, 1997.
Turtles Mollel, Tololwa M. *The Flying Tortoise*. Ross, Gayle. *How Turtle's Back Was Cracked*. Caduto, Michael J., and Joseph Bruchac. "The Earth on Turtle's Back," in *Keepers of the Earth*. Caduto, Michael J., and Joseph Bruchac. "How Turtle Flew South for the Winter," in *Keepers of the Earth*.	***Turtles*** Gerholdt, James E. *Turtles and Tortoises*. Remarkable Reptiles. Edina, MN: Abdo & Daughters, 1994. Papastavrou, Vassili. *Turtles and Tortoises*. Wildlife at Risk. New York: Bookwright Press, 1992. Baskin-Salzberg, Anita, and Allen Salzberg. *Turtles*. New York: Franklin Watts, 1996. Fichter, George S. *Turtles, Toads, and Frogs*. A Golden Junior Guide. Illustrated by Barbara Hoopes Ambler. Racine, WI: Golden Books, 1993. Hirschi, Ron. *Turtle's Day*. Photographs by Dwight Kuhn. New York: Cobblehill Books, 1994.
Insects and Spiders Van Laan, Nancy. "How Spider Caught Flies," in *In a Circle Long Ago*. Kimmel, Eric. *Anansi Goes Fishing*. (spiders) Young, Richard Alan, and Judy Dockrey Young. "Why Anansi Has a Narrow Waist," in *African-American Folktales for Young Readers*. (spiders) McCarthy, Tara. "How the Beetle Got Her Colors," in *Multicultural Fables and Fairy Tales*. Wood, Douglas. *The Windigo's Return*. (mosquitoes) Ross, Gayle. *The Legend of the Windigo*. (mosquitoes)	***Insects and Spiders*** Markle, Sandra. *Outside and Inside Spiders*. New York: Bradbury Press, 1994. Sterry, Paul. *Spiders: A Portrait of the Animal World*. New York: Smithmark, 1996. Souza, Dorothy M. *Eight Legs*. Creatures All Around Us. Minneapolis, MN: Carolrhoda Books, 1991. Johnson, Jinny. *Simon and Schuster Children's Guide to Insects and Spiders*. New York: Simon & Schuster Books for Young Readers, 1996. Macquitty, Miranda. *Amazing Bugs*. Inside Guides. New York: Dorling Kindersley, 1996. Souza, Dorothy M. *Insects in the Garden*. Creatures All Around Us. Minneapolis, MN: Carolrhoda Books, 1991. Still, John. *Amazing Beetles*. Eyewitness Juniors. New York: Alfred A. Knopf, 1991. Patent, Dorothy Hinshaw. *Mosquitoes*. New York: Holiday House, 1986.

Table 2.6. Life Cycles of Organisms (129)
Content Standard C: Life Science

Pourquoi Tales	Nonfiction sources for students' inquiry-based research
Life cycles	*Life cycles*
Bruchac, Joseph. *The Great Ball Game.* (why birds fly south in winter)	Gans, Roma. *How Do Birds Find Their Way?* Let's-Read-and-Find-Out Science. Illustrated by Paul Mirocha. New York: HarperCollins, 1996.
Oliviero, Jamie. *The Day Sun Was Stolen.* (bear hibernation, animals' winter fur)	Crewe, Sabrina. *The Bear.* Life Cycles. Austin, TX: Raintree Steck-Vaughn, 1997.
Bernhard, Emery. *The Tree That Rains.* (planting seeds, growing food, having children)	Pascoe, Elaine. *Seeds and Seedlings.* Photographs by Dwight Kuhn. Woodbridge, CT: Blackbirch Press, 1997.
	Gibbons, Gail. *From Seed to Plant.* Illustrated by the author. New York: Holiday House, 1991.
Mayo, Margaret. "Raven and the Pea-Pod Man," in *When the World Was Young.* (plants, animals, balance in nature, need for sunlight, having children)	Lauber, Patricia. *Who Eats What? Food Chains and Food Webs.* Let's-Read-and-Find-Out Science. Illustrated by Holly Keller. New York: HarperCollins, 1995.
	Regguinti, Gordon. *The Sacred Harvest: Ojibway Wild Rice Gathering.* We Are Still Here Series. Photographs by Dale Kakkak. Minneapolis, MN: Lerner, 1992.
Haley, Gail E. *Two Bad Boys.* (the need to plant seeds and harvest, hunting animals for food)	McMillan, Bruce. *Nights of the Pufflings.* Photographs by the author. Boston: Houghton Mifflin, 1995. (life/reproductive cycle of puffins)
Rohmer, Harriet. *The Legend of Food Mountain.* (the need to grow food with seed and rain)	Guiberson, Brenda Z. *Into the Sea.* Illustrated by Alix Berenzy. New York: Henry Holt, 1996. (life/reproductive cycle of sea turtle)
	Fleisher, Paul. *Life Cycles of a Dozen Diverse Creatures.* Brookfield, CT: Millbrook Press, 1996.
Bruchac, Joseph. "Waynabozho and the Wild Rice," in *Native Plant Stories.* (harvesting & life cycle of wild rice)	Llamas Ruiz, Andres. *Metamorphosis.* Cycles of Life Series. New York: Sterling, 1997.
	Pringle, Laurence. *An Extraordinary Life: The Story of a Monarch Butterfly.* Illustrated by Bob Marstall. New York: Orchard, 1997.
Mayo, Margaret. "Tortoise's Big Idea," in *When the World Was Young.* (why people must die)	George, Jean Craighead. *Look to the North: A Wolf Pup Diary.* Illustrated by Lucia Washburn. New York: HarperCollins, 1997.
	Pfeffer, Wendy. *A Log's Life.* Illustrated by Robin Brickman. New York: Simon & Schuster Books for Young Readers, 1997.

Table 2.7. Organisms and Their Environments (129)
Content Standard C: Life Science

Pourquoi Tales	Nonfiction sources for students' inquiry-based research
Ocean organisms and environment	**Ocean organisms and environment**
Crespo, George. *How the Sea Began*. (origin of the sea) Jaffe, Nina. *The Golden Flower*. (origin of the sea and its creatures) Adler, Naomi. "Sedna and King Gull," in *The Dial Book of Animal Tales from Around the World*. (origin of sea creatures) Wood, Audrey. *The Rainbow Bridge*. (origin of dolphins) Mayo, Margaret. "The Magic Millstones," in *When the World Was Young*. (why the sea is salty) French, Vivian. *Why the Sea Is Salt*.	Savage, Stephen. *Animals of the Oceans*. Animals by Habitat. Austin, TX: Raintree Steck-Vaughn, 1997. Kovacs, Deborah, and Kate Madin. *Beneath Blue Waters: Meeting with Remarkable Deep-Sea Creatures*. Photographs by Larry Madin. New York: Viking, 1996. Pringle, Laurence. *Coral Reefs: Earth's Undersea Treasures*. New York: Simon & Schuster Books for Young Readers, 1996. Simon, Seymour. *Oceans*. New York: Morrow Junior Books, 1990. Pringle, Laurence. *Dolphin Man: Exploring the World of Dolphins*. Photographs by Randall S. Wells, New York: Atheneum Books for Young Readers, 1995. Markle, Sandra. *Pioneering Ocean Depths*. New York: Atheneum Books for Young Readers, 1995. Lambert, David. *The Kingfisher Young People's Book of Oceans*. New York: Kingfisher, 1997. Johnson, Jinny. *Simon & Schuster Children's Guide to Sea Creatures*. New York: Simon & Schuster Books for Young Readers, 1998.
Other habitats	**Other habitats**
Jackson, Ellen. *The Precious Gift*. (desert) Esbensen, Barbara Juster. *The Star Maiden*. (forest) Wood, Douglas. *The Windigo's Return*. (forest) Esbensen, Barbara Juster. *The Great Buffalo Race*. (prairie) Norman, Howard. *How Glooskap Outwits the Ice Giants*. (shoreline) Crespo, George. *How Iwariwa the Cayman Learned to Share*. (rain forest) Adler, Naomi. "Magic in the Rainforest," in *The Dial Book of Animal Tales from Around the World*. (rain forest) Flora. *Feathers Like a Rainbow*. (rain forest)	*Eyewitness Encyclopedia of Nature*. 2d. CD-ROM. New York: Dorling Kindersley, 1997. Lauber, Patricia. *Fur, Feathers, and Flippers: How Animals Live Where They Do*. New York: Scholastic, 1994. Arnold, Caroline. *Watching Desert Wildlife*. A Carolrhoda Nature Watch Book. Photographs by Arthur Arnold. Minneapolis, MN: Carolrhoda Books, 1994. Taylor, Barbara. *Forest Life*. Look Closer. Photographs by Kim Taylor and Jane Burton. New York: Dorling Kindersley, 1993. Patent, Dorothy Hinshaw. *Prairies*. Photographs by William Muñoz. New York: Holiday House, 1996. Taylor, Barbara. *Shoreline*. Photographs by Frank Greenaway. New York: Dorling Kindersley, 1993. Goodman, Susan E. *Bats, Bugs, and Biodiversity: Adventures in the Amazonian Rain Forest*. Photographs by Michael J. Doolittle. New York: Atheneum Books for Young Readers, 1995. Grupper, Jonathan. *Destination: Rain Forest*. New York: National Geographic Society, 1997.

Table 2.8. Evolution (185)
Content Standard C: Life Science

Pourquoi Tales	Nonfiction sources for students' inquiry-based research
Creation	*Evolution*
Anderson, David A. *The Origin of Life on Earth*. Caduto, Michael J., and Joseph Bruchac. "The Earth on Turtle's Back," in *Keepers of the Earth*. French, Fiona. *Lord of the Animals*. Gerson, Mary-Joan. *People of Corn*. Goble, Paul. *Remaking the Earth*. Hamilton, Virginia. "The Woman Who Fell from the Sky," in *In the Beginning*. Mayo, Margaret. "The Girl Who Did Some Baking," in *When the World Was Young*. Mayo, Margaret. "Raven and the Pea-Pod Man," in *When the World Was Young*. Rohmer, Harriet. *How We Came to the Fifth World*.	Bailey, Marilyn. *Evolution: Opposing Viewpoints*. San Diego, CA: Greenhaven Press, 1990. Campbell, Ann-Jeanette, and Ronald Rood. *The New York Public Library Incredible Earth: A Book of Answers for Kids*. Illustrated by Jessica Wolk-Stanley. New York: Stonesong Press, 1996. Cole, Joanna. *Evolution*. Let's-Read-and-Find-Out Science. Illustrated by Aliki. New York: Thomas Y. Crowell, 1987. Couper, Heather, and Nigel Henbest. *Big Bang*. Illustrated by Luciano Corbella. New York: Dorling Kindersley, 1997. Gallant, Roy A. *Before the Sun Dies: The Story of Evolution*. New York: Macmillan, 1989. Hooper, Meredith. *A Pebble in My Pocket. A History of Our Earth*. Illustrated by Chris Coady. New York: Viking, 1996. Llamas Ruiz, Andres. *Evolution*. Cycles of Life Series. New York: Sterling, 1996. Myers, Lynne Born, and Christopher A. Myers. *Galápagos: Islands of Change*. Photographs by Nathan Farb. New York: Hyperion Books for Children, 1995.

Note: Although the concept of evolution is not listed as a standard until grades 9–12 (185), creation myths may precipitate discussions at earlier grades. If this is a point of interest, there are possibilities for the pairing of literature on this concept.

Table 2.9. Changes in the Earth and Sky (134)
Content Standard D: Earth and Space Science

Pourquoi Tales	Nonfiction sources for students' inquiry-based research
Changes in earth's surface	***Changes in earth's surface***
Jaffe, Nina. *The Golden Flower.* (origin of island of Puerto Rico) Crespo, George. *How the Sea Began.* (origin of four Caribbean islands) Dixon, Ann. *The Sleeping Lady.* (origin of Mount Susitna, Alaska) Bruchac, Joseph. *Between Earth & Sky.* (origin of Great Smoky Mountains, Grand Canyon, Painted Desert, etc.) Oodgeroo. *Dreamtime.* (origin of earth's surface and its contours) Caduto, Michael J., and Joseph Bruchac. "Loo-Wit, the Fire-Keeper," in *Keepers of the Earth.* (origin of Mt. St. Helens and its eruption; the Dalles, Mount Adams, Mount Hood) Taylor, C. J. "The Birth of Niagara Falls," in *How We Saw the World.* (origin of Niagara Falls) Williams, Julie Stewart. *Māui Goes Fishing.* (origin of the islands of Hawaii) Dwyer, Mindy. *Coyote in Love.* (origin of Crater Lake) Varez, Dietrich. *Pele.* (origin of volcanoes)	Lasky, Kathryn. *Surtsey: The Newest Place on Earth.* Photographs by Christopher G. Knight. New York: Hyperion Books for Children, 1992. Myers, Lynne Born, and Christopher A. Myers. *Galápagos: Islands of Change.* Photographs by Nathan Farb. New York: Hyperion Books for Children, 1995. Zoehfeld, Kathleen Weidner. *How Mountains Are Made.* Let's-Read-and-Find-Out Science. Illustrated by James Graham Hale. New York: HarperCollins, 1995. Llewellyn, Claire. *Rocks and Mountains.* Why Do We Have? Series. Illustrated by Anthony Lewis. Hauppauge, NY: Barron's, 1995. Sattler, Helen Roney. *Our Patchwork Planet: The Story of Plate Tectonics.* Illustrated by Giulio Maestro. New York: Lothrop, Lee & Shepard Books, 1995. Lauber, Patricia. *Volcano: The Eruption and Healing of Mount St. Helens.* New York: Bradbury Press, 1986. Clifford, Nick. *Incredible Earth.* Inside Guides. New York: Dorling Kindersley, 1996. (includes waterfalls) Anderson, Peter. *A Grand Canyon Journey: Tracing Time in Stone.* New York: Franklin Watts, 1997. (origin of Grand Canyon) *Volcanoes: Life on the Edge.* CD-ROM. Bellevue, WA: Corbis, 1996. Taylor, Barbara. *Earth Explained: A Beginner's Guide to Our Planet.* New York: Henry Holt, 1997.
Changes in the weather	***Changes in the weather***
Bryan, Ashley. *The Story of Lightning & Thunder.* Climo, Shirley. *Stolen Thunder.* Mollel, Tololwa M. *A Promise to the Sun.* (drought, the need for and formation of rain) Oliviero, Jamie. *The Fish Skin.* (the need for and formation of rain) Taylor, C. J. "The First Tornado," in *How We Saw the World.* Bernhard, Emery. *The Tree That Rains.* (rain and flood) Alexander, Ellen. *Llama and the Great Flood.* (flood myth) Pohrt, Tom. "Coyote Creates a New World," in *Coyote Goes Walking.* (flood myth) Gerson, Mary-Joan. *People of Corn.* (flood myth) Esbensen, Barbara Juster. *The Great Buffalo Race.* (drought, clouds)	Simon, Seymour. *Weather.* New York: Morrow Junior Books, 1993. McMillan, Bruce. *The Weather Sky.* Photographs by the author. New York: Farrar, Straus & Giroux, 1991. Kahl, Jonathan D. W. *Weather Watch: Forecasting the Weather.* Minneapolis, MN: Lerner, 1996. Kahl, Jonathan D. W. *Storm Warning: Tornadoes and Hurricanes.* Minneapolis, MN: Lerner, 1993. Wood, Jenny. *Storms: Nature's Fury.* Wonderworks of Nature. Milwaukee, WI: Gareth Stevens Children's Books, 1991. Kramer, Stephen. *Eye of the Storm: Chasing Storms with Warren Faidley.* Photographs by Warren Faidley. New York: G. P. Putnam's Sons, 1997. Kramer, Stephen. *Tornado.* Minneapolis, MN: Carolrhoda Books, 1992. Lauber, Patricia. *Hurricanes: Earth's Mightiest Storms.* New York: Scholastic, 1996. Kahl, Jonathan D. W. *Wet Weather: Rain Showers and Snowfall.* Minneapolis, MN: Lerner, 1992.

Table 2.9 continues on page 66.

Table 2.9. Continued.

Pourquoi Tales	Nonfiction sources for students' inquiry-based research
Changes in the weather	*Changes in the weather*
Larry, Charles. *Peboan and Seegwun.* (seasons) Bateson-Hill, Margaret. *Lao Lao of Dragon Mountain.* (seasons) Milord, Susan. "The Twelve Months," in *Tales of the Shimmering Sky.* (seasons) Taylor, Harriet Peck. *When Bear Stole the Chinook.* (seasons) Van Laan, Nancy. *Shingebiss.* (seasons)	Lauber, Patricia. *Flood: Wrestling with the Mississippi.* Washington, DC: National Geographic Society, 1996. Vogel, Carole Garbuny. *The Great Midwest Flood.* Boston: Little, Brown, 1995. Leslie, Clare Walker. *Nature All Year Long.* New York: Greenwillow Books, 1991. Gibbons, Gail. *The Reasons for Seasons.* Illustrated by the author. New York: Holiday House, 1995. Elsom, Derek. *Weather Explained: A Beginner's Guide to the Elements.* New York: Henry Holt, 1997.
Objects in the sky	*Objects in the sky*
Bishop, Gavin. *Māui and the Sun.* (path of the sun, proportion of sunlight and night) Simms, Laura. *Moon and Otter and Frog.* (phases of the moon) Moroney, Lynn. *Moontellers.* (moon myths) Rattigan, Jama Kim. *The Woman in the Moon.* (image on the moon) Daly, Niki. *Why the Sun & Moon Live in the Sky.* Mollel, Tololwam. *The Orphan Boy.* (appearance of morning star and evening star) Bruchac, Joseph, and Gayle Ross. *The Story of the Milky Way.* Goble, Paul. *Her Seven Brothers.* (origin of Big Dipper) Milord, Susan. "Great Bear," in *Tales of the Shimmering Sky.* (Big Dipper and other stars)	Vogt, Gregory L. *The Sun.* Brookfield, CT: Millbrook Press, 1996. Gibbons, Gail. *The Moon Book.* Illustrated by the author. New York: Holiday House, 1997. Branley, Franklyn M. *The Sun and the Solar System.* Secrets of Space. New York: Twenty-First Century Books, 1996. Scagell, Robin. *Space Explained: A Beginner's Guide to the Universe.* A Henry Holt Reference Book. New York: Henry Holt, 1996. Lauber, Patricia. *Journey to the Planets,* 4th ed. New York: Crown, 1993. Simon, Seymour. *Our Solar System.* New York: Morrow Junior Books, 1992. Simon, Seymour. *Venus.* New York: Morrow Junior Books, 1992. Gibbons, Gail. *Stargazers.* Illustrated by the author. New York: Holiday House, 1992. Branley, Franklyn M. *The Big Dipper,* rev. ed. Let's-Read-and-Find-Out Science. Illustrated by Molly Coxe. New York: HarperCollins, 1991.

Table 2.10. Changes in Environments (138)
Content Standard F: Science in personal and social perspectives

Pourquoi Tales	Nonfiction sources for students' inquiry-based research
Environmental messages	*Environmental information*
Esbensen, Barbara Juster. *The Great Buffalo Race.* (share available food/resources; don't take more than your share; don't disregard smaller creatures) Gerson, Mary-Joan. *Why the Sky Is Far Away.* (consequences for wastefulness) Caduto, Michael J., and Joseph Bruchac. "Lee-Wit, the Fire-Keeper," in *Keepers of the Earth.* (consequences for not caring for the earth) Haley, Gail E. *Two Bad Boys.* (consequences for wastefulness)	Swanson, Diane. *Buffalo Sunrise: The Story of a North American Giant.* San Francisco: Sierra Club Books for Children, 1996. Love, Ann, and Jane Drake. *Take Action: An Environmental Book for Kids.* Illustrated by Pat Cupples. New York: Tambourine Books, 1992. Lovett, Sarah. *Extremely Weird Endangered Species.* Santa Fe, NM: John Muir, 1992. Peace Child International, in association with the United Nations. *Rescue Mission Planet Earth: A Children's Edition of Agenda 21.* New York: Kingfisher Books, 1994. Pollock, Steve. *The Atlas of Endangered Places.* New York: Facts on File, 1993. Galan, Mark. *There's Still Time: The Success of the Endangered Species Act.* Foreword by Bruce Babbitt. Washington, DC: National Geographic Society, 1997. Patent, Dorothy Hinshaw. *Back to the Wild.* Photographs by William Munoz. New York: Gulliver Books, 1997. Bang, Molly. *Common Ground: The Water, Earth, and Air We Share.* Illustrated by the author. New York: Blue Sky, 1997.

REFERENCES

American Association for the Advancement of Science. 1993. *Benchmarks for Science Literacy*. New York: Oxford University Press.

Brown, Fern G. 1997. *American Indian Science: A New Look at Old Cultures*. New York: Twenty-First Century Books.

Bruchac, Joseph. 1997. *Tell Me a Tale: A Book About Storytelling*. San Diego, CA: Harcourt Brace.

Lemke, Jay L. 1990. *Talking Science: Language, Learning, and Values*. Norwood, NJ: Ablex.

Lewis, Jo Anne Ollerenshaw. 1997. Interview with the author, Iowa City, IA, June 4.

———. "Storytelling As a Performance Assessment in Elementary Science Classrooms." Ph.D. diss., University of Iowa, 1998.

Lewis, Jo Anne Ollerenshaw, Rebecca Monhardt, and Leigh Monhardt. "Ethnoscience and Storytelling." Paper presented at the meeting of the Association for the Education of Teachers of Science, Minneapolis, MN, January 1998.

Lewis, Jo Anne Ollerenshaw, and Steven R. Yussen. "Storytelling As a Vehicle for Elementary School Children to Think and Learn About Scientific Inquiry." Paper presented at the conference, Project on the Rhetoric of Inquiry, Iowa City, IA, January 1998. Available on the World Wide Web: http:\\www.uiow.edu\~poroi

National Research Council. 1996. *National Science Education Standards*. Washington, DC: National Academy Press.

Piaget, Jean. 1960. *The Child's Conception of the World*. Translated by Joan Tomlinson and Andrew Tomlinson. Paterson, NJ: Littlefield, Adams.

Shapiro, Bonnie L. 1994. *What Children Bring to Light: A Constructivist Perspective on Children's Learning in Science*. New York: Teachers College Press.

story themes and topics

This chart is a useful tool for planning grouped tales for storytelling and story hour programs, thematic units for reading classes, and compare-and-contrast activities. Note that concept/theme elements are broader and allow for more sophisticated associations among stories and cultures, whereas topical elements allow for simpler comparisons. To obtain full bibliographic information on the stories, consult chapter 4, "Annotated Bibliography."

Topic	Pourquoi Elements	Title/Author/Culture
Animal characteristics—behavioral and physical		
Alligators	Why alligators wait and watch for dogs	*Why Alligator Hates Dog* (Reneaux) American/Cajun
Bald heads	How the spider gets a bald head	"How Spider Got a Bald Head," in *The Adventures of Spider* (Arkhurst) African (West African)
	How spider (Anansi) gets a bald head	*Anansi* (Gleeson) Central American/Caribbean (Jamaican)
	How buzzards get bald heads	"How Grandmother Spider Stole the Sun," in *Keepers of the Earth* (Caduto/Bruchac) Native American/Muskogee (Creek)
	How buzzards get bald heads	"Bruh Buzzard and Fair Maid," in *When Birds Could Talk & Bats Could Sing* (Hamilton) African American
Bats	Why bats can fly	"How Bat Learned to Fly," in *How Chipmunk Got Tiny Feet* (Hausman) Native American/Koasati Creek
	Why bats hide and fly at night How rain is made	*A Promise to the Sun* (Mollel) African
	Why bats are accepted as animals Why birds fly south in winter	*The Great Ball Game* (Bruchac) Native American/Muskogee (Creek)
	How Bat loses her voice and can only squeak How the birds get their songs	"When Miss Bat Could Sing," in *When Birds Could Talk & Bats Could Sing* (Hamilton) African American
	Origin of the bat Why bats fly in the dark	"How the Bat Came to Be," in *Keepers of the Night* (Caduto/Bruchac) Native American/Anishinabe
	Why bats are skin and bone and short hairs; Why bats are blind; Why bats hide and fly at night	"Still and Ugly Bat," in *When Birds Could Talk & Bats Could Sing* (Hamilton) African American
Bears	Origin of bear from sky constellation; Why bears hibernate	*When Bear Came Down from the Sky* (Gerez) European/Finno-Ugric
	Why bears hibernate; How the sun is brought back to the world	*The Day Sun Was Stolen* (Oliviero) Native American/Haida
	Why bears hibernate; Origin of circular markings around owls' eyes; How spring comes	*When Bear Stole the Chinook* (Taylor) Native American/Siksika (Blackfoot)
Birds	Crow's black feathers Gift of fire; first snow	*Rainbow Crow* (Van Laan) Native American/Lenape
	How birds get rainbow colors How people get fire	*Rainbow Bird* (Maddern) Australian/Aboriginal
	Crow's black color	*Crow Chief* (Goble) Native American/Dakota

Topic	Pourquoi Elements	Title/Author/Culture
Animal characteristics—behavioral and physical		
Birds	How birds get colors Why people hunt birds	*How the Birds Changed Their Feathers* (Troughton) South American Indian
	Origin of pheasants and kingfishers	*Pheasant and Kingfisher* (Berndt) Australian/Aboriginal
	How birds get beaks suited to their tasks; How people get teeth, fingernails, toenails	"How the Birds Got New Beaks and Men Got Teeth," in *Moon Was Tired of Walking on Air* (Belting) South American Indian/Bororo Indians
	How birds of the Amazon rain forest get their colors	*Feathers Like a Rainbow* (Flora) South American Indian/Amazon area
	How birds of the forest get their colors; How raccoons get rings around their eyes	*Brother Wolf* (Taylor) Native American/Seneca
	How the guinea fowl gets spotted feathers	*How the Guinea Fowl Got Her Spots* (Knutson) African (East African)
	How hummingbirds get the whirring sound in their wings How Hummingbird loses her voice	"Hummingbird and Little Breeze," in *When Birds Could Talk & Bats Could Sing* (Hamilton) African American
	How cuckoos get their dark feathers; How cuckoos get their voice	*Cuckoo* (Ehlert) Central American/Mayan
	Why birds fly south in winter; Why bats are accepted as animals	*The Great Ball Game* (Bruchac) Native American/Muskogee (Creek)
	Why different birds construct their nests in their own way	*The Magpies' Nest* (Foster) European/British Isles
	Why ducks sleep on one leg	*Why Ducks Sleep on One Leg* (Garland) Vietnamese
	How the birds get their songs How Bat loses her voice and can only squeak	"When Miss Bat Could Sing," in *When Birds Could Talk & Bats Could Sing* (Hamilton) African American
	How Loon gets her mournful cry; Why deer lose their antlers each fall; Why bears hibernate each winter; How Raven wins back the sun	*How the Loon Lost Her Voice* (Cameron) Native American/Northwest coast
	Buzzard's ill-fitting feathers; Why buzzards fly high, eat rotten fish; How birds get feathers	"How the Birds Got Their Feathers," in *The Boy Who Lived with the Bears* (Bruchac) Native American/Iroquois
	Crow's black color; Why cranes have a croaking voice	"Crane and Crow," in *Crow & Fox* (Thornhill) Australian (in a collection of several cultures)
	Swallow's feet and tail feathers; Why swallows nest near chimneys	"Blue Jay and Swallow Take the Heat," in *When Birds Could Talk & Bats Could Sing* (Hamilton) African American
	How the cardinal gets red feathers Why the kildeer says, "Kill deer!"	"Cardinal and Bruh Deer," in *When Birds Could Talk & Bats Could Sing* (Hamilton) African American

Topic	Pourquoi Elements	Title/Author/Culture
Animal characteristics—behavioral and physical		
Birds	How the owl gets its feathers Why owls come out only at night	"Owl Feathers," in *The Acorn Tree* (Rockwell) Central American/Puerto Rico (in a collection of several cultures)
	Owl's pushed-down head, "ears," brown color, big eyes Owl's nocturnal habits	*Owl Eyes* (Gates) Native American/Kanienkeha ka (Mohawk)
	Owl's large eyes; Owl's nocturnal habits; Meadowlark's necklace and breast markings	"Chipmunk and the Owl Sisters," in *Keepers of the Night* (Caduto/ Bruchac) Native American/Okanagan
	Owl's large eyes Owl's nocturnal habits	"Owl Big Eyes," in *Animal Lore and Legend: Owl* (Browne) Native American/Seneca
	Origin of circular markings around owls' eyes Why bears hibernate How spring comes	*When Bear Stole the Chinook* (Taylor) Native American/Siksika (Blackfoot)
	Why gulls warn people of approaching storms	"The Warning of the Gulls," in *The Monster from the Swamp* (Taylor) Native American/Seneca
	Origin of black crane	*Enora and the Black Crane* (Meeks) Australian/Aboriginal
Buffalo	Origin of buffaloes' humps and heads	*The Great Buffalo Race* (Esbensen) Native American/Seneca
	Origin of buffaloes' humps and heads	"Why Buffalo Has a Hump," in *Animal Lore and Legend: Buffalo* (Midge) Native American/Ojibwa & Seneca
Cats	How the cat gets its purr; Why cats and rats are enemies	*The Cat's Purr* (Bryan) African
	Why dogs still pursue cats	"Why Dogs Chase Cats," in *How Many Spots Does a Leopard Have?* (Lester) Jewish (in a collection of several cultures)
	Why cats and rats are enemies	*Cat and Rat* (Young) Asian/Chinese
	Why the Manx cat has no tail	*How the Manx Cat Lost Its Tail* (Stevens) European/British Isles
Chipmunks	Origin of chipmunks' stripes	"Chipmunk & Bear," in *The Boy Who Lived with the Bears* (Bruchac) Native American/Iroquois
	Why chipmunks have tiny feet	"How Chipmunk Got Tiny Feet," in *How Chipmunk Got Tiny Feet* (Hausman) Native American/Navajo
Coyote	Origin of coyotes' yellow eyes	"How Coyote Got Yellow Eyes," in *How Chipmunk Got Tiny Feet* (Hausman) Native American/Navajo

Topic	Pourquoi Elements	Title/Author/Culture
Animal characteristics—behavioral and physical		
Coyote	Origin of coyotes' yellow eyes	"Coyote," in *How the Animals Got Their Colors* (Rosen) Native American/Zuni (in a collection of several cultures)
Deer	How deer get antlers	"How Deer Won His Antlers," in *How Rabbit Tricked Otter* (Ross) Native American/Cherokee
	Why deer's teeth are blunt	"Why Deer's Teeth Are Blunt," in *How Rabbit Tricked Otter* (Ross) Native American/Cherokee
Dogs, horses	Why dogs and horses are man's helpers; Why man is separate from the other animals	*The Two-Legged Creature* (Walters) Native American/Otoe
	Why dogs are the helpers of humans Origin of horses as helpers of humans	"The Dog," and "The Horse," in *Full Moon Stories* (Turtle) Native American/Cheyenne and Kiowa
Frogs	Why frogs swim	"Why Frogs Swim," in *In a Circle Long Ago* (Van Laan) Native American/Shasta
Hyenas	Origin of hyenas' pushed-in hind legs; Why hyenas slink	*Hyena and the Moon* (McNeil) African/Kenya
	Origin of hyenas' matted fur Why hyenas laugh	*The Mean Hyena* (Sierra) African/Malawi
Jaguars	Origin of jaguars' spots	*Journey of the Nightly Jaguar* (Albert) Central American/Mayan
Lizards	Why lizards bask in the sun	*The Lizard and the Sun* (Ada) Central American/Mexican
Monkeys	Origin of howler monkeys	"The Flood and the Howler Monkeys," in *When Jaguars Ate the Moon* (Brusca/Wilson) South American/Yaruro Indians of Venezuela
	Why monkeys live in trees	"Why Monkeys Live in Trees," in *How Many Spots Does a Leopard Have?* (Lester) African/Ngoni (in a collection of several cultures)
	Why monkeys live in trees	*Tiger Soup* (Temple) Central American/Caribbean (Jamaican)
Necks, long	How giraffes get their long necks	*How Giraffe Got Such a Long Neck . . . and Why Rhino Is So Grumpy* (Rosen) African (East African)
	How ostriches get their long necks	*How the Ostrich Got Its Long Neck* (Aardema) African/Akamba of Kenya
Platypus	Why the platypus has both bird and mammal traits	*Black Duck and Water Rat* (Trezise) Australian/Aboriginal
Rabbits	Why rabbits are always running	"Why Hare Is Always on the Run," in *Tales Alive!* (Milord) African/Ghana (in a collection of several cultures)

Topic	Pourquoi Elements	Title/Author/Culture
Animal characteristics—behavioral and physical		
Rabbits	Origin of rabbits' short tails, split lips, back legs Origin of pussywillows	"Rabbit's Snow Dance," in *The Boy Who Lived with the Bears* (Bruchac) Native American/Iroquois
	Origin of rabbits' short tails, long ears, hopping legs Origin of pussywillows	"Rabbit and the Willow," in *In a Circle Long Ago* (Van Laan) Native American/Seneca
	Why rabbits' ears are long Why rabbits' tails are short	*Why Lapin's Ears Are Long* (Doucet) American/Cajun/Creole
	Origin of rabbits' short tails Origin of pussywillows	*How Rabbit Lost His Tail* (Tompert) Native American/Seneca
	Origin of rabbits' split lips Origin of flint rock pieces	"Flint Visits Rabbit," in *How Rabbit Tricked Otter* (Ross) Native American/Cherokee
	Origin of rabbits' short tails Why otters swim	"How Rabbit Tricked Otter," in *How Rabbit Tricked Otter* (Ross) Native American/Cherokee
	Origin of rabbits' long ears	*Rabbit Wishes* (Shute) Central American/Cuban
	Origin of rabbits' floppy ears and split lips	"How Manabozho Saved the Rose," in *Manabozho's Gifts* (Greene) Native American/Chippewa
Snails	Why snails have a shell Why snails leave a moist trail	*The Precious Gift* (Jackson) Native American/Navajo
	Origin of mark on conk snail's shell	"Leelee Goro," in *Misoso* (Aardema) African/Temne
Snakes	Why pythons change their skin Why people must die	"A Journey of Life and Death," in *African Folktales & Activities* (Orlando) African/Mende of Sierra Leone
Tails	Why the Manx cat has no tail	*How the Manx Cat Lost Its Tail* (Stevens) European/British Isles
	Why rabbits have short tails	"Rabbit's Snow Dance," in *The Boy Who Lived with the Bears* (Bruchac) Native American/Iroquois
	Why rabbits have short tails	"Rabbit and the Willow," in *In a Circle Long Ago* (Van Laan) Native American/Seneca
	Why bears have stubby tails	"Fox and Bear," in *Crow & Fox* (Thornhill) European/Northern European
	Why foxes' tail tips are black	*Llama and the Great Flood* (Alexander) South American/Native Andean
	Why rabbits have short tails	"How the Rabbit Lost His Tail," in *Nho Lobo and Other Stories* (Cabral) African

Topic	Pourquoi Elements	Title/Author/Culture
Animal characteristics—behavioral and physical		
Tails	Why possums have bare tails	"How Grandmother Spider Stole the Sun," in *Keepers of the Earth* (Caduto/Bruchac) Native American/Muskogee/Creek
	Why possums have bare tails Why possums play dead	"Why Possum's Tail Is Bare," in *How Rabbit Tricked Otter* (Ross) Native American/Cherokee
	Why possums have bare tails Why possums play dead Why possums hang by their tails	"How Possum Got His Skinny Tail," in *In a Circle Long Ago* (Van Laan) Native American/Cherokee
	Why possums have bare tails Why possums hang by their tails	"How Possum Lost His Tail," in *How Chipmunk Got Tiny Feet* (Hausman) Native American/Koasati Creek
Tortoises	How tortoises' backs get their pattern Why tortoises pull in their heads and legs	*The Flying Tortoise* (Mollel) African/Nigerian/Igbo
Turtles	How turtles' backs get their pattern	*How Turtle's Back Was Cracked* (Ross) Native American/Cherokee
	How turtles' backs get their pattern	"The Earth on Turtle's Back," in *Keepers of the Earth* (Caduto/Bruchac) Native American/Onondaga
	How turtles' backs get their pattern	"How Turtle Flew South for the Winter," in *Keepers of the Earth* (Caduto/Bruchac) Native American/Dakota (Sioux)
	How turtles' backs get their pattern	"Tortoise and Crane," in *Crow & Fox* (Thornhill) Chinese (in a collection of several cultures)
	How turtles' backs get their pattern	"Turtle Makes War on Man," in *The Boy Who Lived with the Bears* (Bruchac) Native American/Iroquois
	How turtles get their hard shells	*The Leopard's Drum* (Souhami) African/Asante of West Africa
	How turtles' backs get their pattern	*The Fish Skin* (Oliviero) Native American/Cree
Wolves	Why wolves hunt caribou Origin of arctic mammals	*Amorak* (Jessell) Native American/Inuit
Arts, stories, celebration		
Dance	Origin of the buffalo dance	*Buffalo Dance* (Van Laan) Native American/Blackfoot
Game of chess	Origin of game of chess	*The Token Gift* (McKibbon) Asian/Indian
Love, comfort	How hugging came into the world	"Leelee Goro," in *Misoso* (Aardema) African/Temne

Topic	Pourquoi Elements	Title/Author/Culture
Arts, stories, celebration		
Dancing, feast	Origin of yearly dancing feast in honor of the sun	*The Lizard and the Sun* (Ada) Central American/Mexican
Hunting celebrations and rituals	Origin of bear-hunting rituals	*The Girl Who Lived with the Bears* (Goldin) Native American/Pacific Northwest
Music	Origin of seasons by playing pipes Origin of night by playing pipes	"How Averiri Made the Night and the Seasons," in *Moon Was Tired of Walking on Air* (Belting) South American/Campas Indians
	Origin of music	*How Music Came to the World* (Ober) Central American/Mexican (Aztec)
Music, celebration	How singing and celebrations came to the people	*The Eagle's Song* (Rodanas) Native American/Northwest coast
Music, dancing	Origin of music on earth Origin of dancing, laughter, color	*Musicians of the Sun* (McDermott) Central American/Mexican/Aztec
Stories	Origin of stories	*How Stories Came into the World* (Troughton) African (West African)
	Origin of stories	*A Story, A Story* (Haley) African (West African)
	Origin of stories; How spider (Anansi) gets a bald head	*Anansi* (Gleeson) Central American/Caribbean (Jamaican)
Pot making	Why Cherokee potters fire their pots	*Grandmother Spider Brings the Sun* (Keams) Native American/Cherokee
Weaving	How weaving was taught to the Navajo people	*The Magic of Spider Woman* (Duncan) Native American/Navajo
	How weaving was taught to the Navajo people	*The Magic Weaver of Rugs* (Oughton) Native American/Navajo
Balance in nature or in life		
Day and night	Origin of balanced amount of daylight and night	*Māui and the Sun* (Bishop) Australian/New Zealand/Polynesian
Forces of nature	Origin of difficult and gentle aspects of nature (weather, rivers, etc.)	*The Woman Who Fell from the Sky* (Bierhorst) Native American/Iroquois
Size	Why the animals needed to be shrunk down to a size proportional to humans	"How Glooskap Made Human Beings," in *How Glooskap Outwits the Ice Giants* (Norman) Native American/Northeast
Work	Why there is a balance of work for the gifts of food	*Two Bad Boys* (Haley) Native American/Cherokee
	Why there is a balance of work for the gifts of food	"Manabozho and the Maple Trees," in *Keepers of the Earth* (Caduto/Bruchac) Native American/Anishinabe

Topic	Pourquoi Elements	Title/Author/Culture
Balance in nature or in life		
Weather	Origin of balanced amount of sun and rain	*The Fish Skin* (Oliviero) Native American/Cree
Work	Why people must walk the Middle Way	*The Magic of Spider Woman* (Duncan) Native American/Navajo
Conflict, disagreement		
Confusion	Why there is confusion among people Why the stars are scattered in the sky	*How the Stars Fell into the Sky* (Oughton) Native American/Navajo
Crying	How crying came into the world	"Leelee Goro," in *Misoso* (Aardema) African/Temne
Fighting	Why there is fighting among many animals	*The Honey Hunters* (Martin) African
War	How war began on earth	"Coyote and the Blackbirds," in *In a Circle Long Ago* (Van Laan) Native American/Pueblo (Tewa)
Creation		
Cosmic egg	The egg as the beginning of the world	"The Cosmic Egg," in *The Illustrated Book of Myths* (Philip) Asian/Chinese (in a collection of several cultures)
	The egg as the beginning of the world	"Yin, Yang, and the Cosmic Egg," in *Out of the Ark* (Ganeri) Asian/Chinese (in a collection of several cultures)
	The egg as the beginning of the world	"Bursting from the Hen's Egg," in *In the Beginning* (Hamilton) Asian/Chinese (in a collection of several cultures)
Flood	Flood as an agent of re-creation; How an insult causes a flood that destroys all but two people; How humans survive the flood	*The Fifth and Final Sun* (Greger) Central American/Mexican (Aztec)
	Flood as an agent of re-creation How the people and animals survive the flood	*Llama and the Great Flood* (Alexander) South American/Native Andean
	Flood as an agent of creation or re-creation How Coyote creates the world anew after people get too wild	"Coyote Creates a New World," in *Coyote Goes Walking* (Pohrt) Native American
	Flood as an agent of re-creation Why humans must praise creation	*People of Corn* (Gerson) Central American/Mayan

Topic	Pourquoi Elements	Title/Author/Culture
Creation		
Flood	Flood as an agent of re-creation Why people must praise the goddess Origin of howler monkeys	"The Flood and the Howler Monkeys," in *When Jaguars Ate the Moon* (Brusca/Wilson) South American/Yaruro Indians of Venezuela
	Flood as an agent of re-creation How the only good man and woman survive	*How We Came to the Fifth World* (Rohmer/Anchondo) Central American/Mexican (Aztec)
	Flood as an agent of re-creation How the animals and Noah survive How the Manx cat loses its tail	*How the Manx Cat Lost Its Tail* (Stevens) European/British Isles
	Flood as an agent of re-creation How one good person and plants survive Origin of rain for the crops	*The Tree That Rains* (Bernhard) Central American/Mexican (Huichol Indians)
Human beings	Origin of humans from seeds of sacred plant	*The Rainbow Bridge* (Wood) Native American/Chumash
	Origin of humans from clay	"Coyote Creates a New World," in *Coyote Goes Walking* (Pohrt) Native American
	Origin of humans from river mud	*Lord of the Animals* (French Native American/Miwok
	Origin of humans from ground corn	*People of Corn* (Gerson) Central American/Mayan
	Origin of humans	*The Legend of Food Mountain* (Rohmer) Central American/Mexican (Aztec)
	Origin of humans from bones	"Bones in the Basket," in *Bones in the Basket* (Taylor) Native American/Modoc
	Origin of humans using magic	"How Glooskap Made Human Beings," in *How Glooskap Outwits the Ice Giants* (Norman) Native American/Northeast
	Origin of humans from shaping and baking clay	"The Girl Who Did Some Baking," in *When the World Was Young* (Mayo) African/Akan-Ashanti (in a collection of several cultures)
	How humans started from a pea pod	"Raven and the Pea-Pod Man," in *When the World Was Young* (Mayo) Native American/Unalit Eskimo (in a collection of several cultures)
	Why man has strength and woman has power	*Her Stories* (Hamilton) African American
Human beings, world	Origin of humans from earth Origin of world	*And in the Beginning . . .* (Williams) African
	Origin of humans from earth Origin of world, plants Origin of personalities	*The Origin of Life on Earth* (Anderson) African/Yoruba

Topic	Pourquoi Elements	Title/Author/Culture
Creation		
Human beings, world	Origin of earth in a watery world Origin of light	*Cry of the Benu Bird* (Greger) African/Egyptian
Woman who fell through the sky, Earth on turtle's back	Origin of earth in a watery world Origin of animals, plants Origin of hunting Origin of thunder Origin of the two-leggeds	*Remaking the Earth* (Goble) Native American/Algonquian
	Origin of earth in a watery world Origin of plants	"The Woman Who Fell from the Sky," in *In the Beginning* (Hamilton) Native American/Huron (in a collection of several cultures)
	Origin of earth in a watery world Origin of plants, rivers, seasons Origin of human beings Origin of balance between gentle and hard aspects of life	*The Woman Who Fell from the Sky* (Bierhorst) Native American/Iroquois
	Origin of earth in a watery world Origin of moon Origin of plants, rivers, mountains	"Creation," in *Bones in the Basket* (Taylor) Native American/Mohawk
	Origin of earth in a watery world Origin of marks on turtles' backs Origin of plant life	"The Earth on Turtle's Back," in *Keepers of the Earth* (Caduto/Bruchac) Native American/Onondaga
	Origin of earth in a watery world Origin of plant life	"The Mud on Turtle's Back," in *When the World Was Young* (Mayo) Native American/Huron (in a collection of several cultures)
World	Origin of earth after flood Origin of animals from mud	"Coyote Creates a New World," in *Coyote Goes Walking* (Pohrt) Native American
	Origin of earth; Origin of animals; Origin of laws	"The Beginning of Life," in *Dreamtime* (Oodgeroo) Australian/Aboriginal
	Origin of earth in a watery world Origin of animals	*Raven's Light* (Shetterly) Native American/Northwest coast
	Origin of earth in a watery world	"Coyote's Cave," in *Maybe I Will Do Something* (Ude) Native American/Southwest
	Origin of earth in a watery world	"Tirawa Creates the People," in *How the World Was Saved* (Harper) Native American/Pawnee
	Origin of earth from dust Origin of plants, food	"Moon Was Tired of Walking on Air," in *Moon Was Tired of Walking on Air* (Belting) South American/Chorote Indians
	Origin of the present (5th) world through five epochs	*How We Came to the Fifth World* (Rohmer) Central American/Mexican (Aztec)

Topic	Pourquoi Elements	Title/Author/Culture
Creation		
World	How the first people came to the present world from the underworld; How water came to the new land; Origin of several animal traits	*The Precious Gift* (Jackson) Native American/Navajo
Earth/geological formations		
Islands	Origin of island and its forests Origin of the sea Origin of sea creatures	*The Golden Flower* (Jaffe) Central American/Caribbean (Taino)
	Origin of four islands; Origin of the sea; Origin of sea creatures	*How the Sea Began* (Crespo) Central American/Caribbean (Taino)
	Origin of islands of Hawaii	*Māui Goes Fishing* (Williams) Hawaiian
Islands, straits	Origin of Orkney, Shetland, and Faroe Islands, and Iceland Origin of straits in Denmark	"Jamie and the Biggest, First, and Father of All Sea Serpents," in *Mythical Birds & Beasts from Many Lands* (Mayo) European/Scandinavian (Orkney Islands, in a collection of several cultures)
Caves	Origin of wind in Wind Cave, South Dakota	*The Return of the Buffaloes* (Goble) Native American/Lakota
Flint rock	Origin of flint rock pieces Origin of rabbit's split lip	"Flint Visits Rabbit," in *How Rabbit Tricked Otter* (Ross) Native American/Cherokee
Canyons	Origin of Grand Canyon	*A Grand Canyon Journey* (Anderson) Native American/Havasupai and Hualapai
Mountains	Origin of El Capitan	*Two Bear Cubs* (San Souci) Native American/Miwok
	Origin of Mount Susitna, Alaska	*The Sleeping Lady* (Dixon) American/Alaskan
Crater in mountain lake	Origin of Crater Lake	*Coyote in Love* (Dwyer) Native American
Mountains, waterfalls, canyons	Great Smoky Mountains; Hero Twins/El Capitan; Grand Canyon; Niagara Falls	*Between Earth & Sky* (Bruchac) Native American/several nations
Mountains, volcanoes	Origins of Mt. St. Helens, Mt. Hood, Mt. Adams, and the Dalles	"Loo-Wit, the Fire-Keeper," in *Keepers of the Earth* (Caduto/Bruchac) Native American/Nisqually
Volcanic eruptions	Origin of fire in the earth; origin of volcanic eruptions	*Pele* (Varez) Hawaiian
Waterfalls	Origin of Niagara Falls	"The Five Water-Spirits," in *Multicultural Fables and Fairy Tales* (McCarthy) Native American/Canadian (in a collection of several cultures)

Topic	Pourquoi Elements	Title/Author/Culture
Earth/geological formations		
Waterfalls	Origin of Niagara Falls	"The Birth of Niagara Falls," in _How We Saw the World_ (Taylor) Native American/Algonquin
	Origin of White Hair Falls	_The Long-Haired Girl_ (Rappaport) Asian/Chinese
Gift		
Game of chess	Origin of game of chess	_The Token Gift_ (McKibbon) Asian/Indian
Fire, freedom	Gift of fire to the animals from the Great Sky Spirit Gift of freedom to the crow from the Great Sky Spirit	_Rainbow Crow_ (Van Laan) Native American/Lenape
Food	Gift of food from the sky; Why not to waste the gifts of nature	_Why the Sky Is Far Away_ (Gerson) African/Nigerian
Horses	Gift of horses to the people from the Great Chief	_Dance of the Sacred Circle_ (Rodanas) Native American/Blackfoot
	Gift of horses to the people from the Great Spirit	_The Gift of the Sacred Dog_ (Goble) Native American/Great Plains
	Origin of horses to help the people	"How Horses Came into the World," in _How We Saw the World_ (Taylor) Native American/Blackfoot
Music	Gift of song from old mother to the people; Origin of celebration	_The Eagle's Song_ (Rodanas) Native American/Northwest coast
Water	How water came to the new land How the first people came to the present world from the underworld	_The Precious Gift_ (Jackson) Native American/Navajo
Plant life		
Corn	Origin of corn	_People of Corn_ (Gerson) Central American/Mayan
Cranberries	Origin of cranberries	_The Legend of the Cranberry_ (Greene) Native American/Delaware
Medicinal plants	Origin of plants for healing	_Ladder to the Sky_ (Esbensen) Native American/Ojibwa
	Origin of plants for healing	"How Medicine Came," in _The Circle of Thanks_ (Bruchac) Native American
Palm trees	Origin of palm trees	_First Palm Trees_ (Berry) Original
Plants	Origins of many plants	_Hidden Stories in Plants_ (Pellowski) Collection of several cultures

Topic	Pourquoi Elements	Title/Author/Culture
Plant life		
Birch Trees	Why birch trees have stripes	*How the Birch Tree Got Its Stripes* (Ahenakew) Native American/Cree
Plants	Origin of plant life Origin of earth in a watery world Origin of marks on turtle's back	"The Earth on Turtle's Back," in *Keepers of the Earth* (Caduto/Bruchac) Native American/Onondaga
Pumpkins	Origin of pumpkins and other plants	"Pumpkins from Elk Hairs," in *When Jaguars Ate the Moon* (Brusca/Wilson) Native American/Osage
Pussy-willows	Origin of pussywillows Origin of rabbit's short tail, split lip, back legs	"Rabbit's Snow Dance," in *The Boy Who Lived with the Bears* (Bruchac) Native American/Iroquois
	Origin of pussywillows Origin of rabbit's short tail, long ears, hopping legs	"Rabbit and the Willow," in *In a Circle Long Ago* (Van Laan) Native American/Seneca
	Origin of pussywillows Origin of rabbit's short tail	*How Rabbit Lost His Tail* (Tompert) Native American/Seneca
Roses	Why roses have thorns	"How Manabozho Saved the Rose," in *Manabozho's Gifts* (Greene) Native American/Chippewa
Straw-berries	Origin of strawberries	*The First Strawberries* (Bruchac) Native American/Cherokee
Water lilies	Origin of water lilies	*The Silver Cow* (Cooper) European/British Isles (Welsh)
	Origin of water lilies	*Star Maiden* (Esbensen) Native American/Ojibwa
Wild rice	Origin of wild rice planting and harvesting	"Waynabozho and the Wild Rice," in *Native Plant Stories* (Bruchac) Native American/Ojibwa
Yucca	Origin of yucca plant and other plants; Why people must work for their food	"Star Girl Brings Yucca from the Sky," in *When Jaguars Ate the Moon* (Brusca/Wilson) South American/Cayapo of Brazil
Sky phenomena		
Day and night	Origin of night; Origin of morning star; Origin of rooster's crow	*How Night Came from the Sea* (Gerson) South American/Bahia region (African slaves)
	Why there are both nighttime and daytime	"Bear and Coyote," in *Crow & Fox* (Thornhill) Native American/Western Canada (in a collection of several cultures)
	Origin of seasons Origin of night	"How Averiri Made the Night and the Seasons," in *Moon Was Tired of Walking on Air* (Belting) South American/Campas Indians

Topic	Pourquoi Elements	Title/Author/Culture
Sky phenomena		
Day and night	Origin of length of day and night	"The Division of Day and Night," in *Tales of the Shimmering Sky* (Milord) Native American/Creek (in a collection of many cultures)
Day and night, Sun	Origin of proportion of sunlight and night; Origin of the sun's path; Why the sun has rays	*Māui and the Sun* (Bishop) Australian/New Zealand/Polynesian
Moon	Why the moon is in the sky	*Anansi the Spider* (McDermott) African
	How the moon is brought to the sky	*How Raven Freed the Moon* (Cameron) Native American/Northwest coast
	Why the moon has phases Why the moon casts a silvery path on the water Why otters wait for the moon	*Moon and Otter and Frog* (Simms) Native American/Modoc
	Origin of woman's image on the moon	*The Woman in the Moon* (Rattigan) Polynesian/Hawaiian
	Origin of rabbit's image on the moon	"The Rabbit in the Moon," in *The Dial Book of Animal Tales from Around the World* (Adler) Asian/Indian (in a collection of several cultures)
	Origin of man's image on the moon	*Just Rewards* (Sanfield) Asian/Chinese
	Origin of various images on the moon Origin of phases of the moon	*Moontellers* (Moroney) Twelve cultures (in a collection of several cultures)
	Origin of rabbit's image on the moon	"The Hare in the Moon," in *Tales of the Shimmering Sky* (Milord) Asian/Indian (in a collection of several cultures)
	Origin of rabbit's image on the moon Why coyotes howl at the moon	*The Tale of Rabbit and Coyote* (Johnston) Central American/Mexican (Zapotec Indians)
Rainbow	Origin of rainbow as a sign	*How the First Rainbow Was Made* (Robbins) Native American/Northwest
Sky	Why the sky is far away Why people must toil for food	*Why the Sky Is Far Away* (Gerson) African/Nigerian
Sky: going to/from the sky world on a rope or ladder	Origin of fox's face on the moon Why mole hides underground	*Moon Rope* (Ehlert) South American/Peruvian
	Origin of illness and healing	*Ladder to the Sky* (Esbensen) Native American/Ojibwa

Topic	Pourquoi Elements	Title/Author/Culture
Sky phenomena		
Sky: going to/from the sky world on a rope or ladder	Origin of the stars Origin of the ancestor humans	"What Happened When Armadillo Dug a Hole in the Sky," in *Moon Was Tired of Walking on Air* (Belting) South American/Cayapo Indians
	How stories came into the world	*A Story, A Story* (Haley) African (West African)
	Origin of earth in a watery world; Origin of plant life; Origin of personalities; Origin of humans; Origin of life	*The Origin of Life on Earth* (Anderson) African/Yoruba
	Origin of music	*How Music Came to the World* (Ober) Central American/Mexican (Aztec)
Stars	Origin of water lilies from stars	*The Star Maiden* (Esbensen) Native American/Ojibwa
	Origin of the Big Dipper	*Her Seven Brothers* (Goble) Native American/Plains (Cheyenne)
	Origin of the Big Dipper and nearby constellations	"Great Bear," in *Tales of the Shimmering Sky* (Milord) Native American/Mimac (in a collection of several cultures)
	Origin of the Pleiades	"The Boastful Star," in *Tales of the Shimmering Sky* (Milord) Polynesian (in a collection of several cultures)
	Origin of the Pleiades and nearby stars	*The Lost Children* (Goble) Native American/Siksika
	Origin of the Southern Cross	"Mirrabooka," in *Dreamtime* (Oodgeroo) Australian/Aboriginal
	Origin of the morning star	*The Orphan Boy* (Mollel) African/Masai
	Why stars are arranged in shapes of the animals	*Coyote Places the Stars* (Taylor) Native American/Wasco
	Why the stars are scattered in the sky; Why there is confusion among people	*How the Stars Fell into the Sky* (Oughton) Native American/Navajo
	Origin of the Milky Way	*The Story of the Milky Way* (Bruchac/Ross) Native American/Cherokee
	Origin of the Milky Way	*Elinda Who Danced in the Sky* (Moroney) European/Estonian
	Origin of the stars	"What Happened When Armadillo Dug a Hole in the Sky," in *Moon Was Tired of Walking on Air* (Belting) South American/Cayapo Indians

Topic	Pourquoi Elements	Title/Author/Culture
Sky phenomena		
Stars	Origin of the ox, the beast of burden, from the stars	*How the Ox Star Fell from Heaven* (Hong) Asian/Chinese
	Origin of bear from sky constellation; Why bears hibernate	*When Bear Came Down from the Sky* (de Gerez) European/Finno-Ugric
	Origin of the morning star	"Lighting the Way," in *Tales Alive!* (Milord) Australian/Aboriginal (in a collection of several cultures)
	Origin of the morning star	*Bawshou Rescues the Sun* (Yeh) Asian/Chinese (Han)
Stars, moon	Origin of the morning star Origin of the stars Origin of the moon	*How Night Came from the Sea* (Gerson) South American/Bahia region/African slaves
Sun and moon	Why the sun and moon are in the sky	*Why the Sun & Moon Live in the Sky* (Daly) African/Nigerian
	Why the sun and moon are in the sky	"Why the Sun and Moon Live in the Sky," in *How Many Spots Does a Leopard Have?* (Lester) African/Efik-Ibibio (in a collection of several cultures)
	Origin of the sun and moon	*The Fifth and Final Sun* (Greger) Central American/Mexican (Aztec)
	Why the sun and moon do not burn and freeze the earth	"The Traveling Sky Baskets," in *Moon Was Tired of Walking on Air* (Belting) South American/Apanyekra Indians, Ramkokamekra Indians
	Why the sun has rays and the moon does not	"Why Sun Has a Headdress and Moon Has None," in *Moon Was Tired of Walking on Air* (Belting) South American/Ramkoka mekra Indians
	Why the sun makes a daily path across the sky Origin of the moon	"Ra, the Shining Sun God," in *When the World Was Young* (Mayo) African (East African) (in a collection of several cultures)
Sun, obtaining the sun	How the sun is brought to this side of the earth; Why the sun makes rays across the sky	"How Grandmother Spider Stole the Sun," in *Keepers of the Earth* (Caduto/Bruchac) Native American/Muskogee (Creek)
	How the sun is brought to this side of the earth Why the sun makes rays across the sky	"Grandmother Spider," in *The Dial Book of Animal Tales from Around the World* (Adler) Native American/Cherokee (in a collection of several cultures)
	How the sun is brought to this side of the earth	*Grandmother Spider Brings the Sun* (Keams) Native American/Cherokee
	How the sun is found again	*How the Sun Was Brought Back to the Sky* (Ginsburg) European/Slovenian
	How the sun is brought to the world for all the people and animals	*Raven* (McDermott) Native American/Northwest coast

Topic	Pourquoi Elements	Title/Author/Culture
Sky phenomena		
Sun, obtaining the sun	How Raven brings the sun to the world for all people; Origin of the moon; Origin of earth in a watery world; Origin of animals and plants	*Raven's Light* (Shetterly) Native American/Northwest coast
	How Raven brings back the sun Why sea gulls walk as though their feet are sore	"Raven and the Sea Gull," in *Echoes of the Elders* (Smith) Native American/Kwakiutl
	How Raven wins back the sun; How Loon gets her mournful cry; Why deer lose their antlers each fall; Why bears hibernate each winter	*How the Loon Lost Her Voice* (Cameron) Native American/Northwest coast
	How the sun is brought back to the world Origin of the sun's rays	"Greeting the Sun: A Maushop Story," in *Four Ancestors* (Bruchac) Native American/Wampanoag
	How the sun is brought back to the world	*How Snowshoe Hare Rescued the Sun* (Bernhard) Native American/Yuit Eskimo
	How the sun is brought back to the world; Why bears hibernate	*The Day Sun Was Stolen* (Oliviero) Native American/Haida
	How the sun is brought back to the world	"Raven and the Pea-Pod Man," in *When the World Was Young* (Mayo) Native American/Eskimo (in a collection of several cultures)
Spider/Insect characteristics—behavioral and physical		
Butterflies	Why butterflies flutter about	*Coyote and the Laughing Butterflies* (Taylor) Native American/Tewa
Grass-hoppers, Dragonflies	Origin of grasshoppers' long hind legs Why dragonflies have exoskeletons	"The War Party," in *Lessons from the Animal People* (Thomason) Native American
Hornets, blackflies, mosquitoes, stinging insects	Origin of stinging insects	"Beaver Face," in *Echoes of the Elders* (Smith) Native American/Kwakiutl
Mosquitoes	Origin of mosquitoes	*The Windigo's Return* (Wood) Native American/Ojibwa
	Origin of mosquitoes	*The Legend of the Windigo* (Ross) Native American/Algonquian
	Why mosquitoes buzz in people's ears	*Why Mosquitoes Buzz in People's Ears* (Aardema) African

Topic	Pourquoi Elements	Title/Author/Culture
Spider/Insect characteristics—behavioral and physical		
Spiders	Origin of spider web weaving How spiders catch flies	"How Spider Caught Flies," in *In a Circle Long Ago* (Van Laan) Native American/Wishosk
	Origin of spider web weaving	*Anansi Goes Fishing* (Kimmel) African
	Spider web as origin of rays of sun	"How Grandmother Spider Stole the Sun," in *Keepers of the Earth* (Caduto/Bruchac) Native American/Muskogee (Creek)
	Why spiders have a narrow-waisted shape	"Why Anansi Has a Narrow Waist," in *African-American Folktales for Young Readers* (Young/Young) African (in a collection of several cultures)
Survival		
Death	Origin of people killing each other	*The Man Who Knew Too Much* (Lester) African/Baila of Zambia
	Origin of death	"The Origin of Death," in *Keepers of the Earth* (Caduto/Bruchac) Native American/Siksika (Blackfoot)
	Why people and tortoises must die; Why stones do not die	"Tortoise's Big Idea," in *When the World Was Young* (Mayo) African/Nupe of Nigeria (in a collection of several cultures)
	Why people must die Why pythons change their skin	"A Journey of Life and Death," in *African Folktales & Activities* (Orlando) African/Mende of Sierra Leone
Fire	How fire is obtained for the people and animals; Why fire can be got by rubbing sticks together	*Fire Race* (London) Native American/Karuk
	How fire is obtained for the people and animals; Why animals stare at fire from the woods	*How Iwariwa the Cayman Learned to Share* (Crespo) South American/Yanomami
	How fire is obtained for the people; Why fire can be got by rubbing sticks together	*Coyote and the Fire Stick* (Goldin) Native American/Pacific Northwest
	How fire is obtained for the people	"How Humans Claimed Fire," in *African Folktales & Activities* (Orlando) African/San of Botswana
	How fire is obtained for the animals Why fire can be got by rubbing sticks together Origin of the route of the Grande Ronde River	"How Beaver Stole Fire," in *In a Circle Long Ago* (Van Laan) Native American/Nez Percé

Topic	Pourquoi Elements	Title/Author/Culture
Survival		
Fire	How fire is obtained for the people Origin of colorful tail of rainbow bird	*Rainbow Bird* (Maddern) Australian/Aboriginal
	Origin of fire as a gift to the animals	*Rainbow Crow* (Van Laan) Native American/Lanape
	Origin of fire from lightning	*Rainbow Bridge* (Wood) Native American/Chumash
	How fire is obtained for the people	"How Manabozho Stole Fire," in *Manabozho's Gifts* (Greene) Native American/Chippewa
	How fire is obtained for people and animals Why swallows nest near chimneys	"Blue Jay and Swallow Take the Heat," in *When Birds Could Talk & Bats Could Sing* (Hamilton) African American
	How fire is obtained for the animals Origin of crying, hugging Origin of markings on antelope, leopard, elephant, spider, conk	"Leelee Goro," in *Misoso* (Aardema) African/Temne
	How fire was obtained for the animals Why fire can be got by rubbing sticks together	"Catch It and Run!" in *When the World Was Young* (Mayo) Native American/Karok (in a collection of several cultures)
Food	Origin of fruit trees and food plants from the food tree	"Mouse and Tapir," in *Crow & Fox* (Thornhill) South American (in a collection of several cultures)
	Origin of corn, the source of life	*People of Corn* (Gerson) Central American/Mayan
	Why people must work for food	*Why the Sky Is Far Away* (Gerson) African/Nigerian
	Origin of food Why rain is needed to grow food	*The Legend of Food Mountain* (Rohmer) Central American/Mexican
	Origin of wild rice harvesting	"How Manabozho Found Rice," in *Manabozho's Gifts* (Greene) Native American/Chippewa
	Why people must work for their food; Origin of yucca plant and other plants	"Star Girl Brings Yucca from the Sky," in *When Jaguars Ate the Moon* (Brusca/Wilson) South American/Cayapo of Brazil
Greed	Why people must not take more than they need	"Raven and the Pea-Pod Man," in *When the World Was Young* (Mayo) Native American/Unalit Eskimo (in a collection of several cultures)
	Why people must not take more than they need	*Why the Sky Is Far Away* (Gerson) African/Nigerian

Topic	Pourquoi Elements	Title/Author/Culture
Survival		
Greed	Why people must not be greedy Why the sea is salt	"The Magic Millstones," in *When the World Was Young* (Mayo) European/Icelandic (in a collection of several cultures)
Illness & healing	Origin of ginseng for healing	*The Rabbit's Escape* (Han) Asian/Korean
	Origin of bear medicine (healing arts)	"The Bear," in *Full Moon Stories* (Turtle) Native American
Illness & healing, death	Origin of sickness and death Origin of plants for medicine and healing	*Ladder to the Sky* (Esbensen) Native American/Ojibwa (Chippewa)
Water	How water came to the new land How the first people came to the present world from the underworld	*The Precious Gift* (Jackson) Native American/Navajo
Work	Why people must get rain to get food	*The Legend of Food Mountain* (Rohmer) Central American/Mexican (Aztec)
	Why people and oxen must toil on the land for their food	*How the Ox Star Fell from Heaven* (Hong) Asian/Chinese
	Why people must work for their food	*Why the Sky Is Far Away* (Gerson) African/Nigerian
	Why people must work for their food	*Two Bad Boys* (Haley) Native American/Cherokee
	Why there is confusion in the world	*How the Stars Fell into the Sky* (Oughton) Native American/Navajo
	Why people must be resourceful	*Uncegila's Seventh Spot* (Rubalcaba) Native American/Lakota
Water, ocean life		
Dolphins	Origin of dolphins	*The Rainbow Bridge* (Wood) Native American/Chumash
Ocean tides	Origin of ocean tides	*James the Vine Puller* (Stiles) South American/Brazilian (Arawak)
Sea	Origin of the sea; Origin of sea creatures; Origin of four islands	*How the Sea Began* (Crespo) Central American/Caribbean (Taino)
	Origin of the sea; Origin of sea creatures; Origin of island and its forests	*The Golden Flower* (Jaffe) Central American/Caribbean (Taino)
	Why the sea is salty	"Why the Sea Is Salty," in *Stories from the Sea* (Riordan, comp.) European/Finnish (in a collection of several cultures)

Topic	Pourquoi Elements	Title/Author/Culture
Water, ocean life		
Sea	Why the sea is salty	*Why the Sea Is Salt* (French) European/Norwegian
Sea creatures	Origin of whales, seals, walruses, fish, etc.	"Sedna and King Gull," in *The Dial Book of Animal Tales from Around the World* (Adler) Native American/Inuit (in a collection of several cultures)
	Origin of sea creatures	"The Old Man of the Sea," in *Stories from the Sea* (Riordan, comp.) Siberian (in a collection of several cultures)
Whales	Origin of narwhal's tusks	"How the Narwhal Got Its Tusk," in *The Girl Who Dreamed Only Geese* (Norman) Native American/Inuit
Weather phenomena		
Lightning	Origin of lightning from a snake	*Uncle Snake* (Gollub) Central American/Mexican
Lightning & thunder	Why lightning and thunder live in the sky	*The Story of Lightning & Thunder* (Bryan) African (West African)
	Origin of lightning and thunder	*How Thunder and Lightning Came to Be* (Harrell) Native American/Choctaw
	Origin of lightning	*The Rainbow Bridge* (Wood) Native American/Chumash
	Origin of thunder and lightning	*Stolen Thunder* (Climo) European/Norse
Rain	How rain is made with sun, steam, clouds, wind Why bats hide and fly at night	*A Promise to the Sun* (Mollel) African
	Origin of rain from fig tree	*The Tree That Rains* (Bernhard) Central American/Mexican (Huichol Indians)
	Origin of rain after drought Why there is a need for balance between sun and clouds	*The Fish Skin* (Oliviero) Native American/Cree
	Origin of rain	"The Fish at Dragon's Gate," in *Mythical Birds & Beasts of Many Lands* (Mayo) Asian/Chinese (in a collection of several cultures)
Rainbow	Origin of the rainbow	"After the Rain," in *Tales of the Shimmering Sky* (Milord) African/Kenyan (in a collection of several cultures)
Rain, lightning	Why rain is needed to grow food Where lightning comes from	*The Legend of Food Mountain* (Rohmer) Central American/Mexican

Topic	Pourquoi Elements	Title/Author/Culture
Weather phenomena		
Rain, lightning, thunder	Origins of rain, thunder, lightning	*The Woman in the Moon* (Rattigan) Polynesian/Hawaiian
Rain, storms	Origins of rain and storms	"The Green-Clawed Thunderbird," in *Mythical Birds & Beasts of Many Lands* (Mayo) Native American/Blackfoot (in a collection of several cultures)
Rain, storms, thunder, rainbows	Origins of rain, rainbows, thunder, and storms	*Marriage of the Rain Goddess* (Wolfson) African/Zulu
Seasons	Origin of seasons Origin of night	"How Averiri Made the Night and the Seasons," in *Moon Was Tired of Walking on Air* (Belting) South American/Campas Indians
	Origins of winter and spring	*Peboan and Seegwun* (Larry) Native American/Ashinabe Ojibwa
	Origin of length of seasons Why winter does not stay too long Origin of rain, wind, fog	"The Long Winter," in *In a Circle Long Ago* (Van Laan) Native American/Slavey
	How the Chinook wind is restored so that spring comes	*When Bear Stole the Chinook* (Taylor) Native American/Siksika (Blackfoot)
	Origin of winter Origin of spring	*Shingebiss* (Van Laan) Native American/Ojibwa
	How summer came to the north	"The Capture of Summer," in *Little Folk* (Walker) Native American/Abenaki
	Origin of weather of the twelve months	"The Twelve Months," in *Tales of the Shimmering Sky* (Milord) European/Slovakian (in a collection of several cultures)
	Origin of winter and spring	"Spring Defeats Winter," in *Keepers of the Earth* (Caduto/Bruchac) Native American/Seneca
	Origin of winter and spring	*Ishtar and Tammuz* (Moore) Asian/Babylonian
Seasons, snow	Origin of snow and wind	*Rainbow Crow* (Van Laan) Native American/Lenape
	Origin of snowflakes Origin of blossoms & fruits of spring, summer, fall	*Lao Lao of Dragon Mountain* (Bateson-Hill) Asian/Chinese
Snow	Origin of first snowfall in Alaska	*The Sleeping Lady* (Dixon) American/Alaskan
Snow, wind, thunder	Origin of wind, snow, and thunder	*The Miser on the Mountain* (Luenn) Native American/Nisqually

Topic	Pourquoi Elements	Title/Author/Culture
Weather phenomena		
Tornadoes	Origin of the tornado	"The First Tornado," in *How We Saw the World* (Taylor) Native American/Kiowa
	Why tornadoes never come back How Orekeke became a healer	"When Orekeke Wrestled Tornado," in *Moon Was Tired of Walking on Air* (Belting) South American/Teheulces Indians
Wind	Origin of the sea wind and breezes	"Sea Wind," in *Stories from the Sea* (Riordan, comp.) African/Senegalese (in a collection of several cultures)

Chapter 4

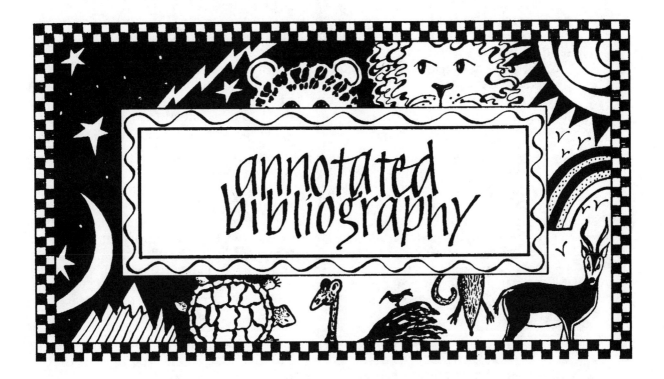

The books in this chapter are arranged by continental areas; some areas are further broken down by country or culture. The last two categories are collections that include two or more cultures and originally written pourquoi stories. Books may also be accessed in chart format in chapter 3, "Story Themes and Topics." The chart provides topical and thematic associations between stories and across cultures.

AFRICAN

Aardema, Verna. *How the Ostrich Got Its Long Neck: A Tale from the Akamba of Kenya.* Illustrated by Marcia Brown. New York: Scholastic, 1995.
Crocodile awakens with a toothache and tries to coax various animals to pull his tooth. Fish Eagle keeps warning, "Don't do it!" but short-necked Ostrich is moved by Crocodile's crying. Once Ostrich's head is inside Crocodile's mouth, Crocodile clamps down. Ostrich pulls and pulls to get free, stretching his neck out. This tale also explains why the ostrich stays in the bush, far from the river. Humorous illustrations and accessible text make this a good choice for younger children.

———. *Misoso: Once Upon a Time Tales from Africa*. Illustrated by Reynold Ruffins. New York: Apple Soup Books, 1994.

A collection of 12 tales representing great variety in types of tales and tribal cultures. The first, "Leelee Goro," is a notable pourquoi tale; it explains the origins of several animals' traits and also crying and hugging. The animals need fire, so they take turns going to the hut of a woman and her daughter, Leelee Goro, to ask for it. The woman tells each animal that he must fight her daughter for the fire. Each time, the mother sings a magic song, and the girl throws the animal high into the air. As each animal lands in defeat, it gets a lasting trait: antelope's cough, leopard's spots, elephant's tusks, spider's crawling legs, and conk snail's shell. Conk wins fire by leaving some slippery slime, which trips the girl. This brings crying into the world, and the mother's hug brings comfort to stop the crying. Use this collection as a read-aloud or as a storytelling source.

———. *Why Mosquitoes Buzz in People's Ears: A West African Tale*. Illustrated by Leo Dillon and Diane Dillon. New York: Dial Press, 1975.

A mosquito is annoying Iguana, who puts sticks in his ears to shut out Mosquito's voice. When a python talks to Iguana, he appears to ignore the snake. Agitated, the python slithers off, upsetting the animals in a chain reaction culminating in the accidental death of an owlet. Mother Owl is too sad to wake the sun. The animals have a council, and King Lion puts together the story piece by piece. When they determine that the mosquito started it all, they decide to punish her. This satisfies Owl, who wakes the sun. Meanwhile, the mosquito buzzes about with a guilty whine and gets what she deserves—a slap. The story, illustrations, and humor of this older Caldecott winner continue to delight.

Anderson, David A./Sankofa. *The Origin of Life on Earth: An African Creation Myth*. Illustrated by Kathleen Atkins Wilson. Mt. Airy, MD: Sights Productions, 1991.

A mood of reverence and mysticism pervades this telling of the creation of the earth and its peoples. Olorun, the supreme being, lives in the sky world with his many orishas (assistants). One orisha, Obatala, has the urge to go to the watery world below and start a new world. With the help of Olorun and the others, he descends to the water world on a golden chain. He brings sand, seeds, and a special egg. He spreads sand to create the earth, and the bird from the egg infuses personality into the soils from which the humans will be made. He shapes people out of the soil, and during a period of carelessness (from drinking wine, which he vows not to do again), he creates some bodies with disabilities. He later becomes the guardian of people with disabilities. Olorun contributes the essence of life to the new people. It is interesting that this Yoruba myth has the same motif as many Native American creation myths: coming down from the sky world to a watery world below. Because of its mystical, serious tone, this story is more suited to middle and upper grades.

Arkhurst, Joyce Cooper. *The Adventures of Spider: West African Folktales*. Illustrated by Jerry Pinkney. Boston: Little, Brown, 1964.

A collection of six pourquoi and trickster tales suitable for independent reading practice by middle grades. Most stories are versions of tales also found in more lavishly illustrated picture book formats, allowing for comparison opportunities. These include "How Spider Helped a Fisherman" (*Anansi Goes Fishing* by Kimmel), "How Spider Got a Bald Head" (*Anansi* by Gleeson), and "Why Spiders Live in Dark Corners" ("tar baby" motif found in many tales including *How Turtle's Back Was Cracked*, by Ross). All are told in an easy, humorous style.

Bryan, Ashley. *The Cat's Purr*. Illustrated by the author. New York: Atheneum, 1985.

Cat and Rat used to be best friends, farming together. Cat's uncle gives Cat a special drum, telling him no one else may play it, and shows Cat the soft *purrum* sound it makes when stroked. Jealousy sets Rat in motion. He fakes a stomachache so he can stay behind and play the drum while Cat toils in the fields. When Cat discovers his friend's betrayal, he opens his mouth in rage. Rat stuffs the drum down Cat's throat. Now, when a cat is stroked, you can hear the gentle sound of the drum. Young students listen eagerly to this story, and those in middle grades can read it independently. Hear Ashley Bryan tell this story on the audiotape (next entry).

———. *Poems & Folktales*. Belfast, ME: Audio Bookshelf, 1994. Audiocassette.
    Ashley Bryan tells his stories with his unique rhythmic style. Four stories and a selection of his poems round out a lively performance. Pourquoi tales include "The Cat's Purr" and "The Story of Lightning and Thunder."

———. *The Story of Lightning & Thunder*. Illustrated by the author. New York: Jean Karl, 1993.
    Ma Sheep Thunder and Son Ram Lightning live in the village. They bring the rains when needed, especially when a drought comes. The village honors them with a harvest festival, where Son Ram Lightning gets rambunctious, showing off and making mischief. Because of his trouble making, the King moves Ma Sheep Thunder and Son Ram Lightning out past the edge of town. Son shows off again, starting a fire with his sparks and causing destruction. The King decrees that for safety's sake, Thunder and Lightning can no longer dwell on earth. They go up the mountain and into the sky.

Butler, Andrea. *Mr. Sun and Mr. Sea: An African Legend*. Illustrated by Lily Toy Hong. Glenview, IL: GoodYearBooks, 1994.
    A very simple telling in the format of an independent-reader "little book" for first graders (Let Me Read, Level 3). Mr. Sun often visits Mr. Sea. One day, Mr. Sun invites Mr. Sea and his children to his house. The house floods with water and sea creatures and Mr. Sun must jump up into the sky, where he stays to this day. Use this book when lower-level reading material is needed. Compare to the more detailed telling by Niki Daly (entry after next).

Cabral, Len. *Nho Lobo and Other Stories*. Cranston, RI: Story Sound Productions. Audiocassette.
    Cabral tells a humorous story, "How the Rabbit Lost His Tail," which also explains why dogs chase rabbits. The tape also includes two trickster stories and some songs.

Daly, Niki. *Why the Sun & Moon Live in the Sky*. Illustrated by the author. New York: Lothrop, Lee & Shepard, 1995.
    In this Nigerian tale, Sun and Moon live on a mountain top in a huge house. Moon stays at home; Sun visits many of the wonders on earth. Sun wishes Moon could see the splendor of his friend the Sea. Sea is invited, along with all her children, but soon Sea and her creatures are flooding the mountain top home. Sun and Moon must flee to the sky. Moon is so annoyed that she moves to the dark side of the earth.

Dayrell, Elphinstone. *Why the Sun and the Moon Live in the Sky*. Illustrated by Blair Lent. Boston: Houghton Mifflin, 1968.
    A simple, easy-to-read version of the same story as Niki Daly's, previous entry. Because it is a Caldecott winner, it is often found on library shelves and is still available from the publisher. Accessible to first-grade readers.

Gerson, Mary-Joan. *Why the Sky Is Far Away: A Nigerian Folktale*. Illustrated by Carla Golembe. Boston: Little, Brown, 1992.
    All ages respond to this tale with its powerful message about the value of nature's gifts and the consequences of wastefulness. The sky used to be near the ground. When people were hungry, they would just reach up, grab a piece of the sky, and eat. They become wasteful, however, taking more than they need and discarding the rest. The sky gets tired of this and decrees that people must no longer waste or the sky's gifts

would no longer be theirs. People are careful, for a while. Then one particularly greedy woman gets careless, and lightning strikes. The sky moves up high, out of reach. This tale explains not only why the sky is far away, but also why people must toil for their food. The bright illustrations add to the appeal of this book.

Greger, C. Shana. *Cry of the Benu Bird: An Egyptian Creation Story*. Illustrated by the author. Boston: Houghton Mifflin, 1996.

Egyptian gods create the earth, sunlight, and humans. The Benu Bird symbolizes protection from the dark and is the sun god Re's soul. In the beginning, when the world is a still ocean, the Benu Bird arises to light the world. The creator Atum begins his work. Land begins to form from the god Shu. Atum makes humans from his tears to take care of the gods. Several other gods play their parts. Because of the complexity of the gods and their roles, this myth is for older grades.

Haley, Gail E. A *Story, A Story: An African Tale*. New York: Atheneum, 1970.

In this well-known Caldecott winner, Anansi wants all the stories of the world, but they are kept by Nyame, the Sky God. Nyame assigns Anansi three seemingly impossible tasks, which Anansi accomplishes through his tricky plotting. He is awarded the box of stories and opens it, allowing the stories to float up and out to the whole world.

Kimmel, Eric. *Anansi Goes Fishing*. Illustrated by Janet Stevens. New York: Holiday House, 1992.

A humorous trickster tale with a pourquoi ending. Anansi, pictured as a spider, goes fishing with Turtle. Turtle tells Anansi that he can choose to be the one who does the work, or he can choose being tired. Anansi, alarmed, does not want to get tired. He becomes irritated when he realizes he is doing all the work. His skill at weaving fishnets is still evident today in all spiders' webs.

Knutson, Barbara. *How the Guinea Fowl Got Her Spots: A Swahili Tale of Friendship*. Illustrated by the author. Minneapolis: Carolrhoda Books, 1990.

Guinea Fowl and Cow are friends, and they watch out for each other as they forage for food. Twice, Guinea Fowl sees Lion stalking Cow, and she creates a distraction, saving her friend's life. In gratitude, Cow spatters drops of her creamy white milk all over Guinea Fowl, creating a camouflage. Text is large and easy to read for primary students.

Lester, Julius. *The Knee-High Man and Other Tales*. Illustrated by Ralph Pinto. New York: Dial Press, 1972.

A collection of six short tales. "Why Dogs Hate Cats" is a particularly humorous story of Cat and Dog, who jointly own a piece of ham. After Dog sings "Our Ham" and Cat sings "My Ham," Cat climbs a tree and eats the whole thing. An effective read-aloud for primary and middle grades.

———. *The Man Who Knew Too Much: A Moral Tale from the Baila of Zambia*. Illustrated by Leonard Jenkins. New York: Clarion Books, 1994.

A somewhat frightening story. A woman takes her baby with her to work in the fields, where it cries and cries. She can't get her work done because she needs to keep comforting the child. An eagle flies down and sits on the baby. The mother is terrified that her child is injured or worse, but the baby is fine and does not cry after the eagle's visit. This happens again the next day. That evening, the woman tells her husband, who doesn't believe her. Next day, he follows her out to the field and hides with his bow and arrows. When the eagle comes, the man shoots at the eagle but accidentally kills his child. The eagle tells the man that from now on, people will kill each other.

Martin, Francesca. *The Honey Hunters: A Traditional African Tale.* Illustrated by the author. Cambridge, MA: Candlewick Press, 1992.

In this short, cumulative story, a boy hears the birdsong of the honey guide and follows. Soon other animals (rooster, leopard, antelope, lion, etc.) follow, too. When they find the honey, the boy divides the honeycomb among pairs of animals, and soon they are all fighting. "The damage is done"; now there is fighting among those animals. But there is still harmony between the honey guide and other animals. The text is readable for younger students.

McCoy, Sarah. *Why the Sky Is Far Away and Other African/African American Tales.* Cleveland, OH: Wonderstorms, 1991. Audiocassette.

An energetic, compelling storyteller, Sarah McCoy tells six lively tales. Pourquoi tales include "Why the Sky Is Far Away" and "Why the Spider Has a Small Waist."

McDermott, Gerald. *Anansi the Spider: A Tale from the Ashanti.* Illustrated by the author. New York: Henry Holt, 1972.

This tale, featuring the trickster Anansi, explains how the moon was placed in the sky. Anansi gets into trouble, and his six sons use their clever and unique powers to rescue him. Back home that night, Anansi finds a glowing orb and wants to give it to the son who rescued him. He asks the god Nyame to help him decide. Nyame and Anansi see that each son played an equal part. Nyame places the ball of light into the sky for everyone's benefit; it is the moon. Simply written in large text for primary grades.

McNeil, Heather. *Hyena and the Moon: Stories to Listen to from Kenya.* World Folklore Series. Englewood, CO: Libraries Unlimited, 1995. Audiocassette.

Expertly performed by storyteller Heather McNeil, these six tales have an authentic dramatic effect. McNeil's use of an African accent and voices for her characters contribute to a professional and entertaining storytelling experience for all ages. "Hyena and the Moon" tells about a group of hyenas piled on top of each other in an attempt to reach the moon; their failed attempt results in their pushed-in hind legs and their slinking behavior.

Mollel, Tololwa M. *The Flying Tortoise: An Igbo Tale.* Illustrated by Barbara Spurll. New York: Clarion Books, 1994.

Both a trickster tale and a pourquoi tale, this story features a trick played on the trickster. Mbeku the tortoise used to have a smooth shell, and like many tricksters, he is always scheming to get food. When he hears that the birds have been invited to a feast in the Skyland, he convinces the birds that he should go, too, because he can provide special advice on Skylanders. He gets the birds and his friend Lizard to make him some wings to fly to Skyland. He tells the birds that Skylanders like special names, and his new name is "Aaallll-of-You." At the Skylanders' feast, the King says that the feast is for "Aaallll of you." Tortoise explains to the birds that he, the spokesman, is fed first. Tortoise eats all the food, and the Skylanders vanish in the mist. The infuriated birds tear off Tortoise's feathers so he can't fly home. He cries piteously, and the birds agree to help him get home by constructing a pile of soft things for him to land on. One bird overhears Tortoise calling all the birds fools, so in countertrickster fashion, the birds construct a pile of hard things instead. When Tortoise lands on the pile, he cracks his shell. His embarrassment is the reason tortoises pull their heads inside their shells. Text and illustrations are very appealing to primary and middle grades.

———. *The Orphan Boy: A Maasai Story.* Illustrated by Paul Morin. New York: Clarion Books, 1990.

Stunning illustrations convey the mood of this sober tale of the origin of the planet Venus. An old man notices a star is missing from the skies. He meets an orphan boy and offers to share his home. The boy completes difficult chores with the cattle herd in little time. A drought burns up the grass and water supply. The boy says he has his father's power over drought, but it must remain secret. Despite the scorching landscape, the boy helps the herd remain fat and full of milk. Eventually, the old man's curiosity gives way to betrayal of the trust they shared. He spies on the boy, and as a consequence, the boy is transformed into a star, and the herd is dry and emaciated. Now the boy appears as Venus (the "Orphan Boy") at dawn to take the herd out and again in the evening to bring it back.

———. *A Promise to the Sun: An African Story*. Illustrated by Beatriz Vidal. Boston: Little, Brown, 1992.

During a scorching drought, the birds congregate to pick someone to find rain. Their cousin Bat must go. Bat flies off on an unfolding series of missions, beseeching Moon, who sends her to the Stars, then the Clouds, who say they need Winds, who say they need Sun to bring steam to the sky. Sun agrees to help, but for a favor in return. Sun wants a nest in the treetops to rest each evening. Bat gets the birds to eagerly agree to the task, but after the renewing rains come, they lose interest in their promise. Bat cannot get the birds to help and so hides from Sun in fear ever after. This useful, well-told story explains why bats live in caves and also provides scientific knowledge about the formation of rain. Readable by second-graders and up.

Orlando, Louise. *African Folktales & Activities*. New York: Scholastic Professional Books, 1995.

A professional resource book, this volume contains 13 tales to read aloud. Each is accompanied by two or three pages of cultural information and suggestions for activities and curricular tie-ins. Most are origin tales of African animals, including the giraffe, elephant, stork, leopard, and zebra. Two tales explain why humans have to die. "How Humans Claimed Fire" is amusing and ends with a statement of cultural pride for the San people. A useful collection for grades 2–5.

Rosen, Michael. *How Giraffe Got Such a Long Neck . . . and Why Rhino Is So Grumpy*. Illustrated by John Clementson. New York: Dial Books for Young Readers, 1993.

In this tale from East Africa, Giraffe was not tall in the beginning. But then there is drought and nothing is left to eat except for the green, juicy leaves that are too high in the trees. Giraffe and Rhino seek the help of Man, who promises to prepare a magic herb. Rhino forgets to show up, and Giraffe waits, but then eats all of it. Giraffe's neck grows long, and she eats the leaves. Rhino is angry with Man and with Giraffe and remains so to this day. Easy text and appealing colorful illustrations make this tale especially accessible for primary grades.

Sierra, Judy. *The Mean Hyena: A Folktale from Malawi*. Illustrated by Michael Bryant. New York: Lodestar Books, 1997.

Mean Hyena, playing a trick on Tortoise, picks him up, sticks him in a tree, and leaves him stranded there. The next day, Tortoise decides to make something of his predicament, so from his place in the tree, he offers to give the animals new coats. He paints stripes on the plain white zebra and spots on the plain leopard, both of whom live in the bush so the others will leave them alone in their beauty. Hyena now wants a new coat, too, so Tortoise takes the opportunity to trick him. He dabs blobs of sticky tree gum all over his fur; this attracts sticks and burrs and forms mats of fur. When others laugh at him, Hyena laughs back, as though he meant to make everyone laugh. The story ends with a lesson to the listener to think before playing tricks or it could also happen to you. A simple story for primary grades, with pourquoi explanations for the traits of several animals.

Souhami, Jessica. *The Leopard's Drum: An Asante Tale from West Africa*. Illustrated by the author. Boston: Little, Brown, 1995.

The lowly tortoise tricks the leopard and wins a hard shell in this tale. Proud Osebo, the leopard, has a large drum that is coveted by all the animals. Nyame, the

Sky-God, wants the drum so badly he promises a reward to the animal who can get it. Many animals try but are intimidated by Osebo's fearsome presence. The little soft-shelled tortoise tricks Osebo into proving he can fit inside his own drum. The tortoise seals up the drum with a pot and takes it to the Sky-God. When Nyame offers his reward, the tortoise asks for a tough, hard shell as protection from the larger animals. Short, simply told, and brightly colored, this book is accessible to primary-grade readers.

Troughton, Joanna. *How Stories Came into the World: A Folk Tale from West Africa.* Illustrated by the author. New York: Peter Bedrick Books, 1990.
This book contains five stories within a story. It begins and ends with the story of mouse, who goes everywhere and gets all the stories. She weaves the stories into a story picture. On the last page, Lightning, angry at being banished, breaks Mouse's door, and the stories go out into the world. Between the two pages of the simple story of Mouse are five other stories, simply told but not clearly set off from each other: "Why the Sun and Moon Live in the Sky," "How All Animals Came on Earth," "Why the Hippo Lives in Water," "Rubber Girl," and "The Story of Lightning and Thunder." These are usable as additional material. Students who need simpler reading levels could benefit from this book. For example, some students could read Ashley Bryan's *Story of Lightning & Thunder* while students with special needs read the two-page Troughton version.

Williams, Sheron. *And in the Beginning. . . .* Illustrated by Robert Roth. New York: Atheneum, 1992.
This is a creation myth set in small, dense text. It explains, in a colloquial storytelling style, the origins of the world and particularly of the first human beings. Mahtmi, the Blessed One, takes the darkest, richest soil from Mt. Kilimanjaro and fashions a man, Kwanza, to his liking. While this man starts on his adventures, the Creator also makes people out of red soil and sand. Kwanza gets a little jealous, so Mahtmi gives him one more sign of his favored status: tightly curled hair. A skillful read-aloud would make the most of this myth for upper grades.

Wolfson, Margaret Olivia. *Marriage of the Rain Goddess: A South African Myth.* Illustrated by Clifford Alexander Parms. New York: Marlowe, 1996.
The central plot of this Zulu myth is the rain goddess's search for and testing of a man to become her partner; it also features this goddess as the source of rain, rainbows, thunder, and storms. Mbaba Mwana Waresa, the rain goddess beloved by earth people, is in search of a partner to share her joy in life. She transforms herself into a ray of sunlight and then a cloud, looking over both gods and mortals. She decides on Thandiwe, a cattle-herder, but he must be tested. She sends him a dream, in which he meets his betrothed, and she devises a challenging test of recognition. During a worrisome thunderstorm, he must wait for his bride outside the bridal hut he has built, and then a beautiful, decorated woman approaches him. He knows that the lovely woman is not his betrothed and chooses a woman in rags and ashes. The story and the author's notes provide interesting details on bead ornament love letters and other Zulu customs. For upper grades.

AFRICAN AMERICAN

Hamilton, Virginia. *Her Stories: African American Folktales, Fairy Tales, and True Tales.* Illustrated by Leo Dillon and Diane Dillon. New York: Blue Sky Press, 1995.
This handsome collection offers a wide array of folktale types, all featuring female heroes. One is a notable pourquoi tale: "Woman and Man Started Even." God created Woman and Man equal in strength, words, and other ways. One day, Man gets tired of having a woman he can't win over. So he goes to God and asks to have more strength than Woman. God gives it to him, and this makes Woman furious. This anger gives the

devil an opportunity to influence Woman. He tells her to get a set of "power keys" near the pearly gate. Then she must lock the doors to the kitchen, bedroom, and children's room because Man is always wanting to eat, sleep, and pass his name on through his children. Man becomes angry, but God can't take away what he has given and Woman isn't interested in making a trade with Man. Thus Man still has the strength, but Woman still has the power. Told with a sophisticated humorous flair, this feminist tale is effective with older students.

———. *When Birds Could Talk & Bats Could Sing: The Adventures of Bruh Sparrow, Sis Wren, and Their Friends.* Illustrated by Barry Moser. New York: Blue Sky Press, 1996.
  Rich in all aspects—language, illustrations, pourquoi elements—this is a collection to treasure. Hamilton's African American storytelling style is masterful in its humor, dialect, and characterizations. Moser's illustrations cause spontaneous gasps of awe and laughter. These eight tales, all featuring birds, are filled with numerous pourquoi explanations and state a sassy moral at the end. In "Still and Ugly Bat," Missy Bat used to have seven layers of feathers and was very beautiful. She is so haughty, however, she decides she cannot be like other birds and sheds any feathers that resemble theirs. Soon she is skin and bone. The moral is "Stars do fall!" In "Blue Jay and Swallow Take the Heat," two birds steal fire from Firekeeper, and we learn why swallows build nests near chimneys. "Bruh Buzzard and Fair Maid" explains Buzzard's bald head. "Cardinal and Bruh Deer" is a bloody explanation for cardinal's color. Save this volume for reading aloud to groups to fully enjoy the dialect and art. Although young children could enjoy some of these tales, the subtle and sophisticated humor is better suited to middle and older grades.

Young, Richard Alan, and Judy Dockrey Young. *African-American Folktales for Young Readers: Including Favorite Stories from African and African-American Storytellers.* Little Rock, AR: August House 1993.
  Many of the 31 stories from the oral tradition in this collection are credited to well-known storytellers. Both African and African American, these short tales can be told or read aloud to students. "Why Anansi has a Narrow Waist" is especially successful. A good resource for teachers and librarians.

AMERICAN

Dixon, Ann. *The Sleeping Lady.* Illustrated by Elizabeth Johns. Anchorage, AK: Alaska Northwest Books, 1994.
  Giant people known for their peaceful ways used to live near Cook Inlet, Alaska. A young man and woman have to wait to be married because of an impending attack by warriors. Susitna waits on a hill while her man goes off to battle, and after days, she goes to sleep there and becomes a mountain. This sad tale explains the origin of Alaska's first snowfall, and the origin of the mountain still known as the Sleeping Lady. According to the best of the reteller's research, this is a modern-day folk legend and probably not actually a native legend. The text is easily accessible to middle grades.

Doucet, Sharon Arms. *Why Lapin's Ears Are Long: And Other Tales from the Louisiana Bayou.* Illustrated by David Catrow. New York: Orchard Books, 1997.
  Three humorous tales from the Cajun and Creole tradition. Compère Lapin (French for Brother Rabbit) is the cunning trickster in these tales with pourquoi elements. In "Why Lapin's Ears Are Long," Compère Lapin wants to be bigger so he can get some respect. He asks Madame Tortue, who is learning how to do *gris gris* (magic) to work a spell on him. Hoping to be rid of him, she first requires three impossible tasks, which Lapin accomplishes by trickery. When she still can't perform the magic, she pulls on his ears until they are long and then stumbles backward into her own conjure pot.

In "Why Lapin's Tail Is Short," Lapin plays two tricks and gets caught short in the end. He offers to teach sleepy Alligator what "trouble" is. He pours syrup between Alligator's toes to attract the wasps and bees to Alligator's softest flesh. Later he starts a bragging contest about who has more relatives and gets the alligators to line up across the bayou to count them. He just wants an easy bridge to the other side of the water, but at last, Compère Alligator snaps at Rabbit's fine long tail, leaving it a mere puff of fur to this day. Cajun dialect and humorous illustrations make this a read-aloud delight for all ages.

Reneaux, J. J. *Gumbo Ya-Ya.: Cajun Stories & Songs*. Music by Cayenne. Comer, GA: Story Theater South, 1989. Audiocassette.
    J. J. Reneaux's distinctive style of music and storytelling is strongly Cajun. Two entertaining stories are pourquoi tales suited to child audiences: "Why Onions Make Us Cry" and "Why Alligator Hates Dog" (see the next entry).

———. *Why Alligator Hates Dog: A Cajun Folktale*. Illustrated by Donnie Lee Green. Little Rock, AR: August House LittleFolk, 1995.
    Cajun pronunciations of four words enhance the flavor of this telling. M'su Cocodrie (Mr. Alligator) has the respect of everyone except that taunting, barking dog. But one day, Dog forgets himself in the frenzy of chasing a rabbit and finds himself face-to-face with M'su Cocodrie. Dog slyly diverts M'su Cocodrie by promising him the "juicy scraps" fed to him by Man. Once Alligator gets up on Man's porch, Dog barks for Man, who beats M'su Cocodrie with a broom. M'su Cocodrie gets away and lies in wait for Dog to this very day. Told briefly, simply, and with Cajun flair, this is a humorous trickster/pourquoi tale. Students can hear Reneaux tell this tale on her tape *Gumbo Ya-Ya* (previous entry).

ASIAN

Babylonian

Moore, Christopher. *Ishtar and Tammuz: A Babylonian Myth of the Seasons*. Illustrated by Christina Balit. New York: Kingfisher Books, 1996.
    Ishtar is the all-powerful, sometimes terrible, goddess of creation. When she sends Tammuz, her son, to live on earth, plants and animals spring forth and grow in abundance. Ishtar becomes jealous of the attentions given to Tammuz, so she has him killed. He descends to the underworld, which is ruled by Ishtar's sister, Allatu. With Tammuz gone, the plants of the earth wither and die, and the people hunger. Their prayers reach Ishtar, who relents and goes to the dark underworld to fight her sister and regain Tammuz for the earth. Allatu allows Ishtar and Tammuz to leave her kingdom on the condition that Tammuz returns for six months every year. This six-month cycle becomes the cycle of the seasons; while Tammuz walks the earth, spring and summer bring life and growth. The elegant illustrations, the joy of springtime, and the reunion of mother and son soften the harshness of this ancient myth. For middle and upper grades.

Chinese

Bateson-Hill, Margaret. *Lao Lao of Dragon Mountain*. Illustrated by Francesca Pelizzoli. London: De Agostini Editions, 1996.
    An old woman named Lao Lao earns the admiration of people for miles around for her Chinese paper cuts. The greedy emperor hears of her art and sends his guards to capture her and imprison her in a high tower on a mountain top. There, she is ordered to make "jewel" papercuts from a huge stack of paper. As she toils, fashioning diamond-shaped designs, the Ice Dragon senses something is wrong. The dragon picks up the old woman, and she rides on his back, scattering her diamond paper cuts. The

paper turns into sparkling snowflakes. She continues to ride on the dragon's back to this day, cutting papers that cover springtime trees and summer fields with flowers and autumn trees with fruits and nuts. The tower atop the mountain is replaced by three ice pillars, which are the transformed bodies of the guards and the emperor. This tale, containing both pourquoi and transformation elements, is readable by second- or third-graders and works as a read-aloud for all ages.

Han, Carolyn. *Why Snails Have Shells: Minority and Han Folktales from China.* Translated by Jay Han. Illustrated by Li Ji. Honolulu: University of Hawaii Press, 1993.
A collection of 20 tales of minority cultures of China, including Tibetan, Yao, Yi, and others. Each is one or two pages long, with a colorful illustration. Many are pourquoi tales, with a few trickster tales and cautionary tales; all feature animals. Many of these tales are variant tellings of similar motifs found in other cultures, such as "The Flying Frog" (compare to "How Turtle Flew South for the Winter" in *Keepers of the Earth*). These amusing tales are suitable for independent reading by older grades, and listening by younger grades.

Hong, Lily Toy. *How the Ox Star Fell from Heaven.* Illustrated by the author. Morton Grove, IL: Albert Whitman, 1991.
The origin of the ox as an agricultural work animal is explained by this Chinese tale. The oxen used to live with the Emperor of All the Heavens and lie about in silk. The people on earth work hard to grow food, often going as long as five days without a meal. The Emperor of All the Heavens decrees that people can eat at least once every three days. He dispatches Ox Star with the message, but Ox Star inverts the message to: "eat three times a day." The Emperor is angry and banishes the oxen to earth, where to this day they toil in the fields. Now the people have a part of heaven on earth, helping them to get their work done so they can eat. Delightfully told and illustrated, this tale can be read by primary and middle-grade students.

Rappaport, Doreen. *The Long-Haired Girl: A Chinese Legend.* Illustrated by Yang Ming-Yi. New York: Dial Books for Young Readers, 1995.
The virtue of selflessness, as seen in the deeds of a brave young woman, is explained in this tale about the origins of the waterfall known as White Hair Falls. During a terrible drought, a young woman named Ah-mei trudges up a mountain in search of herbs and finds some green leaves. When she pulls the long turnip out, sweet, cold water trickles out. After she drinks, the turnip places itself back in the hole, and the God of Thunder roars his anger at Ah-mei. He threatens to kill her if she tells anyone about his secret spring. Ah-mei returns to her mother's home and worries daily about the village's desperate need for water. Her complexion turns pale, and her hair turns white. Finally, after watching the anguish of an old man, Ah-mei takes action. She calls out to the villagers, leading them to the secret place in the mountain. They chop at the hole until water races out in a torrent. The God of Thunder takes Ah-mei away. She begs the god to let her see her mother one last time; then she will return as commanded to lay at the bottom of the waterfall, where the water will fall on her body forever. As she is walking back to fulfill her orders, the old man stops her and shows her a stone statue that looks like her. He takes Ah-mei's white hair and magically transfers it to the statue. He places the statue at the bottom of the falls, and Ah-mei's hair grows back beautiful and black. Ah-mei is safe, and from then on, the people have the cold waters of White Hair Falls. This book is for middle grades.

Sanfield, Steve. *Just Rewards, or Who Is That Man in the Moon & What's He Doing Up There Anyway?* Illustrated by Emily Lisker. New York: Orchard, 1996.
In this Chinese tale, two farmers, one kind and one greedy, are neighbors. The kind farmer finds an injured sparrow and nurses it back to health while the neighbor scoffs. But the sparrow rewards the kind farmer with a seed that grows into a watermelon vine. The melons contain jewels, coins, and pearls. The greedy neighbor is jealous. He

sets out to find an injured sparrow, and when he cannot, he wounds one on purpose. He takes it home, reminding it to reward him. The sparrow gives a seed to this farmer, but his vine grows straight up to the moon. He climbs it, and the vine withers, exiling him on the moon. The stingy man's face can be seen on the moon to this day. Appealing to all ages; independent reading by middle grades.

Yeh, Chun-Chan, and Allan Baillie. *Bawshou Rescues the Sun: A Han Folktale*. Illustrated by Michelle Powell. New York: Scholastic, 1991.

Both transformational and pourquoi elements are found in this complex plot told with spare, efficient language. A man and his wife contentedly wait for the birth of their first child, but their serenity ends when a strong wind comes and steals the sun. The King of the Devils is behind it, and the young man decides to find the sun. He journeys for months with a golden phoenix while, back home, his wife gives birth to their son, Bawshou. When the phoenix returns alone, the wife sees a new star in the sky—her husband, the morning star. Suddenly, the baby, Bawshou, transforms into a grown, giant man. Guided by the phoenix, he embarks on harrowing adventures in search of the sun. Eventually, Bawshou finds the kingdom of the Devils, and he finds where they hid the sun. Bawshou and the phoenix pull the sun out, and the King of the Devils is burned out of the sky. This tale explains the origin of the morning star, as well as the pink-gold cloud seen at dawn, the Phoenix. No source notes.

Young, Ed. *Cat and Rat: The Legend of the Chinese Zodiac*. Illustrated by the author. New York: Henry Holt, 1995.

The Emperor announces a race for the animals; each of the first 12 to cross the finish line will be named as a year in the Chinese calendar. Cat and Rat are good friends and want to win. They collaborate and talk Buffalo into letting them ride on his back. When the race takes them across the river, Rat pushes Cat off into the water. She struggles while, one by one, 12 animals finish the race before her. This is why cats hate rats, and why there is no Year of the Cat in the zodiac.

Hmong

Xiong, Blia. *Nine-in-One Grr! Grr! A Folktale from the Hmong People of Laos*. Adapted by Cathy Spagnoli. Illustrated by Nancy Hom. San Francisco: Children's Book Press, 1989.

Tiger, hoping for babies, visits the god Shao in the sky. She humbly tells Shao of her loneliness and asks how many cubs she will have. Shao tells her she will have nine in one year and cautions her to remember what he has said. As Tiger travels back to earth, she chants a song as a memory aid. When Bird finds out this news, she goes to Shao to complain that nine cubs per year will soon eat all the birds. Shao says his word is good as long as Tiger remembers. Bird goes back to earth and distracts Tiger so that she forgets "nine-in-one"; she replaces the chant with "one-in-nine." This is why we don't have very many tigers today. The large, simple text is readable by younger students. The bright illustrations enhance the story.

Indian

McKibbon, Hugh William. *The Token Gift*. Illustrated by Scott Cameron. Toronto: Annick Press, 1996.

This tale of trickery recounts the origins of the game of chess and dramatizes a mathematical principle as well. An old man who lives in a castle has the title Rajrishi, the "wise one." He recalls that as a young man, he pursued his love of games to the point of devising his own game of strategy. He fashioned game pieces on a board with 64 squares and called it Chaturanga. It became popular all over the country, and its production made him wealthy. Now, the King summons the Rajrishi to the palace, commending the Rajrishi for his invention and asking him to name a suitable reward. At first, the Rajrishi tells the King he has no wants, but the King is insulted, demanding that the Rajrishi name a reward. The Rajrishi tells the King he would like one grain of rice for the first square of the game board, two grains for the second, four, eight, and so on. As the request is fulfilled, it becomes evident that a doubling of the rice 64 times results in more rice than there is in the world. The King, distressed that he cannot fulfill the promise, steps down and installs the Rajrishi as king. The Rajrishi-as-king makes one decree: reinstate the original king as King. Why? Because the Rajrishi tricked the King with cleverness, and he believes that honor is more important.

Japanese

Hamilton, Morse. *Belching Hill.* Illustrated by Forest Rogers. New York: Greenwillow Books, 1997.
   Humorously told and brightly illustrated with numerous ogres, this Japanese tale explains the source of the rumbling from a hill named Geppuyama. An old woman lives happily, cooking rice dumplings for herself and her pig. One day, a hot dumpling drops and rolls down the hill. A hand comes out from a hole and grabs the dumpling. The old woman crawls into the hole to demand it back. Rude and dull-witted ogres live down there, and they demand that she cook more dumplings for them. They give her a pinch of rice and a magic spoon. Her dumplings sate them, and while they sleep, she escapes. With her new pot and magic spoon, she continues to make dumplings, and once in a while, one rolls down the hill to the ogres. For primary grades.

Korean

Han, Suzanne Crowder. *The Rabbit's Escape.* Illustrated by Yumi Heo. New York: Henry Holt, 1995.
   Written bilingually with Korean characters and western English. Illustrations are fanciful and surreal. The Dragon King of the Sea is ill and can be cured only with the fresh raw liver of a rabbit. The sea creatures have never seen a rabbit, and travel to land is dangerous. Turtle is selected for the mission, and when he brings Rabbit to the sea kingdom, Rabbit states he has not brought his liver with him. He tricks his way back to land, where a god gives Turtle some ginseng roots to cure the King. This trickster tale doubles as a pourquoi tale, explaining the origin of the use of ginseng as a medicine.

Heo, Yumi. *The Green Frogs: A Korean Folktale.* Illustrated by the author. Boston: Houghton Mifflin, 1996.
   Two green frogs are exceptionally disobedient, mischievous, and contrary as their tired mother tries to raise them. When she grows old and ill, she asks her sons to bury her near the stream. For once, they obey her. But then it rains long and hard, and the frogs cry and worry that their mother's grave will wash away. Both humorous and startlingly sad, this tale explains why frogs sit and cry by the stream when it rains and why disobedient children in Korea are called green frogs.

Vietnamese

Garland, Sherry. *Why Ducks Sleep on One Leg.* Illustrated by Jean Tseng and Mou-sien Tseng. New York: Scholastic, 1993.
   When the world was newly created, all animals were pleased except three ducks who had one leg each. They write a petition to the Jade Emperor, the ruler of all spirits, and ask the guardian spirit of the village to intercede on their behalf. They negotiate a deal to receive the extra three legs from his incense burner. Because these legs are made of gold, they are admonished to take care of them. The ducks use the golden legs well, but every night they tuck their legs under their wings so no one will steal them.

AUSTRALIAN/NEW ZEALAND/POLYNESIAN

Australian/New Zealand

Berndt, Catherine. *Pheasant and Kingfisher: Originally Told by Nganalgindja in the Gunwinggu Language.* Illustrated by Arone Raymond Meeks. Greenvale, NY: Mondo, 1994.

Two men are traveling through the land: Bookbook the Pheasant and Bered-bered the Kingfisher. They find a place to stay by a bamboo-lined stream. One day, a man visits, warning the two that they are on land belonging to a group of men who are coming to kill them. The two defend themselves with spears but are outnumbered, so they grow feathers and fly away. The warriors on the ground turn to stone and can still be seen today. Told in simple text, this tale explains the origins of the pheasant and kingfisher.

Bishop, Gavin. *Māui and the Sun: A Maori Tale.* Illustrated by the author. New York: North-South Books, 1996.

In this New Zealand telling of a Polynesian tale, the sun races across the sky too fast. Māui and his brother need the sun to move across the sky more slowly so that they have more daylight to go fishing. Māui talks his brothers into helping him catch the sun. They gather flax to make ropes and travel for weeks until they get to the pit where the sun sleeps. They stretch their rope net over the pit and hold tight as the sun rises. Māui beats on the sun with his enchanted weapon (the jawbone of his grandmother). The sun cries and reveals his secret name. Now that Māui knows the sun's secret name, he has the power to make the sun move slowly, but things are not quite right, yet. The sun goes so slowly, it stays out for months, scorching everything. Māui gets angry. He ties a rope around the sun and ties the other end around the moon, obtaining a balance of night and day. This humorous tale is well suited to middle grades.

Maddern, Eric. *Rainbow Bird: An Aboriginal Folktale from Northern Australia.* Illustrated by Adrienne Kennaway. Boston: Little, Brown, 1993.

Long ago in the Dream Time, Crocodile Man had one thing that no one else had: fire. Bird Woman wants fire, but Crocodile Man is too mean. Once, when Crocodile Man yawns a great yawn, Bird Woman swoops down and grabs some firesticks and gives fire to the people. She puts the firesticks in her tail and becomes the Rainbow Bird.

Meeks, Arone Raymond. *Enora and the Black Crane.* Illustrated by the author. New York: Scholastic, 1991.

A young man named Enora lives with his people in the rain forest. Enora witnesses magical colors among the birds and kills a crane to bring proof to his family. Black feathers grow on Enora's body, and he becomes a black crane. The Australian Aboriginal artist/author bases his original story on folk elements passed on to him from his Aboriginal grandfather.

Oodgeroo. *Dreamtime: Aboriginal Stories.* Illustrated by Bronwyn Bancroft. New York: Lothrop, Lee & Shepard, 1993.

The first half of this collection presents childhood stories from the Aboriginal author's life. The second half has folktales of the old Dreamtime and the new Dreamtime. A strength of this collection is that it is a source of authentic folktales illustrated by an Aboriginal artist. A notable story is "The Beginning of Life," in which a female Rainbow Serpent awakes and starts shaping the earth and bringing the animals forth. The water for the earth comes from the awakening frogs, who were storing it. The short "Mirrabooka" is about the Southern Cross constellation. Text is dense, and some tellings are complex.

Trezise, Percy, and Mary Haginkitas. *Black Duck and Water Rat.* Illustrated by the authors. Milwaukee, WI: Gareth Stevens, 1988.

Originally published in Australia, this tale relates the biological origin of the unusual platypus, that is, a marriage between a black duck and a water rat. In the Dreamtime, Mara the black duck lives with others of her species in a lily lagoon. One day, she wanders too far and is captured by a water rat, who forces her to marry him and live with him. Later, she escapes back to her own people. When it is time for the black ducks to lay eggs, Mara lays only two, which hatch into different creatures. They have webbed feet and duck bills, but they have furry animal bodies. The duck people reject the strange creatures, so Mara takes them far away to a muddy pool in the rain forest, where they play and eventually have families of their own. Simply told in large typeface, this tale would work with primary and intermediate grades.

Hawaiian

Rattigan, Jama Kim. *The Woman in the Moon: A Story from Hawai'i.* Illustrated by Carla Golembe. Boston: Little, Brown, 1996.

This Polynesian tale not only explains the origins of the image on the moon and rain and storms but also takes up issues of women's rights and freedoms. Hina makes the finest tapa cloth in Hawai'i, cloth so beautiful that people stop making their own, wanting only hers. She is so busy making tapa, she cannot attend the feasts and festivals. Most husbands cook and help prepare tapa bark, but Hina's husband is either gone or lazy. She tires of her husband's demands and also questions why many things in the community are *kapu,* or forbidden to women: certain foods, praying or eating with their husbands, going with them on adventures. She wanders the island to search for a place where she would be happier. She tries a mountain top (too cold), climbs a rainbow (too hot), and finally climbs a moon bow to the moon, where she can watch over the things she loves. Thus Hina's image is on the moon. Children say that when it rains, Hina is sprinkling joy, and thunder and lightning are the sounds of her work making tapa cloth. This thoughtful, well-illustrated story would work with all ages.

Varez, Dietrich, and Pua Kanaka'ole Kanahele. *Pele: The Fire Goddess.* Illustrated by Dietrich Varez. Honolulu: Bishop Museum Press, 1991.

This classic myth tells of the birth and adventures of Pele, the Goddess of volcanoes. Pele is born to a large family; her brothers and sisters play in the water, but Pele is different, avoiding the water. Her uncle Lonomakua is the keeper of the flame and knows that Pele will someday keep the fire that burns underground. Pele's older sister has many arguments with her, holding Pele responsible for hot spots on the island. The family decides to send Pele to another island, but some of her siblings come with her. Lonomakua gives Pele a magic stick to help her locate the right fire island. Finally she finds a volcanic island and names it Hawai'i. On this new island, Pele has many adventures, challenges, interactions with gods and magic, and a dream about a man who dances the hula. She falls in love with this man, Lohi'au, a chief on the island of Kaua'i, and sends a sister, Hi'iaka, to bring him to her. Hi'iaka's journey is long and difficult, and when she reaches the island of Kaua'i she finds out that Lohi'au is dead. Hi'iaka performs a ritual that brings Lohi'au back to life. Since Hi'iaka's journey takes longer than expected, Pele grows suspicious and impatient and starts a volcanic eruption. The lava flows over the home of another sister and turns her to stone. When Hi'iaka returns and finds her sister turned to stone, she embraces Lohi'au, making Pele even more furious. Pele sends lava and flames over Lohi'au. Finally, both sisters cool off and realize the damage that their anger has wrought. Pele brings Lohi'au back to life, and the sisters let him choose his mate. He chooses Hi'iaka. Pele is sad, but keeps her promise to keep peace with her sister. Pele remains on the island of Hawai'i to this day. Because the story is long and complicated, it is a good choice for middle and upper grades, and it is well worth the effort.

Williams, Julie Stewart. *Māui Goes Fishing*. Illustrated by Robin Yoko Burningham. Honolulu, HI: University of Hawaii Press, 1991.

The clever boy, Māui, brings the islands of Hawaii into being in this trickster/ pourquoi tale. He fishes daily with his three brothers but never catches anything. After much teasing by his brothers, Māui starts catching fish: He slyly slips the hooks out of his brothers' catches and claims them as his own. His brothers tire of this and refuse to take him with them anymore. So Māui makes a magic fishhook and asks to go with his brothers once again. When the fishing line begins to pull, he instructs his brothers to paddle home steadfastly and not look back to see what is on the line. When they feel the pull, it is powerful and the sea turns rough. Māui yells to keep paddling, but then the brothers look back to see what's going on. At that moment the line breaks. What they see is land! Because the brothers look too soon, the land does not rise fully out of the water; it remains as several peaks instead of a land mass. Māui has fished up the peaks that are the islands of Hawaii. For primary and middle grades.

CENTRAL AMERICAN

Caribbean

Crespo, George. *How the Sea Began: A Taino Myth*. Illustrated by the author. New York: Clarion Books, 1993.

When the islands of Puerto Rico, Cuba, Jamaica, and the Dominican Republic/Haiti were still four mountains on land, the village's best hunter, Yayael, was out hunting one day. The goddess of hurricanes came, and Yayael disappeared in the storm. His revered bow and arrows were found, however, and brought back to his home. They are now kept in a gourd hanging from the ceiling in case Yayael's spirit visits. Without Yayael, there is never enough food for the villagers. One night, Yayael's family takes the gourd down, and fresh fish pour out. For once, everyone's stomach is full. The next day, four boys take the gourd down. In their hurry to put it back up, they do not tie it securely, and it falls and breaks. Out floods water—tasting like tears and full of ocean creatures—that turns the four mountains into islands. With the sea nearby, the people finally have enough to eat. The author's note gives valuable information on the Taino people and the significance of "burying" Yayael's belongings. For middle grades. Compare with Jaffe's telling of the Taino origin tale of the sea.

Gleeson, Brian. *Anansi*. Illustrated by Steven Guarnaccia. Rowayton, CT: Rabbit Ears Books/Saxonville, MA: Picture Book Studio, 1992.

An easy Jamaican style, punctuated by "Yah, mahn," makes this an entertaining read-aloud. The volume presents two trickster Anansi stories; the first doubles as a pourquoi tale. In the first tale, Tiger has all the stories, and tiny, insignificant Anansi is jealous. He wants the stories, so Tiger gives him a dangerous task: He must bring Tiger the big, big snake. Anansi appeals to Snake's pride to trick him into capture, so he gets the stories. Compare this telling to *A Story, A Story* by Haley.

Jaffe, Nina. *The Golden Flower: A Taino Myth from Puerto Rico*. Illustrated by Enrique O. Sánchez. New York: Simon & Schuster Books for Young Readers, 1996.

This unique creation myth of the origin of the sea and the island and forests of Puerto Rico is simply told and beautifully illustrated. Long ago, when there was no water, only a dry mountain on a plain, a child collects seeds and plants them atop the mountain, where they grow into a forest. One plant grows into a vine with a stunning golden flower. The blossom develops into a growing yellow ball—a pumpkin. Some people are afraid of what's inside. Two men want to own it, fighting over it until it breaks open. Out pours the sea and its creatures. People fear the rising waters and flee to the mountain top; the waters stop when they reach the forest at the top of the mountain. Now the people have water, fish to eat, and the beautiful tropical island known as Puerto Rico. End notes provide valuable information on the history of the people and the tale. Readable by second grade and up. Compare with the earlier entry on Crespo's tale of the sea's origin.

Shute, Linda. *Rabbit Wishes*. Illustrated by the author. New York: Lothrop, Lee & Shepard, 1995.
    In this Cuban tale, *Tio Conejo* (Uncle Rabbit) complains to the Creator that he wishes he were bigger. *Papa Dios* considers the request, assigning three difficult tasks to the rabbit. The rabbit uses trickery to accomplish the tasks. He is rewarded only with longer ears, which he has to this day. Both a trickster tale and a pourquoi tale, the book includes a Spanish glossary and background information.

Temple, Frances. *Tiger Soup: An Anansi Story from Jamaica*. Illustrated by the author. New York: Orchard, 1994.
    This delightful trickster/pourquoi tale reveals a double trick: both stealing the food and passing on the blame. Anansi lures Tiger away from the soup he is making, ostensibly to teach Tiger to swim. Once Tiger is in the water, Anansi slurps down Tiger's soup. Anansi then goes on to teach the little monkeys a fun little song: "We ate the tiger soup!" Tiger angrily chases the monkeys into the trees, and this is why monkeys live in trees to this day. This book makes for an entertaining read-aloud, especially for primary students.

Latin American

Aldana, Patricia, ed. *Jade and Iron: Latin American Tales from Two Cultures*. Translated by Hugh Hazelton. Illustrated by Luis Garay. Toronto: Groundwood Books, 1996.
    Complex retellings, dense text, and some adult themes make this collection suited to older students. For example, "The Legend of Manioc" explains the origin of the staple food of the native peoples of southern Brazil, but it comes from a rejected daughter who asks to be buried alive. "When Mountains Became Gods" tells of the transformation of people into mountains, but it involves a complex situation with lovers. "The Gods of Light" is a usable tale of the origin of flint and fire. A strength of this book is the assembling of tales from the two main cultures that struggle to coexist in Latin America: the native and the Hispanic.

Mayan

Albert, Burton. *Journey of the Nightly Jaguar: Inspired by an Ancient Mayan Myth*. Illustrated by Robert Roth. New York: Atheneum Books for Young Readers, 1996.
    One line of free verse per page provides a poetic explanation for the jaguar's spots. At sunset, the largest raindrops turn into the marks on the jaguar. A short read and appealing artwork for all ages.

Ehlert, Lois. *Cuckoo: A Mexican Folktale* (Cucú: Un Cuento Folklórico Mexicano). Translated by Gloria de Aragón Andújar. Illustrated by the author. San Diego: Harcourt Brace, 1997.
    Enhanced by Ehlert's characteristic folk-art-inspired illustrations, this tale traces the deed that changes the colorful, tuneful Cuckoo into a black bird with her limited song. The other birds view Cuckoo as too self-absorbed to help collect the seeds they need to save for next year's planting. While the others rest in preparation for this chore, Cuckoo detects a fire that will destroy the seeds. Mole tells Cuckoo she can save the seeds by dropping them in his hole. Cuckoo's brave work leaves her feathers and voice

scorched, but the food supply is safe. The tale ends with the lesson that you can't judge a bird by its feathers. Also told in Spanish, this easy-to-read text is accessible to primary grades.

Gerson, Mary-Joan. *People of Corn: A Mayan Story*. Illustrated by Carla Golembe. Boston: Little, Brown, 1995.

    This creation myth tells of the origin—and fine-tuning—of human beings and the origin of life-giving corn. The tale also includes the flood motif, in which a flood cleanses the earth of unsatisfactory human beings so that the creators can start over. The two creation gods make the earth and its creatures but are still trying to fashion creatures who will voice appreciation, love, and praise for creation. The first humans are made of wood and have no hearts. So the gods send floods to eradicate the imperfect world. On the highest mountain, they find a field of corn planted by Grandmother of Light. The two gods gather and grind the corn, and from this corn they mold the "first true people." Afterward, the gods still need to adjust humans so that they cannot see everything beyond. But humans can still see deeply into the mysteries of the world when they sleep. Although this story is told in simple language, its mystical nature makes it more suited to upper grades.

Lattimore, Deborah Nourse. *Why There Is No Arguing in Heaven: A Mayan Myth*. Illustrated by the author. N.p.: Harper & Row, 1989.

    A story of the creation of the earth and human beings. Several Mayan gods argue and try to create beings to worship them. The mud people and the wood people, the first two attempts, do not satisfy and are flooded away. The Maize God steps forth, assembling the right variety and balance of materials and combining these with spirits. These new beings work hard and worship the gods. The Maize God takes his place next to Hunab Ku, the first Creator. The illustrations reveal Lattimore's research into Mayan art and stonework. The telling is straightforward, but because of the complexity of the gods and their interactions, this is a book for upper grades.

Mexican

Ada, Alma Flor. *The Lizard and the Sun: An Old Mexican Folktale*. Translated by Rosalma Zubizarreta. Illustrated by Felipe Dávalos. New York: Doubleday Books for Young Readers, 1997.

    This simple bilingual story tells of a time when the sun disappears. The animals search but cannot find it. Finally, a lizard sees a glowing rock. With the help of the emperor and a woodpecker she investigates, and together they find the sun is sleeping behind the rock. In order to stay fully awake, the sun needs music and dancing. So the people have a great festival at the highest pyramid. From that time, the people have had an annual dancing feast to keep the sun shining. This also explains why lizards still bask in the sun. For primary grades and up.

———. *Mediopollito: Half-Chicken*. Illustrated by Kim Howard. New York: Doubleday Books for Young Readers, 1995.

    With light-hearted humor, accessible text, and bright, stylized illustrations, this is a Mexican tale of the origin of the weathervane. One newly hatched chick is different from the rest: one leg, one wing, one eye. Although he grows up somewhat vain, he is helpful, which saves his life at one point. When the wind returns a favor by blowing him up to a rooftop, out of harm's way, he stays there, pointing the direction of his friend the wind. Written bilingually in Spanish.

Bernhard, Emery. *The Tree That Rains: The Flood Myth of the Huichol Indians of Mexico*. Illustrated by Durga Bernhard. New York: Holiday House, 1994.

    An overall reverence for the earth and its life-giving food pervades this myth. Watakame works hard clearing, planting, and tending his fields. Something is definitely odd, because every night for four nights, the trees he chops down grow right back. Watakame discovers a small, old woman rising out of the earth. She is Great-Grandmother Earth, who makes everything grow. She warns Watakame that a flood is coming because the people no longer honor the gods. She instructs him to make a boat and get five grains of each kind of corn, beans, squash seeds, five hot coals, and his dog. She rides the boat with Watakame for five years. After the flood, Great-Grandmother Earth goes back to making things grow, and Watakame plants his seeds. A huge fig tree spouts water for the crops. Watakame finds out that inside the skin of his faithful dog is a woman. She becomes his wife, and they have many children. The people remember that Great-Grandmother Earth has given them the tree that rains, showering the crops.

Gollub, Matthew. *Uncle Snake.* Illustrated by Leovigildo Martinez. New York: Tambourine Books, 1996.

Both transformation and pourquoi elements come into play in this somewhat frightening tale from Mexico. Ignoring the warnings of his elders, a boy ventures into a cave. The cave is full of snakes, who say they are enchanted children. When the boy returns to his family, his head has changed into a snake head. The father takes him to healers and a worker of magic. The boy must wear a mask and dance every year at the fiesta. Twenty years later, he is told to stay in the cave for three days and take off the mask. He turns into a snake body with a human head. Then he takes off into the sky as lightning. For middle or upper grades.

Greger, C. Shana. *The Fifth and Final Sun: An Ancient Aztec Myth of the Sun's Origin.* Illustrated by the author. Boston: Houghton Mifflin, 1994.

Organized into one- or two-page chapters, this Aztec myth recounts the rivalries between the various gods to be the sun. The fourth sun is a woman, the Goddess of the Waters, and during this time, the earth becomes green, water-filled, and Man and Woman are created. The God of the Night becomes jealous of the Goddess's success and insults her; she cries a flood that destroys all but two people. Finally, a contest of self-sacrifice decides the birth of the Fifth and Final Sun, as well as the Moon. The complexities of plot and names make this a choice for older students.

Johnston, Tony. *The Tale of Rabbit and Coyote.* Illustrated by Tomie dePaola. New York: G. P. Putnam's Sons, 1994.

This delightful folktale of the Zapotec Indians incorporates many motifs from the African American Brer Rabbit stories and Native American and Mexican trickster stories. Rabbit repeatedly tricks, torments, and foils Coyote, who keeps thinking he will finally capture and devour him. Humorous text and illustrations keep the reader or audience chuckling. Rabbit's final trick is to climb a ladder to the moon and hide the ladder. Coyote can't pursue Rabbit anymore, and this is why Coyote howls at the moon and also why people in Mexico say you can still see the image of Rabbit in the moon.

McDermott, Gerald. *Musicians of the Sun.* Illustrated by the author. New York: Simon & Schuster Books for Young Readers, 1997.

This brief, somber tale from the Aztecs relates the transformation of a world from a dark, silent, joyless place to a world filled with light and music. The Lord of the Night is determined to give the people the joy of dancing, light, laughter, and music. He sends the Wind to go to the house of the Sun and rescue the four musicians: Red, Yellow, Blue, and Green. The Wind is fearful of the Sun, a warrior who uses fire against others. The Lord of the Night gives Wind three objects (shield, thunder, clouds) to arm and protect him on his quest. Wind confronts Sun and finally gains the advantage by unleashing clouds and thunder. The musicians are brought to earth, and they bring such happiness that even Sun pours down its light on the world. Compare to the telling by Ober (next entry). For all ages.

Ober, Hal. *How Music Came to the World: An Ancient Mexican Myth*. Illustrated by Carol Ober. Boston: Houghton Mifflin, 1994.

Two Aztec gods, the sky god and the wind god, want music to come to the earth. The wind god (Quetzalcoatl) travels to the sky world on a rope bridge to take the musicians from the Sun. The wind god creates a storm which overpowers the Sun's hold on the musicians. The earth is relieved and beautified by music. A fairly simple telling, suitable for second grade and up.

Rohmer, Harriet. *The Legend of Food Mountain/La Montaña del Alimento*. Illustrated by Graciela Carrillo. San Francisco: Children's Book Press, 1988.

The people have just been created by the god Quetzalcoatl. They need food. The gods don't know what to give them. Then a huge ant brings kernels of corn, which she got from far-off Food Mountain. The people are nourished and strengthened. Quetzalcoatl tries unsuccessfully to move Food Mountain to the people. The gods decide that the Lightning God must open the mountain up. Finally, it opens, but the rain dwarfs steal all the food. From then on, the people must get rain to bring them food. The story is simply told and has a powerful message.

Rohmer, Harriet, and Mary Anchondo. *How We Came to the Fifth World/Cómo Vinimos al Quinto Mundo: A Creation Story from Ancient Mexico*. Illustrated by Graciela Carrillo. San Francisco: Children's Book Press, 1988.

This story recounts the cyclical flourishing and destruction of the Aztec people. In each of the four historical periods, the people live peacefully with plenty of food until they become greedy and combative and are destroyed by one of the gods—the first time by floods, the second epoch by wind, the third by fire, and the fourth by total darkness. At the end of each period, only one good man and woman are left. They are guided by a god to survive into the next epoch. The people are now in the fifth world. Middle grades would enjoy this story and take to heart its message of the importance of kind and cooperative behavior.

EUROPEAN

British Isles

Cooper, Susan. *The Silver Cow: A Welsh Tale*. Illustrated by Warwick Hutton. New York: Margaret K. McElderry, 1983.

The origin of water lilies unfolds in this haunting tale. Readers empathize with Huw, a young boy who must work hard for his cruel and stingy father. The boy takes good care of the black Welsh cattle, sometimes playing his harp in the pasture against his father's orders. One day, while playing his music, Huw sees a new, silver cow in the herd. The cow gives great quantities of rich milk, eventually making Huw's father wealthy with its offspring. Years later, the miserly father plans to have the cow butchered, and he locks up Huw's harp. When the butchering begins, the Tylwyth Teg, the magic people in the lake, call all the silver cows back to them. The father's money vanishes, and water-lilies appear on the lake.

Foster, Joanna. *The Magpies' Nest*. Illustrated by Julie Downing. New York: Clarion Books, 1995.

A perfect nature lesson, this tale explains why all the birds build different kinds of nests. In the spring, the birds call out that it's time to lay their eggs. The robin asks where to put them; how do you build a nest? The magpies answer and demonstrate, one step at a time, with all the materials they use: mud, sticks, grasses for weaving, soft fibers for the lining. But some birds are present only for the explanation of one step and thereafter use only that one method. The flamingoes use only mud. Eagles use sticks. Orioles weave grasses. Cuckoos and cowbirds don't care for the work, so they sneak their eggs into others' nests. Light and educational, this story appeals to primary and middle grades.

Stevens, Janet. *How the Manx Cat Lost Its Tail.* Illustrated by the author. San Diego: Harcourt Brace Jovanovich, 1990.
Cats on the Isle of Man, in the Irish Sea, don't have tails. This story shows the scene on Noah's Ark just as Noah is about to close the door—but the Manx cat is missing. At the last minute, Noah's wife calls the cat in, but his tail gets cut off by closing the door.

Estonian

Moroney, Lynn. *Elinda Who Danced in the Sky: An Estonian Folktale.* Illustrated by Veg Reisberg. San Francisco: Children's Book Press, 1990.
In this Estonian tale, Elinda is born from a tiny egg and grows up to be a beautiful and kind woman who cares for the birds. She has many suitors—the North Star, the Sun, the Moon—but refuses them. But then she agrees to marry Prince Borealis, and they dance in the sky. He promises to return for her, but the sky spirits won't let him. Elinda weaves her wedding veil with delicate iridescent threads. As the days and months pass, the veil reaches the ends of the earth, and her tears fill the rivers. Finally, the birds carry her into the sky, where she reigns. Sometimes she dances with Prince Borealis, and sometimes you can see her veil across the sky; it is the Milky Way.

Finno-Ugric

de Gerez, Tree. *When Bear Came Down from the Sky.* Illustrated by Lisa Desimini. New York: Viking, 1994.
This story of how Bear came to live on earth is told partially in verse. According to this tale from the Finnish and Hungarian languages, Bear used to live as a star constellation in the sky. Bear is curious about earth, and Sky Father warns him that once he goes, he cannot return to the sky. Bear makes a ladder, but it is too short, and he makes the rest of the trip in a basket. Sky Father reminds him to sleep half the winter. Tellervo, the Lady of the Green Dress, welcomes Bear to the forest. Bear learns about earth, and when the snows come, he remembers to sleep. Simple text and illustrations are appealing to primary grades.

Norse

Climo, Shirley. *Stolen Thunder: A Norse Myth.* Illustrated by Alexander Koshkin. New York: Clarion Books, 1994.
Climo starts this tale with two and a half pages of background, in storytelling style, to help readers understand the setting and characterizations encountered in this piece of Norse mythology, thereby successfully avoiding potential pitfalls sometimes associated with mythology for children. When Thor, the Thunder-maker, awakes one morning to discover that Mjolnir, his magic hammer, is missing, he enlists the help of mischievous Loki. Loki goes to Thrym, the Frost King, who has stolen Thor's Thunder. Thrym wants the goddess Freya for his bride in exchange for the hammer. Loki devises a plan which requires Thor to dress up in women's clothes to pose as Freya. This masquerade is not only humorous but successful. This tale explains the origin of lightning and thunder as well as the expression "stolen thunder." Climo's telling is accessible to middle and upper grades.

Norwegian

French, Vivian. *Why the Sea Is Salt*. Illustrated by Patrice Aggs. Cambridge, MA: Candlewick Press, 1993.

A light and humorous telling of a resourceful girl who receives and shares a magical churn. It produces whatever a person wishes for, such as food for her large, starving family. A wealthy, greedy uncle grabs it for himself but with disastrous results, as he doesn't know or care about the magic words to stop the churn. Now that the girl's family is well off, they move to live by the sea. A man on a boat makes a plea to the girl, who freely gives the churn to help him out. The man is actually the same greedy uncle. He wishes for salt on his food, but without the magic words, the salt keeps coming until it sinks the boat and makes the entire sea salty. Read aloud to all ages; independent reading by middle grades.

Slovenian

Ginsburg, Mirra. *How the Sun Was Brought Back to the Sky: Adapted from a Slovenian Folk Tale*. Illustrated by Jose Aruego and Ariane Dewey. New York: Macmillan, 1975.

The illustrations and text of this simple story hold appeal for primary-aged children. The sun has been covered by big gray clouds, so little chicks go off in search of it. In cumulative-tale fashion, they ask one animal after another and eventually find the sun, groaning and sluggish. They help the sun to spruce up and shine again.

NATIVE AMERICAN

Ahenakew, Freda, trans. and ed. *How the Birch Tree Got Its Stripes: A Cree Story for Children*. Illustrated by George Littlechild. Saskatoon, Saskatchewan: Fifth House, 1988.

Written by students in a Cree language course, this is the English version of a linguistics project. The telling is brief and easy to understand. A man catches some ducks and prepares to cook them. But he tests himself, trying to keep from eating as long as possible. The man asks two birch trees to hold on to him and not let go. Other animals come to take advantage. The man gets angry and asks the trees to let him go, but they don't. Finally, the man sleeps, and the animals devour his meal. Once free, the man takes willow branches and whips the trees. That is why birches have stripes. Accessible to primary grades and up.

Anderson, Peter. *A Grand Canyon Journey: Tracing Time in Stone*. A First Book. New York: Franklin Watts, 1997.

Primarily a nonfiction narrative, this book includes brief summaries of two creation myths explaining the origins of the Grand Canyon. This book takes the reader on a guided hiking tour down into the Grand Canyon, explaining the geological history, pointing out rock formations, and observing the heat and plant life. From the rim at the top, down to the Colorado River, the book-tour is good reading. The chapter "Tall Tales" includes two Native American myths. The first is from the Havasupai, "people of the blue-green water," descendants of the Anasazi who are the only people to continue to live at the bottom of the Canyon. The story relates a quarrel between two gods; one god threatens to flood the world, so the other god builds a boat so his daughter will survive. The flood comes in a wall of water, which carves a deep canyon in the earth. The daughter is saved in her boat, but the world is dark and there are no other people. The sun rises and fathers her first child, and a waterfall fathers a second. The blue-green waters are still found at the foot of Havasu Falls. The other story is from the Hualapai people, who also tell of a great flood. A giant named Packithaawi swims in the flood. With his knife and a club, he cuts a gash in the earth to drain off the flood to the sea. When the waters recede, the Canyon is left behind. This book is an excellent resource for combining pourquoi tales with the study of science. For fourth grade and up.

Bernhard, Emery. *How Snowshoe Hare Rescued the Sun: A Tale from the Arctic.* Illustrated by Durga Bernhard. New York: Holiday House, 1993.

This Yuit Eskimo legend is derived from a Siberian Eskimo legend. Selfish demons steal the sun and keep it under the earth. The animals have a council meeting, organized by Owl. They send animals, one by one, to rescue the sun, but no one is successful until fast-running Snowshoe Hare goes. Sun is restored to the Arctic.

Bierhorst, John. *The Woman Who Fell from the Sky: The Iroquois Story of Creation.* Illustrated by Robert Andrew Parker. New York: William Morrow, 1993.

A woman falling from the sky world is an element seen in several Native American accounts of creation. Many Native American tales include the existence of parallel worlds in the sky and on the earth, and students should be acquainted with this idea in order to understand these tales. A woman in the sky world falls through a hole to the watery world below. The animals must dive and bring up some mud to spread on Turtle's back; this will grow into the earth. The story goes on to include the creation of many other features of nature. The woman has two sons who help create and have an interesting way of achieving balance between their personalities. Compare this telling to those in Caduto/Bruchac's *Keepers of the Earth*; Hamilton's *In the Beginning*; and Taylor's *Bones in the Basket*.

Bruchac, Joseph. *Between Earth & Sky: Legends of Native American Sacred Places.* Illustrated by Thomas Locker. San Diego: Harcourt Brace, 1996.

Each two-page spread of this stunning book presents a brief telling of a legend accompanied by Locker's glowing oil paintings. Each legend is an origin story about an earth feature—mountains, canyons, waterfalls—and relates it to one of the Seven Directions. This book can be used at many levels with many disciplines: as a work of art, for a deeper cultural understanding of Native American reverence for nature, as a geographical reference to relate to studies of the regions of the United States, as a complement to science studies of geological formations. The legends are contained within a story of a boy and his uncle walking, the young man learning from the elder. Some of the places featured include Niagara Falls, the Grand Canyon, the Painted Desert, and the Great Smoky Mountains. A map relates the stories and sites to the tribes. For middle and upper grades.

———. *The Boy Who Lived with the Bears and Other Iroquois Stories.* Illustrated by Murv Jacob. New York: HarperCollins, 1995.

This handsome collection, written and illustrated by people of Native American descent, is well suited for those in middle grades to read themselves or for reading aloud to younger children. Five of the six stories contain pourquoi elements, and all the stories teach lessons in the gentle way that is characteristic of good, humorous storytelling. "How the Birds Got Their Feathers" focuses on Buzzard, who is brave but vain. "Turtle Makes War on Man," tells of the origin of three animal characteristics: Skunk's flat head, Rattlesnake's flat head, and Turtle's cracked back. The last two stories deal with Chipmunk's stripes and Rabbit's tail. This book is a delightful, authentic, and basic "must-have" for pourquoi tales. Students can hear the author telling these same tales on the audiocassette by the same title (next entry). This collection is used as a core title for a language arts thematic unit in chapter 2, "Activities."

———. *The Boy Who Lived with the Bears and Other Iroquois Stories.* New York: Caedmon, 1991. Audiocassette.

This distinguished author and storyteller entertains with a gently humorous style, voice adjustments for characters, songs that are part of some of the stories, and some drum playing. All six of the stories on the tape are found in the book by the same title (previous entry). Bruchac's tellings are quite close to those in his book. This recording would be an enjoyable treat after students have read the stories and would present an opportunity to observe the differences between storytelling and reading aloud.

———. *The Circle of Thanks: Native American Poems and Songs of Thanksgiving.* Illustrated by Murv Jacob. N.p.: BridgeWater Books, 1996.
These 14 poems express gratitude and appreciation for the gifts of nature. One poem, "How Medicine Came," depicts medicine as a gift from the plants.

———. *The First Strawberries: A Cherokee Story.* Illustrated by Anna Vojtech. New York: Dial Books for Young Readers, 1993.
This easy-to-read tale not only conveys pourquoi elements but also raises issues of sex roles, anger, and reconciliation. The first man and woman live happily together until one day, the man comes home hungry only to find his wife is out picking flowers. He speaks angrily to her of his hunger; she in turn is hurt and angry, for she only wished to share the beauty of the flowers with him. She leaves. The Sun observes and offers to help the man, who is now sorry. The Sun shines in front of the woman's path, and berries grow up. She finally sees the berries and picks them to share with her husband. Strawberries are, to this day, a reminder of the sweetness of kindness and respect.

———. *Four Ancestors: Stories, Songs, and Poems from Native North America.* Illustrated by S. S. Burrus, Jeffrey Chapman, Murv Jacob, and Duke Sine. N.p.: BridgeWater Books, 1996.
Written by a prolific and talented Native American storyteller, this is a rich and useful collection of 31 songs and poems. The stories are grouped into four sections: Fire, Earth, Water, and Air. Most of the stories are pourquoi tales explaining the origins of the four elements and filled with a sense of deep respect for nature. Some tales hold gentle humor or a lesson to be quietly learned. The uses for this book are many: as nature lessons to incorporate into science classes, as examples of regional tribal culture to incorporate into social studies classes, and as a rich addition to the study of pourquoi tales.

———. *The Great Ball Game: A Muskogee Story.* Illustrated by Susan L. Roth. New York: Dial Books for Young Readers, 1994.
Native Americans sometimes used a ball game to settle a dispute instead of going to war, and such is the case with this Muskogee (Creek) tale. Bruchac chooses stickball, a traditional lacrosse-like game. The birds claim that the feathered creatures are better than the other animals; the others claim that those with teeth are better. They agree that a stickball game will decide. Bat has both wings and teeth; after being jeered at by the birds, he sides with the toothed side. The game goes on for hours, into the night. It is so dark that no one can see anymore, but Bat does not need to see and steals the ball. He zigzags around and wins for the animals. He gets to set the penalty for the birds and sends them south. This entertaining tale explains how bats have come to be accepted as an animal and why birds fly south for the winter. This appealing story is readable by primary grades. Collage illustrations are attractive.

———. *Keepers of the Earth: Native American Stories.* Golden, CO: Fulcrum, 1991. Audiocassettes.
A two-cassette set of Joseph Bruchac telling the stories from the book *Keepers of the Earth* by Caduto and Bruchac. Bruchac's storytelling style is relaxed and smooth, laced with moments of gentle humor and quiet solemnity as the moods of the stories change. Short musical interludes add to the authenticity. These tapes bring the stories alive in a personal way.

————. *Native American Stories.* Illustrated by John Kahionhes Fadden. Golden, CO: Fulcrum, 1991.

The stories in this collection are the same ones found in *Keepers of the Earth* by Caduto and Bruchac. This collection contains just the stories; the Caduto/Bruchac *Keepers* also contains discussions about nature. See the Caduto and Bruchac annotation further on for information on the stories.

————. *Native Plant Stories.* Illustrated by John Kahionhes Fadden and David Kanietakeron Fadden. Golden, CO: Fulcrum, 1995.

A collection of stories also published in *Keepers of Life* (Fulcrum, 1994) by Caduto and Bruchac. "Waynabozho and the Wild Rice" provides details about wild rice planting and harvesting, emphasizing the life cycle of plants.

————. *Tell Me a Tale: A Book About Storytelling.* San Diego: Harcourt Brace, 1997.

Tips for storytellers accompany 14 short stories to tell. Tales come from a variety of contemporary and older sources. Four tales are pourquoi stories: "Coyote's Name," "How the Adirondacks Got Their Name," "Yiyi the Spider and the Stick Sap Man," and "The Creation of Gluskabe." This is a resource book for tellers.

Bruchac, Joseph, and Gayle Ross. *The Story of the Milky Way: A Cherokee Tale.* Illustrated by Virginia A. Stroud. New York: Dial Books for Young Readers, 1995.

The people depend on their cornmeal as a basic food staple, but one day an elderly couple discover their cornmeal is being stolen and scattered. A boy hides at night and sees a light, in the shape of a large dog, eating the cornmeal. The people consult an elder, Beloved Woman, who tells them to hide and wait and then make a great noise with their rattles to scare the dog away. The dog leaps into the sky, and the cornmeal trailing from its mouth makes a track of stars across the night sky. The Cherokee call the Milky Way "the place where the dog ran." Told and illustrated by people of Native American descent, this tale is appealing and accessible for primary-grade reading or listening.

Brusca, María Cristina, and Tona Wilson. *When Jaguars Ate the Moon and Other Stories About Animals and Plants of the Americas.* Illustrated by the author. New York: Henry Holt, 1995. (See the annotation under "South American.")

Caduto, Michael J., and Joseph Bruchac. *Keepers of the Earth: Native American Stories and Environmental Activities for Children.* Illustrated by John Kahionhes Fadden and Carol Wood. Golden, CO: Fulcrum, 1988.

A large collection of well-told stories matched with nature activities and discussions. The 24 tales, told by Bruchac, work well as read-alouds to middle and upper grades; some work well with younger grades as well. Notable tales include "Loo-Wit, The Fire-Keeper," "How Grandmother Spider Stole the Sun," "How Raven Made the Tides," and "How Turtle Flew South for the Winter." The same stories, minus the nature discussions, can be found in *Native American Stories* by Bruchac. This author team also collaborated on *Keepers of the Animals* (1991), *Keepers of Life* (1994; plant stories and discussions), and the next title, all published by Fulcrum.

————. *Keepers of the Night: Native American Stories and Nocturnal Activities for Children.* Illustrated by David Kanietakeron Fadden, Jo Levasseur, and Carol Wood. Golden, CO: Fulcrum, 1994.

Seven Native American stories accompanied by activities and nature information. Notable stories include "How the Bat Came to Be" and "Chipmunk and the Owl Sisters."

Cameron, Anne. *How the Loon Lost Her Voice.* Illustrated by Tara Miller. Madeira Park, British Columbia: Harbour, 1985.

The author learned this story from a native storyteller on Vancouver Island. It recounts how Raven rescues the sun from evil spirits and how the gentle Loon sacrifices her lovely voice in the rescue effort. The Loon used to have the most beautiful voice. Her singing helps make the world a happy place until the day the evil spirits steal the sun. The animals have a meeting, where Raven informs them the light is locked in a box surrounded by a wall of ice. One by one, the animals try to invade the wall of ice. Deer crashes and breaks off his antlers; Bear gets pummeled and falls down exhausted. Loon and Mole make a quiet plan to tunnel in, but the spirits catch Loon and swing her around by the neck, ruining her voice. Raven gets mad and moves in to finish the job, hiding the light under his wing. This tale also explains why the deer loses its antlers in the fall and why bears hibernate each winter.

———. *How Raven Freed the Moon.* Madeira Park, British Columbia: Harbour, 1985 (Box 219, Madeira Park, B.C., Canada V0N 2H0).

This simple tale, delightfully told, shows Raven acting for everyone's benefit and yet mischievous as ever. Raven loves shiny bright objects and has heard of an old fisherwoman and her daughter who live on a northern island. It is said that these two keep a bright thing called Moon in a carved box. Raven transforms herself into a baby and lays down at the door of the old fisherwoman, crying piteously. When the old woman and girl find her, the woman lets the girl keep the baby, with instructions to care for it and keep it quiet so she can sleep; she has a hard day of fishing ahead. The baby's fits of crying and the woman and girl's reactions are told with gentle humor. The baby cries more and more insistently, reaching for the carved wooden box. The woman and girl try to keep the baby from their secret, but in exasperation, they let the baby look at the box, and they fall asleep. The baby opens the box, and the bright light awakens the woman and daughter. They realize now the baby is Raven! The trickster flies off with Moon through the smoke hole. She flies far, but Moon is heavy, and Raven almost drops it in the ocean. She tosses it into the sky, where, the old woman agrees, it looks better than it did in the box. For all ages.

Duncan, Lois. *The Magic of Spider Woman.* Illustrated by Shonto Begay. New York: Scholastic, 1996.

The origin of the Navajo art of weaving is traced in this story, which also teaches people to live their lives in balance. The Spirit Being creates the Navajo people and teaches them how to survive in the earth world. But strong-willed Wandering Girl is off herding her sheep at the time. When she comes back in the winter, she needs the help of Spider Woman, who teaches her to weave warm blankets. She is warned that as a Navajo girl she must walk the Middle Way and live her life in balance. Eventually, Wandering Girl (now called Weaving Woman) becomes obsessed with weaving a large, colorful, perfect blanket, and she weaves her spirit into the blanket. To cure her weaving sickness, a shaman advises her to make her blanket less perfect. By pulling a strand loose, a pathway for the spirit is opened, and Weaving Woman is saved. She learns her lesson, to live in balance and not to allow pride to master her. To this day, Navajo weaving is done with one thread pulled free.

Dunn, Anne M. *When Beaver Was Very Great: Stories to Live By.* Illustrated by Sharon L. White. Mount Horeb, WI: Midwest Traditions, 1995.

A collection of both old folktales and new personal stories. Some tales are life lessons, and some are origin tales. The author's Anishinabe heritage provides a gentle undercurrent to the tellings. Pourquoi tales include "Muskrat's Tail," "The Thrush," and "How Turtle Cracked His Shell." This extensive collection is useful as a storyteller's source book or for selective reading aloud.

Dwyer, Mindy. *Coyote In Love.* Illustrated by the author. Seattle, WA: Alaska Northwest Books, 1997.

In this short, sweet, vibrantly illustrated story, Coyote is seen not so much as a trickster but as the character who always insists on getting what he wants, whether it is accessible or not. Coyote falls in love with a beautiful blue star and goes to the top of a high mountain to get close enough to touch her. She only makes fun of him. She pulls him into the sky and then drops him. He falls into the top of the mountain, making a huge hole. He lays in the hole, crying blue tears. This becomes Crater Lake in Oregon.

Eagle Walking Turtle. *Full Moon Stories: Thirteen Native American Legends*. Illustrated by the author. New York: Hyperion Books for Children, 1997.

Thirteen stories, one for each moon of the year. The author frames the stories in the context of the first time his grandfather told them to him when he was a young boy on the Wyoming plains. A strong sense of family pervades each tale; the reader sees the cluster of grandchildren gathering around the wood stove as Grandpa gets ready to tell a story and Grandma provides food. "The Magpie" explains why the magpie is the friend of humans and why it has a rainbow in its tail. "The Horse" explains how horses came to the people. "The Dog" explains why dogs are special friends and helpers to people. "The Bear" explains the origins of bear medicine, a body of knowledge about healing of mental and physical ailments. Many of these stories are examples of the Native American tradition of taking cues and lessons from the natural world. The author comes from the Arapaho people, but the stories are from several Native American tribes. These stories are most effective as read-alouds to all ages.

Esbensen, Barbara Juster. *The Great Buffalo Race: How the Buffalo Got Its Hump*. Illustrated by Helen K. Davie. Boston: Little, Brown, 1994.

This Seneca tale tells of drought, conflict, and its consequences: the physical characteristics of buffaloes. During a great drought, the buffaloes are starving. Young Buffalo wants to travel to new grasslands. Old Buffalo says they should wait for the rain that is coming, and they shouldn't travel because this would take food from other herds. They have a fight, and Young Buffalo wins, so they travel westward. One group, led by Old Buffalo's son, stays back and waits. Old Buffalo's group steps carefully, watching for small creatures and nests, but Young Buffalo's group is not so careful. All the buffaloes who follow westward drop and die from thirst. The Great Spirit scolds Young Buffalo and Old Buffalo and gives them a hump as a way to remember their mistake. Then the Great Spirit pushes the buffaloes' heads in and down to make sure they watch out for the small creatures on the ground. Finally, the Great Spirit transforms Old Buffalo into a cloud to watch over the other buffaloes and Young Buffalo into the Red Buffalo of the under-earth. The environmental message is strong, as is the feel of life on the Great Plains. For middle and upper grades.

———. *Ladder to the Sky: How the Gift of Healing Came to the Ojibway Nation*. Illustrated by Helen K. Davie. Boston: Little, Brown, 1989.

The people are healthy, and no one ever dies. When a person gets old, a spirit-messenger comes down the magic vine and carries the old one into the sky. A spirit-messenger becomes friendly with a young man, making others jealous. When the spirit takes the man into the sky, his grandmother climbs up the vine after him—a forbidden act. After this, people get sick and feel pain. The spirits come down from the sky, and explain that the people will have sickness, but they will also have the power to heal. The spirits teach the gifts of healing, using the plants and flowers, to chosen persons who become the Medicine People.

———. *The Star Maiden: An Ojibway Tale*. Illustrated by Helen K. Davie. Boston: Little, Brown, 1988.

The origin of water lilies in the northern lake country is explained in this gentle, enchanting tale. One night, the people see a bright star that seems to fall to earth. A man is sent out to investigate. In his dreams, a shining silver maiden tells him she wants to live on earth. The chief says she may choose what form she will become. She tries out a hillside flower and then a prairie flower, but these are not satisfactory. Finally, she calls to all her star sisters to settle in the waters of the lake. The next morning, the people find the lake scattered with water lilies.

French, Fiona. *Lord of the Animals: A Miwok Indian Creation Myth.* Illustrated by the author. Brookfield, CT: Millbrook Press, 1997.

Pourquoi, trickster, and transformation elements are present in this short, simple tale of the origin of humans. Coyote is a creator in this story, having just created the world and its creatures. He calls a meeting to decide how to make the Lord of the Animals. The animals all speak up in turn, stating that one of their own traits is the most important attribute for the Lord of the Animals. Finally, Coyote tells the animals that they will all shape a model of the Lord of the Animals out of a lump of mud from the river and then choose one. All the animals get started on the project, but nighttime comes, and they fall asleep. Coyote stays awake and finishes, allowing the other clay models to melt away in the river. Coyote indeed incorporates many of the characteristics suggested by the other animals, such as smoother skin than a fish for swimming, two legs like a bear, and a voice for singing. But Coyote assembles these in a new way, as evidenced by the illustration: He shapes a man and gives him life as the Lord of the Animals. For primary and middle grades.

Gates, Frieda. *Owl Eyes.* Illustrated Yoshi Miyake. New York: Lothrop, Lee & Shepard, 1994.

This Kanienkehaka story (Mohawk of Upper New York State) traces the origin of the owl's features. Its humor can bring giggles, as children may recognize themselves in Owl's pesky personality. Raweno, "Master of all spirits and everything," is finishing some of his creative efforts. He has shaped the woodland animals out of clay, and now each animal gets to tell Raweno what he or she wants to look like. While Raweno works on Fox, Sparrow, and others, Owl keeps interrupting and criticizing. Then, when it is Owl's turn, he keeps changing his mind. Owl is really getting on Raweno's nerves. Raweno tells Owl to face the other way and stay quiet, but he continues to interfere. Exasperated, Raweno takes Owl, stuffs his head down, pulls his ears up, puts him in mud, and shakes him so much his eyes grow big in fright. The Creator tells Owl he will be a night creature so that the Creator can work in peace during the day. The author's notes explain details of tribal groups and names in this area. Enjoyable for all ages.

Goble, Paul. *Crow Chief: A Plains Indian Story.* Illustrated by the author. New York: Orchard Books, 1992.

According to this Dakota tale, crows used to be white. The crows' leader, the Crow Chief, is friendly with buffaloes but not with humans because he wants to be chief of all creatures. When the people get ready to hunt, Crow Chief warns the buffaloes, so the people go hungry. Finally, the people get the help of Falling Star, a man who travels to help people. He devises a plan resulting in the discovery and capture of Crow Chief. Then, the people have a successful hunt. They tie Crow Chief to the top of a tipi and make him smell the smoke of the cooking fire and watch the people eat. In that delicious smoke, his feathers turn black. From then on, crows are black as a reminder to share and care for one another.

———. *The Gift of the Sacred Dog.* Illustrated by the author. Scarsdale, NY: Bradbury Press, 1980.

A tale of the Great Plains, recounting how the Great Spirit makes a gift of the first horses to the people. The people are hungry and cannot find any buffalo to hunt. A boy leaves camp to seek the help of the Great Spirit. Clouds gather in the sky, and someone approaches, riding a magnificent animal called Sacred Dog. As the boy returns to the plain, the sky is full of thunder as numerous Sacred Dogs gallop out of the sky. The horses, Sacred Dogs, will help the people hunt the buffalo.

————. *Her Seven Brothers*. Illustrated by the author. New York: Bradbury Press, 1988.
  Combining pourquoi and transformation elements, this tale describes the origin of the stars that form the Big Dipper. A young woman is skilled at embroidering clothes with porcupine quills. She is decorating six sets of clothing and a smaller seventh outfit, mystifying her mother. The girl is making clothes for seven brothers from the north, whom she has seen in her mind. She makes the long journey and finds a little boy with special powers and his six older brothers. The brothers readily welcome the girl as their sister. One day, the brothers refuse the buffaloes' demand to take their sister away, so the buffaloes stampede. The seven brothers and their sister flee up a tree, which grows taller until it takes them into the sky. The last page shows the Big Dipper, which has a seventh smaller star (the little brother) close to his sister. For middle and upper grades. Chapter 2 provides shadow puppets to dramatize this tale.

————. *The Lost Children: The Boys Who Were Neglected*. Illustrated by the author. New York: Bradbury Press, 1993.
  Six children are orphans and are neglected by the tribe. Only the camp dogs like them. In their sadness, they don't want to be people anymore, and they discuss what they would like to be. They decide to be stars because stars endure. One child leads the way into the sky, warning the others not to look back. One looks back and turns into Smoking Star, a comet. In the sky world, Sun Man and Moon Woman take care of them. They become the Pleiades. The camp dogs howl at the sky. Now there are also hundreds of small stars near the Pleiades; they are the camp dogs, reunited with their children. Large typeface and a simple telling make this readable by second graders.

————. *Remaking the Earth: A Creation Story from the Great Plains of North America*. Illustrated by the author. New York: Orchard Books, 1996.
  An Algonquian creation myth of the "Earth Diver" category, this story takes into account the creation of virtually all aspects of life on earth: earth, animals, birds, plants, the Thunderbirds (for thunderstorms), the two-leggeds, horses, hunting, the buffalo. The world is covered with water, and Earth Maker instructs the water animals to dive down and find earth. Finally little Coot (a water bird) brings up mud, which is spread on Turtle's back. Several pages of text include asterisks providing further explanations of origins in the style of a theatrical "aside," for example, why turtles walk slowly. The one-page essay prior to the story provides informative and reflective comments on the nature of the creation myth. The story ends on a somewhat unique and sobering note: Bull Buffalo is instructed by Earth Maker to push against the mountains, which hold back the waters of the sea. When Bull Buffalo gets old and loses all his hair, the mountains will crumble and the waters will again flood the earth; and Bull Buffalo is weak and most of his hair is already gone.

————. *The Return of the Buffaloes: A Plains Indian Story About Famine and Renewal of the Earth*. Illustrated by the author. Washington, DC: National Geographic Society, 1996.
  The origins of the wind found in Wind Cave, in the Black Hills of South Dakota, are revealed in this tale of reverence for the buffalo. When the buffalo do not return in the spring and the people are in danger of starving to death, two young men are sent out to search. On their journey, they suddenly smell buffaloes and turn to find a mysterious woman standing at the door to a cave, which is her tipi dwelling. The author's note states that this woman is one of the Buffalo People, transformed into human form to bear their message of love and provision for the people. She tells the men she will send her Buffalo People. The people come to the cave and bring gifts. Later, back in the camp, the people are awakened by the thundering of a frenzied buffalo stampede. Goble ends with information about modern-day National Park Service tours of Wind Cave, where the breath of the buffaloes can still be felt. For third grade and up.

———. *Star Boy*. Illustrated by the author. Scarsdale, NY: Bradbury Press, 1983.
   The concept of parallel worlds in the sky and on earth is a foundation for this Blackfoot (Siksika) tale. A young woman admires Morning Star in the sky; a handsome man appears, introduces himself as Morning Star, and takes her to the Sky World to meet his father, the Sun, and his mother, the Moon. They marry and have a child. She is instructed never to dig up a certain plant, but in curiosity she does. The plant leaves a hole in the sky through which she can see the earth world. The woman is punished and sent to earth with her son. The son's face bears an ugly scar that, after a long quest for forgiveness, is erased. The tale explains the appearance of Star Boy in the sky, traveling with the Morning Star and the Evening Star low over the horizon. Well-told and captivating, this tale is interesting to compare with San Souci's *Legend of Scarface* (Doubleday, 1978). The hole in the sky, left by the plant, is also seen in Caduto/Bruchac's *Keepers of the Earth* ("The Earth on Turtle's Back") and Bierhorst's *The Woman Who Fell from the Sky*.

Goldin, Barbara Diamond. *Coyote and the Fire Stick: A Pacific Northwest Indian Tale*. Illustrated by Will Hillenbrand. San Diego: Gulliver Books, 1996.
   Long ago, the people had no fire, so they ask Coyote to help get fire from the three evil spirits who have it. With a plan in mind, Coyote climbs the mountain to the evil spirits' dwelling and hides to watch the fire. When the coast is clear, Coyote grabs a burning stick and flees, with the spirits chasing after him. Just as the spirits grab his tail, Coyote throws the stick to Mountain Lion. A relay-race ensues among the animals, ending with Frog in the river. Frog spits the fire onto a tree. The spirits are confounded, unable to get fire away from the tree. Once they are gone, Coyote shows the People how to rub two sticks together to get fire. Compare to the popular *Fire Race* by Jonathan London.

———. *The Girl Who Lived with the Bears*. Illustrated by Andrew Plewes. San Diego: Gulliver Books, 1997.
   This transformation tale explains the origin of bear-hunting ceremonies and rituals among the peoples of the Pacific Northwest. The daughter of a chief has a spoiled and complaining nature. She resents the bears' presence in the woods as she gathers berries and ignores her friends' warnings not to anger the bears with her comments. Two men approach her when it is dark, offering to help her find her home. They take her to a village that is not her own and keep her there. She learns that the man who has brought her there is the nephew of the bear chief and she is being held as a slave by the Bear People. Mouse Woman teaches the young woman a trick to seemingly transform her slave food into copper. This gets her out of her slave quarters, but then she must marry the chief's nephew. In time, she grows to love her husband, but she does not like to see him don his bearskin; she prefers his human form. She has two children, twins who have a human form but can become bears by wearing bearskins. The bear-husband senses that the young woman's brother is near and will kill him. The young woman wishes to intervene, but the bear-husband instructs her to allow the killing so that his bear-spirit can be released to watch over her. He teaches her songs and rituals that must be performed every time a human kills a bear so that the Bear People do not get angry with humans. It is a reminder to treat all animals with respect.

Greene, Ellin. *The Legend of the Cranberry: A Paleo-Indian Tale*. Illustrated by Brad Sneed. New York: Simon & Schuster, 1993.
   Featuring giant mastodons and woolly mammoths, this tale explains the origin of cranberries as both a food and a sign from the Great Spirit. Long ago, the woolly mammoths, known as Yah-qua-whee, were created to help the People. But now they start harming people and other animals, so the animals have a meeting. The Great Spirit tells the People to help the animals kill the Yah-qua-whee. The People dig pits covered with branches. The huge beasts fall in and are buried with stones. The remaining Yah-qua-whee stampede, creating bogs into which the beasts sink and drown. The

battle and the ensuing winter kill many people. The next summer, the bogs are covered with pink blossoms that mature into cranberries. Thereafter, the People use the berries at feasts as a sign of the Great Spirit's love for the People. They use the berries in pemmican, poultices, and dye. There is a useful author's note at the end. Accessible for second grade and up.

Greene, Jacqueline Dembar. *Manabozho's Gifts: Three Chippewa Tales*. Illustrated by Jennifer Hewitson. Boston: Houghton Mifflin, 1994.

Manabozho, great-grandson of the moon, has special powers beyond humans yet is not a god. All three tales bear a powerful concept of Manabozho as one who causes many things to be, often acting for the greater benefit of the people. The first tale describes how Manabozho brings fire to the people. The second describes Manabozho's arduous vision quest for food for his people. He is rewarded with the discovery of wild rice harvesting. In the third tale, Manabozho rescues the rose from extinction, protecting it with thorns. He also marks rabbits with floppy ears and split mouths because of the harm they did to the roses. The stories are striking and well told and can be read by fourth graders and up.

Haley, Gail E. *Two Bad Boys: A Very Old Cherokee Tale*. Illustrated by the author. New York: Dutton Children's Books, 1996.

Children can readily relate to this tale of two boys' mischief and its sobering consequences. Hunter and Corn Mother, the first people, live with their son and provide meat and vegetables. One day while out playing, Boy discovers another boy in the river. He pulls him out and plays with him day after day. Boy's parents catch the new boy and name him Wild Boy. Wild Boy leads Boy into endless mischief. Against the admonition of Father, Wild Boy lures Boy to follow Father and find out where the meat comes from. When they discover the secret cave of the animals, they let all the animals loose. In despair and disappointment, Father tells the boys that from now on, all meat must be obtained with difficulty by hunting. Then Father must leave the family and go to the Western Land. After a hard and hungry winter, Wild Boy initiates the same adventure to find out where Mother gets the corn and vegetables. When Corn Mother discovers the boys in her storage building, she tells them their lives will never be the same. From now on, they must use the seeds in their hands to plant, and they must work and tend their crops for food. She, too, departs for the West. This story delivers a lesson on peer pressure, obedience, and consequences and explains why people must hunt and work for their food.

Harper, Piers. *How the World Was Saved & Other Native American Tales*. Illustrated by the author. Racine, WI: Golden Books, 1994.

A collection of eight illustrated tales, most two to three pages in length. Four are pourquoi tales; two others are about death. These tellings are variants of tales found in other books and do not contain some of the details that help the plot. Use these tales for comparison.

Harrell, Beatrice Orcutt. *How Thunder and Lightning Came to Be: A Choctaw Legend*. Illustrated by Susan L. Roth. New York: Dial Books for Young Readers, 1995.

This tale was told to the author by her Choctaw mother and other relatives. The Great Sun Father wants to send a warning to the people when he sends rain and wind. He asks two silly birds to think of a warning. One bird, the male, makes a few clumsy trials. The female bird lays her eggs in the soft clouds and then asks the male to keep them from rolling off. They continue to roll around, making a rumbling sound. The male streaks down from the sky to chase the falling eggs, making sparks. Although their attempts are clumsy, the Sun Father likes the noisy and bright warning.

Hausman, Gerald. *How Chipmunk Got Tiny Feet: Native American Animal Origin Stories.* Illustrated by Ashley Wolff. New York: HarperCollins, 1995.

A collection of seven animal stories describing the events that result in their characteristics. Each tale is illustrated with a colorful border imitating the art of the tribe from which the tale comes. In each tale, Mother Earth makes an appearance to help set things right. This appearance of Mother Earth, rather like a fairy godmother, may be problematic for some. One-line sources are listed for each tale, but no background information is given.

Jackson, Ellen. *The Precious Gift: A Navajo Creation Myth.* Illustrated by Woodleigh Marx Hubbard. New York: Simon & Schuster Books for Young Readers, 1996.

A telling of a portion of the Navajo myth of how the people and water came to the present world. A strong message from this story is how precious and rare fresh water is in the arid Southwest. The first people have just come to the present world from the underworld through a reed in the ocean. First Man could make a river or lake if he just had one drop of fresh water. Armed with a water flask, Beaver and Otter are the first to offer to fetch fresh water, but they get distracted by the plant life in the ocean, and they fail. Henceforth, they will always live in the swamps. Next, Frog and Turtle go, and although they fail, their adventure leaves them with the physical characteristics they have to this day. Finally, little Snail goes with the flask and finds the reed in the ocean that leads back to the underworld. She returns with sweet, fresh water, but the water slowly leaks out. First Man finds her just as the last drop is leaking out, but it is enough to make a river. As a reward, Snail gets to keep the flask on her back (her shell), and she always leaves a moist trail. For middle grades.

Jessell, Tim. *Amorak.* Illustrated by the author. Mankato, MN: Creative Editions, 1994.

This tale is simply and quietly yet dramatically told, with effective, dark illustrations. However, no source notes are give for this Inuit legend explaining the origin of Arctic mammals, especially the relationship of the wolf to the caribou. The Great Being of the Sky tells the first woman to cut a hole in the ice. Out come the animals of the north; the last, the caribou, she is told, is the greatest gift because it will provide sustenance. The caribou herd grows, but the woman's sons hunt the strong and healthy ones. Soon there is concern that only weak and sickly caribou will remain. The woman talks to the Great Being, who sends Amorak the wolf. The wolves hunt the weaker caribou, leaving the strong ones to multiply. For middle grades.

Keams, Geri. *Grandmother Spider Brings the Sun: A Cherokee Story.* Illustrated by James Bernardin. Flagstaff, AZ: Rising Moon Books for Young Readers, 1995.

Half the world is in darkness, and the animals have a meeting to see about obtaining a piece of sun from the other side. Several animals, each in their turn, make the journey and fail. Possum carries sun in his tail; possums have skinny bare tails to this day. Buzzard tries and gets a burned bald spot on his head. Grandmother Spider makes a pot to carry the sun in; the Sun Guards don't notice her as she steals a piece. As she brings the pot back through a cave, the pot grows harder and the sun grows larger and bounces into the sky. The author's note explains that the symbolism of this story reflects the way Cherokee potters create their pots and fire them to make them hard. For primary and middle grades.

Larry, Charles. *Peboan and Seegwun.* Illustrated by the author. New York: Farrar, Straus & Giroux, 1993.

A short, simple telling of the origins of winter and spring, illustrated with oversize paintings. A young man, Seegwun, meets an old man, Peboan, who is alone in his lodge. Each speaks in turn of the effects he has on nature when he breathes or tosses his hair. Peboan's breath makes water become still and hard; Seegwun's breath causes flowers to grow. Streams begin to flow from the eyes of Peboan, Old Man Winter, and soon he melts away. The author's notes not only give the source of the story but also fill in valuable information about the Anishinabe people of Michigan, Wisconsin, and Minnesota, called Ojibway by others. For all ages.

London, Jonathan. *Fire Race: A Karuk Coyote Tale About How Fire Came to the People.* Illustrated by Sylvia Long. San Francisco: Chronicle Books, 1993.
The animals have no fire because it is kept by the Yellow Jacket Sisters at the top of the mountain. Coyote persuades the Sisters to let him in by promising to make them pretty by drawing black stripes around their bodies using a charred piece of wood. Once he has the burning wood in his mouth, he makes a run for it. What ensues is much like a relay race with all the animals doing their part to escape with the fire. In the end, the fire is swallowed by the willow tree. From then on, fire can be gotten from wood by rubbing two sticks together. This trickster/pourquoi tale also teaches the value of teamwork and cooperation. Compare to *How Iwariwa the Cayman Learned to Share* by Crespo.

Luenn, Nancy. *Miser on the Mountain: A Nisqually Legend of Mount Rainier.* Illustrated by Pierr Morgan. Seattle: Sasquatch Books, 1997.
This tale from the Pacific Northwest teaches the true meaning of wealth and shows spirits as the bringers of snow, thunder, and wind. At the base of the mountain Ta-co-bet (Mt. Rainier) lives a miserly man, Latsut, who is obsessed with acquiring barter shells called *hiaqua*. He has a vision in which his totem, Elk, speaks to him and advises him to journey to the top of the mountain to seek hidden wealth. Latsut, single-minded and inconsiderate, leaves his family for the dangerous climb. At the summit, he finds the three-rock formations that Elk instructed him to find. At the base of the elk-shaped peak, Latsut digs and finds a bottomless cache of *hiaqua* shells. He grabs all he can carry, ignoring the giant thumping otters that surround him. He offers no thanks or gift for the mountain as he leaves, vowing to return for more. The spirits of wind, thunder, and snow bellow and lash at Latsut, trying to make him realize his blind greed. Frozen and exhausted, he begins to leave strings of shells for the otters and spirits. Finally he realizes his foolishness, recognizing that life is more important, giving up the rest of his shells. He sleeps in a lodge built by his guardian, Elk, and awakens a white-haired old man. He returns to his wife, gathers his people to him in a feast, and advises his descendants on the true meaning of wealth. For middle and upper grades.

Max, Jill, ed. *Spider Spins a Story: Fourteen Legends from Native North America.* Illustrated by six Native American artists. Flagstaff, AZ: Rising Moon Books for Young Readers, 1997.
A collection of 14 tales from various tribal traditions, all featuring the spider. In the tales, Spider acts variously as helper, magical agent, trickster, and Grandmother of the Earth. "How the Tewas Found Their True Home" recounts how the Tewas wander the world in darkness and how mole and Grandmother Spider help them find a place to live in the Blue Sky World. It is the story of the origin of corn and the life of the Tewas on the earth. "Spider, the Fire Bringer" (Cherokee), tells not only of the origin of fire but also of the origin of several animals' traits as a result of attempts to retrieve fire. Other pourquoi tales in this collection include "How the Spider Got Its Web" (Wiyat), "Spider Woman Creates the Burro" (Hopi), and "How the Half-Boys Came to Be" (Kiowa). Tellings are sophisticated, and typeface is small, so this collection may best be used as a read-aloud source to middle and upper grades.

Mayo, Gretchen Will. *Earthmaker's Tales: North American Indian Stories About Earth Happenings.* New York: Walker, 1989.
A collection of 17 tales about earth and weather phenomena. These tales may be used as additional versions of tales for comparison studies. Also by this author: *Star Tales: North American Indian Stories About the Stars* (Walker, 1987).

McDermott, Gerald. *Coyote: A Trickster Tale from the American Southwest.* Illustrated by the author. San Diego: Harcourt Brace, 1994.
This trickster story ends with pourquoi elements. Coyote wants to fly like the crows, so the crows decide to toy with him. They poke their feathers into Coyote's forelegs, but he still cannot fly. They re-poke the feathers to balance him, and he becomes boastful. The crows, angered now, take Coyote out for another flight, and he falls so fast his tail catches fire. To this day, Coyote is a dusty color with a blackened tail tip.

———. *Raven: A Trickster Tale from the Pacific Northwest.* Illustrated by the author. New York: Harcourt Brace Jovanovich, 1993.
In this classic tale of the Native Americans of the Northwest Coast, Raven decides to bring the gift of light to the creatures of earth, who are living in a world of darkness. He uses his powers of transformation to become a pine needle, and later becomes a human baby in the lodge of the sky chief. Behaving like any child who insists on his own way, Raven steals the light and brings it to earth. After introducing students to this simpler telling, compare it to Susan Shetterly's *Raven's Light.* For primary grades.

Medicine Story. *The Children of the Morning Light: Wampanoag Tales As Told by Manitonquat (Medicine Story).* Illustrated by Mary F. Arquette. New York: Macmillan, 1994.
A collection of 11 creation tales. Each tale is fairly long, told in a congenial storytelling style, and most tales are interconnected to those that went before. Many refer to names from earlier tales, including the two brothers born from the sky spirit who fell from the sky. The sophistication of these stories makes them more suitable for older students or for background material.

Midge, Tiffany, and Vic Warren. *Animal Lore and Legend: Buffalo.* Illustrated by Diana Magnuson. New York: Scholastic, 1995.
A useful combination of nonfiction information and folktales written in large, readable text for second to fourth grade. Three short sections contain both factual information and pourquoi tales such as "The Coming of the Buffalo" and "Why Buffalo Has a Hump." The teller is Native American. Other titles in this series: *Owl* (1995), *Bear* (1996), and *Rabbit* (1996).

Norman, Howard. *The Girl Who Dreamed Only Geese: And Other Tales of the Far North.* Illustrated by Leo Dillon and Diane Dillon. New York: Gulliver Books, 1997.
A collection of 10 tales of the Inuit and Eskimo peoples of northern North America. The product of many years of storytelling, transcription, and editing, this unique collection is drawn directly from the oral tradition, from personal friends of Howard Norman who spent hours around kitchen tables telling and evolving the tales. The stories are rather long and reflect the personal experiences of the tellers, imparting a sense of immediacy and of the folk process. One tale is notable as a pourquoi tale: "How the Narwhal Got Its Tusk," in which a boy's aunt is transformed into a narwhal, and his harpoon becomes her tusk.

———. *How Glooskap Outwits the Ice Giants and Other Tales of the Maritime Indians.* Boston: Joy Street Books, 1989.
A collection of six stories from the Native Americans of the coast of New England and Canada. Glooskap is a giant who creates human beings and performs amazing feats of strength and endurance in order to protect them. He brings balance into the lives of the creatures. For middle and upper grades.

Oliviero, Jamie. *The Day Sun Was Stolen.* Illustrated by Sharon Hitchcock. New York: Hyperion Books for Children, 1995.
This Haida (Northwest Coast) legend has elements of pourquoi, trickster, and transformation tales. Illustrated with Haida totem symbols by a Haida artist, this

simply told tale recounts how Bear steals Sun and how a boy disguises himself as a fish to get Sun back. Raven appears briefly at the beginning as the creator of the animals. Bear's coat is too hot, so to relieve the effects of the sun, he manages to take Sun in his mouth by holding snow in his mouth first. Bear hides Sun in a hole. A boy makes a plan with his grandmother's help: He puts on her magic fish skin, gets caught by Bear, waits for Bear to sleep, and shaves off some of Bear's fur so that he, too, will know what it means to be cold. The boy leaves Bear's cave with the fur in a sack, but the sack has a hole through which some fur scatters. Bear becomes cold and releases Sun so he can warm up. Some of the other animals use the scattered fur for their own warmth, which is why some animals grow extra fur in the winter. This also explains why Bear sleeps each winter to stay warm. This tale is a very successful, easy-to-read and easy-to-understand example of Haida folklore. Compare with *When Bear Stole the Chinook*, by Harriet Peck Taylor.

———. *The Fish Skin.* Illustrated by Brent Morrisseau. New York: Hyperion Books for Children, 1993.
    This Cree story from northern Canada contains both pourquoi and transformation elements. The people are tired of the clouds. When they ask the sun to stay, it gets too hot and dry, and everything begins to die. A boy wants to help, so he visits the Great Spirit in the forest. The Spirit gives him a fish skin. When he dons the fish skin, he is transformed into a fish. He drinks volumes of water until he becomes huge. He calls to a cloud and blows all his water at the cloud. The water falls back to earth as rain. This rain-origin story provides discussion material for the role of air moisture in rain formation. In addition, turtle's back is cracked from the heat, as he was too slow to get refreshed by the rain.

Oughton, Jerrie. *How the Stars Fell into the Sky: A Navajo Legend.* Illustrated by Lisa Desimini. Boston: Houghton Mifflin, 1992.
    First Woman is carefully placing the stars in the sky as a way to write the laws so everyone knows what to do. Coyote wants to help but soon tires of the tedious task. He picks up the blanketful of stars and scatters them all over the sky. This Navajo tale explains why there is confusion in the world today.

———. *The Magic Weaver of Rugs: A Tale of the Navajo.* Illustrated by Lisa Desimini. Boston: Houghton Mifflin, 1994.
    A story of how the art of weaving came to the people. Everyone is cold, so two women go off to pray for help. Spider Woman hears them and spins a web to bring the two up to her high canyon wall. She teaches the women how to build a loom, shear the sheep, and go through all the steps, advising patience. They must have beautiful thoughts while they weave. The women tire and worry about their cold families. For revenge, they deliberately weave in a mistake. Spider Woman approves of the error, for perfection is only for a god. Spider Woman keeps the rug, and the women despair as they head home. Later they realize that weaving provides warmth and prosperity. A sober tale conveying a reverence for weaving. For middle grades.

Pohrt, Tom. *Coyote Goes Walking.* Illustrated by the author. New York: Farrar, Straus & Giroux, 1995.
    In this collection of four short Coyote stories, the first, "Coyote Creates a New World," explains the origins of animals and land. It is interesting because it contains the flood motif (similar to the Noah's ark story) as well as the "earth-diver" creation motif. Coyote sees that the creatures have become "too wild," so he decides to create the world anew. He sings for the rains to come, rides a raft, and from his creation kit, turtle is sent down to bring mud up from the bottom of the water. From this mud, the earth is created, and then the animals and people. Compare this creation story to "Earth on Turtle's Back," from *In the Beginning*, and Shetterly's *Raven's Light*.

Robbins, Ruth. *How the First Rainbow Was Made: An American Indian Tale.* Illustrated
by the author. Oakland, CA: Parnassus Press, 1980.

The winter rains on Mt. Shasta are so strong that the people cannot get food. They
ask Coyote to help them approach Old-Man-Above for help. Coyote devises a plan with
the cooperative help of the animals and people. They shoot a hole in the sky and blow
two spiders up and through the hole. Old-Man-Above likes hearing about the cooperative effort and agrees to give them a break in the weather and a rainbow as a sign. The
text is accessible for second or third graders.

Rodanas, Kristina. *Dance of the Sacred Circle: A Native American Tale.* Illustrated by
the author. Boston: Little, Brown, 1994.

This Blackfoot legend, in straightforward text accessible to middle-grade readers,
tells how the first horses came to the Plains Indians. A boy with a scarred face wants to
help his people, who are suffering from hunger because the buffalo herds have become
scarce. He learns about the Great Chief in the sky and travels and dreams his way to
meet him. The Great Chief uses mud to fashion an animal similar to a dog for the boy.
Then, one by one, the other creatures suggest and contribute other qualities to make
the animal more suitable. Fir Tree gives it a tail, Turtle gives it harder feet, Elk makes
it bigger, and so on. As the boy rides home, suddenly there are hundreds of horses
following. At the next hunt, the horses enable the men to ride far and get enough meat.
The boy is now keeper of the gift.

———. *The Eagle's Song: A Tale from the Pacific Northwest.* Illustrated by the author.
Boston: Little, Brown, 1995.

This tale explains the origin of social celebrations, music, and sharing. Long ago,
the people used to live in isolated dwellings, never gathering or speaking together.
Three brothers live in one home and have plenty of provisions because two of the
brothers are skilled hunters. It never occurs to them to share their food or furs. The
youngest brother, Ermine, does not hunt but carves and decorates boxes and bowls for
their supplies. When the two brothers fail to return from a hunting trip one day, Ermine
goes out looking for them. He sees an eagle approach, and it turns into a young man.
The eagle-man speaks to Ermine about his brothers' heartless killing and their attempt to
get the eagle's feathers as a trophy. The eagle takes the boy on his back and flies to the
home of his eagle-mother, a tired, aged woman. She teaches Ermine music, drumming,
singing, dancing, and the joy of being with others. She says when the people learn the
gift of music, she too will get a gift. Ermine returns to his village and teaches his people
the joy of celebration and music. At a festival filled with throbbing drumbeats, Ermine's
brothers return, escorted by the eagle-man. Ermine discovers that the old woman has
been restored to a young eagle. The lives of the people are transformed from isolation
into joyful celebration.

Ross, Gayle. *How Rabbit Tricked Otter and Other Cherokee Trickster Stories.* Illustrated
by Murv Jacob. New York: HarperCollins, 1994.

A collection of 15 stories featuring the Cherokee trickster, Rabbit. Told and illustrated by people of Cherokee descent, these humorous stories have many parallels with
the Brer Rabbit stories of African Americans. Five tales are pourquoi stories, including "Why
Possum's Tail is Bare," "How Deer Won His Antlers," and "How Rabbit Tricked Otter."
The stories are accessible for independent reading by middle grades and listening by
younger grades. Some of these tales are found on Ross's storytelling tape (next entry).

———. *How Rabbit Tricked Otter and Other Cherokee Trickster Stories.* New York:
Caedmon, n.d. Audiocassette.

Experienced storyteller Gayle Ross tells nine tales from the Cherokee tradition.
Her style is smooth and even, and flute music provides pleasant interludes between
stories. Six of the stories are pourquoi tales, some doubling as trickster stories. Six of

the stories on the tape are found in her book by the same title (previous entry); "How Turtle's Back Was Cracked" is also separately published as a picturebook (see next entry). Her tellings follow the books fairly closely. These tellings would be enjoyable for children to hear after reading and to see how storytelling differs from reading aloud.

————. *How Turtle's Back Was Cracked: A Traditional Cherokee Tale.* Illustrated by Murv Jacob. New York: Dial Books for Young Readers, 1995.

Possum picks persimmons for his friend Turtle, and when Wolf steals some, Possum throws a persimmon hard and chokes wolf to death. Turtle gets so worked up about it, he begins to believe it was he who conquered Wolf, and so he goes about the village boasting with his wolf-ear spoons. The other wolves find out about Turtle's insulting actions and capture him. They threaten him with death by fire, then death by boiling. Using the same trickery as Brer Rabbit when he says, "please don't throw me in the briar patch," Turtle gets himself thrown in the river, exactly where he wants to go—but not before his shell hits a rock, cracking it. Told and illustrated by people of Cherokee descent.

————. *The Legend of the Windigo: A Tale from Native North America.* Illustrated by Murv Jacob. New York: Dial Books for Young Readers, 1996.

When members of the community mysteriously disappear, people begin to suspect the Windigo, a terrible monster that is made of stone. A boy gets an idea: If stones in a fire pit can get hot enough to crack, maybe they could burn the Windigo. The people dig a pit and cover it with branches to trap him. When he falls in, they cast firewood and a hot coal in and burn him until he cracks. They hear him scream, and then they hear another, tiny sound. A little voice is in everyone's ear, the voice of mosquitoes, the voice of the Windigo, remaining to eat people forever. A captivating story for all ages. Compare to the telling by Douglas Wood.

Rubalcaba, Jill. *Uncegila's Seventh Spot: A Lakota Legend.* Illustrated by Irving Toddy. New York: Clarion Books, 1995.

Uncegila is a huge, evil, serpentine creature with spots down her back. If a warrior could shoot at the seventh spot, the tribe would know no hunger or fear. Two brothers, one blind, set out on the mission, aided by Ugly-Old-Woman. When Blind-Twin embraces Ugly-Old-Woman, she is transformed into Beautiful-Young-Girl, and she equips the men with magic arrows. Prosperity and complicated rituals follow, and eventually, the tribe decides to give up being bound to the rituals and thereby also to give up the guarantee of prosperity. "Now they could grow strong and resourceful." This tale explains why life has uncertainties that may be overcome by resourceful behavior.

San Souci, Robert D. *Two Bear Cubs: A Miwok Legend from California's Yosemite Valley.* Illustrated by Daniel San Souci. El Poral, CA: Yosemite Association, 1997.

The scenery and wildlife of Yosemite provide a stunning setting for this suspenseful tale. A mother loses her two grizzly bear cubs, and finally Red-tailed Hawk sights them on a rock above the rim of Yosemite valley. The animal people try to rescue them, unsuccessfully, until Measuring Worm makes his way up. This story of courage tells how a rock becomes the famous landmark, El Capitan. The winning team of San Souci and San Souci produce a dramatic book that will captivate all ages.

Shetterly, Susan Hand. *Raven's Light: A Myth from the People of the Northwest Coast.* Illustrated by Robert Shetterly. New York: Atheneum, 1991.

Using the sources of the Tlingit, Kwakiutl, Haida, and Tsimshian peoples of the Pacific Northwest, Shetterly tells an extended version of how Raven brought light to the earth world. It begins with the concept of parallel worlds in the sky and the earth. Raven flies over the watery world below with a heavy sack containing animals, trees, and the materials for the earth. He flies into the sky world through a rip in the sky and steals the sun from the sky chief. Compare the obtaining of light to McDermott's *Raven* and the creation of the world to Pohrt's *Coyote Goes Walking.*

Simms, Laura. *Moon and Otter and Frog*. Illustrated by Clifford Brycelea. New York: Hyperion Books for Children, 1995.

An air of mystery and loneliness pervades this Modoc tale. The haunting blue-gray illustrations give it a dreamlike quality. This tale explains the changing phases of the moon and tells why otters still wait for the moon. Grizzly-bear clouds take bites out of the moon, making it smaller. Moon visits the otters, and they become old friends. Moon wants a wife and meets many pretty frogs but chooses to marry the ugliest one. She goes to live in the sky with the moon, and her comb makes a silvery trail in the water. The jealous bear-clouds still chew on the moon, and the otters still wait for the moon. For middle and upper grades.

Smith, Don Lelooska. *Echoes of the Elders: The Stories and Paintings of Chief Lelooska*. Illustrated by the author. Edited by Christine Normandin. New York: DK Ink, 1997. Book and CD.

Don Lelooska Smith was a Cherokee whose study and artistic practices led him to be adopted by the chief of the Southern Kwakiutl of the Northwest Coast and entrusted with the right to use the stories and masks of the tribes. The five tales, enriched by the paintings and Lelooska's own voice, represent a preservation and passing on of a legacy that might otherwise have been lost. Lelooska worked with the editor to refine the work before his death in 1996. Two tales contains pourquoi elements. The trickster/pourquoi tale, "Raven & Sea Gull" explains why the gull still walks around as though his feet are sore. It is also a story of how Raven brings Sun back to earth, after Sea Gull steals it. "Beaver Face" tells of the origins of stinging, biting insects, much like the legend of the Windigo: the ashes of Tsonoqua the Timber Giant are transformed into biting blackflies, hornets, and mosquitoes. This work of art is a tribute to Chief Lelooska for all ages to treasure.

Steptoe, John. *The Story of Jumping Mouse*. Illustrated by the author. New York: Lothrop, Lee & Shepard, 1984.

Messages of hope, perseverance, and selflessness are communicated in this tale from the Plains Indians, telling of the origin of the eagle. A young mouse wants to pursue a dream to go to the far-off land he has heard about in stories. On his journey he meets Magic Frog, who gives the mouse powerful legs to jump high. Later on his quest, he travels the prairie and meets a bison who is blinded and hopeless. Jumping Mouse tries the same magic the frog used, giving the bison the name "Eyes-of-a-Mouse." Now the bison has the mouse's eyesight, but the mouse is blind. The bison protects the mouse until they come to the mountains, where Jumping Mouse meets a wolf who has lost his sense of smell and his hope. The mouse gives his sense of smell to the wolf, who happily protects him for a time. Without sight or smell, Jumping Mouse wonders how he will survive. Magic Frog appears again and commends the mouse's selflessness. He tells him to jump high and gives him a new name: Eagle. Somber and simple, this is a story for primary and middle grades.

Taylor, C. J. *Bones in the Basket: Native Stories of the Origin of People*. Illustrated by the author. Plattsburgh, NY: Tundra Books, 1994.

A collection of seven creation stories from different tribes. Each is one to three pages in length, accompanied by full-page paintings. It is interesting that in two of the tales ("From Darkness to Light" and "Bones in the Basket"), the people come to earth from *underground*. In many creation stories, the people come to earth from the sky world, as in "Creation" in this collection. Suitable for middle and upper grades.

———. *How We Saw the World: Nine Native Stories of the Way Things Began*. Illustrated by the author. Plattsburgh, NY: Tundra Books, 1993.

A collection of creation stories in the same format as the previous book. Notable stories include "The Birth of Niagara Falls" and "The First Tornado." Compassion is shown in the story "How Horses Came into the World," whereas there is surprising cruelty in "How Eagle Man Created the Islands of the Pacific Coast." The brief "How the World Will End" warns that if people do not keep the earth in balance, Great Beaver will gnaw through the pole holding the earth up.

————. *The Monster from the Swamp: Native Legends of Monsters, Demons and Other Creatures*. Illustrated by the author. Plattsburgh, NY: Tundra Books, 1995.
Eight tales about fearsome monsters who are challenged and overcome by people for the good of all. "The Warning of the Gulls" tells of a Seneca girl who kills a monster bird, releasing a flock of seagulls. From then on, gulls promise to warn the people of approaching storms. "The Snake That Guards the River" explains why the Cheyenne people make an offering to the snakeman before crossing the Mississippi River. "How Muddy Lake Got Its Name" ends with a fierce battle between a young man and an evil monster, which leaves the water of the lake muddy to this day. "The Revenge of the Blood Thirsty Giant" is a violent telling of the legend of the Windigo.

Taylor, Harriet Peck. *Brother Wolf: A Seneca Tale*. Illustrated by the author. New York: Farrar, Straus & Giroux, 1996.
Wolf gives the birds their colors in the wake of trickster Raccoon's antics in this tale geared for primary-grade children. Raccoon taunts and teases Wolf, and later, while Wolf is sleeping, he covers Wolf's eyes with sticky tar and clay. When Wolf wakes, he howls in dismay, and the birds come. Wolf asks the birds to peck off the plaster and he will reward them. The birds want to be painted with the colors of the flowers. After he gives the birds their colors, he paints the black circles around Raccoon's eyes.

————. *Coyote and the Laughing Butterflies*. Illustrated by the author. New York: Macmillan Books for Young Readers, 1995.
Both a trickster and pourquoi tale, this legend of the Tewa explains why butterflies flutter about rather than fly straight. Coyote's wife asks him to travel the day-long journey to the salty lake to collect salt crystals for cooking. Three times, Coyote starts his trip, but eventually he needs to take a nap. Butterflies see him and decide to play a trick on him, so they grab bits of his fur, lifting him and carrying him back home. He awakes at home empty-handed and in ill favor with his wife. On his third attempt, Coyote makes it to the lake and fills his sack before taking his nap, and this time, the butterflies take pity on him and bring him home with his full sack. To this day, butterflies flutter because they are laughing about the trick they played. The text is readable by second or third graders.

————. *Coyote Places the Stars*. Illustrated by the author. New York: Bradbury Press, 1993.
Coyote decides to go adventuring in the sky. He shoots arrows into the moon and constructs a ladder to climb to the moon. Then he shoots arrows into the stars to move them about and form shapes of his animal friends. He comes back to earth and howls for the animals to come and see. A simply told tale for primary grades.

————. *When Bear Stole the Chinook: A Siksika Tale*. Illustrated by the author. New York: Farrar, Straus & Giroux, 1997.
The coming of spring is delayed in this Siksika (Blackfoot) tale explaining weather influences and the origin of animal traits. Winter's grip is lasting too long, so a boy meets with the animals to decide what they can do. Magpie flies off to ask his relatives in the mountains and reports that Bear has stolen the Chinook, the warm wind that blows east from the Rocky Mountains to melt the snows in western Canada. The boy and the animals journey up the mountain to find Bear. The first to look in Bear's cave is Owl, who gets poked in the eyes by Bear. To this day, owls have circular markings around their eyes. After other attempts, the boy blows pipe smoke into Bear's cave through the smoke hole, causing Bear to fall asleep. Then Coyote sneaks into the cave and steals the bag containing the Chinook. Prairie Chicken pecks at the straps until the

warm winds of the Chinook are released. The boy and animals flee as Bear awakens and chases after them. The melting river ice holds the smaller creatures, but Bear cannot cross. The boy returns to his village, where the people stand about in appreciation of the change in the weather. Since then, bears sleep through the cold months. Taylor's batik illustrations and story are appealing to primary and middle grades. Compare to *The Day Sun Was Stolen* by Jamie Oliviero.

Thomason, Dovie. *Lessons from the Animal People.* Music by Ulalí. Cambridge, MA: Yellow Moon Press, 1996. Audiocassette.

Nine Native American stories expertly and appealingly told by a storyteller of Lakota and Kiowa Apache descent. Between each story is a vocal selection by women singers in spirited harmony and rhythm. "The Making of the Animals" tells how the Creator lovingly finishes shaping the animals but gets irritatingly and repeatedly interrupted by an unfinished animal. The Creator loses patience with the interrupter and gives him characteristics opposite of those asked for. This becomes Owl, with its short neck, muddy feathers, and eyes wide with fear. The first animal hops away in distress before it is finished; this becomes rabbit with its folded hind legs. In "Ant Dances for Light," Ant and Bear debate whether there should be daylight or darkness. Bear dances for dark, while Ant fasts, prays, and asks that each animal gets what it needs. Ant keeps fasting and pulling her belt tighter. The story tells how both day and night came to be and why Ant has such a small waist. "Mouse and the Moon" tells how the Mouse People used to live on the moon, nibbling and nibbling away each month. Mice still nibble to this day, and Bear is the only great animal who will not eat Mouse. "The War Party" tells why Grasshopper has long hind legs and why Dragonfly looks like his skeleton is inside out. "Turtle Learns to Fly" explains the cracks on Turtle's back and also why Turtle doesn't interrupt anymore; he's learned how to keep his mouth shut. "Two Chipmunks" explains the origins of Chipmunk's stripes.

Tompert, Ann. *How Rabbit Lost His Tail.* Illustrated by Jacqueline Chwast. Boston: Houghton Mifflin, 1997.

The origin of Rabbit's short tail and of pussy willows are explained by this Seneca tale. Long-tailed Rabbit races round and round a willow tree, snow falling faster and faster. He decides to rest and finds a branch on the willow for his nap. While he sleeps, the snow melts, and Rabbit finds himself high up in the tree, the deep snow having vanished. He asks the other animals to help him down. They finally convince him to jump, but on the way down, his long tail gets caught in a branch. Ever since rabbits have had short, stubby tails, and willow trees have had tiny furry tails on them as a reminder. Illustrations and text are well suited to second grade readers and up. Similar tellings of this tale are found in Van Laan's *In a Circle Long Ago* and Bruchac's *The Boy Who Lived with the Bears.*

Ude, Wayne. *Maybe I Will Do Something.* Illustrated by Abigail Rorer. Boston: Houghton Mifflin, 1993.

A collection of seven Coyote tales. These are longer stories with few illustrations, suitable for additional material or for older readers. The tellings are humorous and sophisticated. One notable tale, "Coyote's Cave," is an earth-diver creation story starting with Coyote and Wolf riding a raft. Turtle dives down and brings up a bit of earth that eventually grows into land.

Van Laan, Nancy. *Buffalo Dance: A Blackfoot Legend.* Illustrated by Beatriz Vidal. Boston: Little, Brown, 1993.

This is the story of how the buffalo dance originated, a dance that is done before and after a buffalo is killed. The people are hungry; no buffalo have come to the piskun, the buffalo jump, and winter is coming. A young woman sees a herd and begs them to jump, but they do not. She promises to marry a buffalo if only they will jump and give meat to her people. Many jump, but then she is afraid of her promise and what it means. The buffalo chief takes her, and when her father comes looking for her, the buffalo trample him to death. The daughter sings and works her strongest medicine and brings her father back to life. The buffalo chief lets her return to her people, but first he teaches her the buffalo dance so that the buffalo, too, may live on. For middle and upper grades.

———. *In a Circle Long Ago: A Treasury of Native Lore from North America.* Illustrated by Lisa Desimini. New York: Apple Soup Books, 1995.
A collection of 25 stories and poems organized into seven regions of North America. The book includes a simple map to identify the regions. Most of the stories are pourquoi tales about animals and the origins of their characteristics. The typeface is large, and text is accessible for independent reading by middle grades and listening by primary grades. Illustrations are lively and break up the text. A very useful collection. This collection is used as a core title for a language arts thematic unit in Chapter 2, "Activities."

———. *Rainbow Crow: A Lenape Tale.* Illustrated by Beatriz Vidal. New York: Dragonfly Books, 1989.
Told in accessible text readable by second- and third-graders, this Lenape tale explains the origins of winter snow, fire, and the crow's black feathers and "crackly" voice. Rainbow Crow has long, colorful plumage and a tuneful voice. Snow comes for the first time, and it begins to concern the animals. Rainbow Crow goes to the Great Sky Spirit for help. The Sky Spirit cannot stop the snow before its time, but he does give the gift of fire. As Rainbow Crow flies back with fire, his feathers become black and charred and his voice becomes hoarse. Crow is sad, but the Sky Spirit comforts him with the gift of Freedom: The Two-Legged would soon come to earth, but they would never hunt or capture Crow, and his black feathers reflect all the colors.

———. *Shingebiss: An Ojibwe Legend.* Illustrated by Betsy Bowen. Boston: Houghton Mifflin, 1997.
The fearless determination of the little merganser duck, Shingebiss, in the face of the fierce cold of Winter Maker, is not only a story but also a model for behavior and survival. This tale tells of the origins of winter and spring and features Shingebiss, who is a diver-duck and a "spirit teacher" who can transform himself from spirit to man to duck. The cold of the Lake Superior region is palpable as Winter Maker repeatedly tries to defeat the little duck's attempts to break the ice and find fish to eat. Finally, Shingebiss sings a song inviting Winter Maker either to come into his home or to leave him alone. Winter Maker comes in, thinking he will freeze Shingebiss out, but the warmth of the wigwam melts Winter Maker a little bit. Winter Maker decides to leave Shingebiss alone. The story ends with a reminder that people who follow Shingebiss's example will find the food and warmth to last the frigid winters of the Lake Superior region. Additional background reading and effective woodcut illustrations make this book a valuable resource for its tale and Ojibwe culture. For all ages.

Walters, Anna Lee. *The Two-Legged Creature: An Otoe Story.* Illustrated by Carol Bowles. Flagstaff, AZ: Northland, 1993.
Back when the animals lived in peace with each other and the two-legged creature (Man), Man learned from the animals how to live. But then Man begins to act differently. He does not heed the warnings of Bear, who teaches him how to go ice fishing and rescues him from freezing. Man becomes rude, complaining, and destructive. The animals have a meeting, and finally Dog and Horse volunteer to stay with Man and be his helper. This explains why Man lives separately from the animals' ways and why dogs and horses live close to humans. Written by an author of Pawnee-Otoe descent, this story is simply told and is readable by second graders and up.

Wood, Audrey. *The Rainbow Bridge: Inspired by a Chumash Tale*. Illustrated by Robert
  Florczak. New York: Harcourt Brace, 1995.
  This creation myth takes place on an island off the California coast. The earth
goddess, Hutash, wants to share life with other beings, so she creates the people of the
Chumash tribe by scattering seeds from a sacred plant. Over time, the number of
people grows until the island is too crowded. Hutash arranges for some of the people
to move to the mainland; she constructs a rainbow bridge for the people to cross. Some
of the people fall off the bridge, and the earth goddess hears their cries and turns them
into dolphins. The Chumash believe to this day that the dolphins are their brothers and
sisters. This tale also briefly describes the origin of the Milky Way, lightning, and fire.

Wood, Douglas. *The Windigo's Return: A North Woods Story*. Illustrated by Greg Couch.
  New York: Simon & Schuster Books for Young Readers, 1996.
  An intriguing Ojibwe (Anishinabe) tale of a legendary creature that strikes fear
among the People. The People are faring well until something strange happens. One
by one, people go out to the woods but do not return. The People gather and remember
the stories of the Windigo, the forest giant who can turn himself into anything. They
meet to decide what to do. A girl suggests a trap, a deep pit in the ground, covered with
branches. The trap works, and the People throw hot coals into the pit, burning the
Windigo to ashes. They take the ashes and throw them into the wind from a high hill.
The People are relieved, the seasons pass, and the Windigo does not return . . . until
the next summer when, one evening, the air fills up with a cloud of ashes. The ash-beings
land on the people's skin, bite them, and make them itch. The girl declares the Windigo
has returned to eat them all . . . as mosquitoes! Compare with the telling by Gayle Ross.

SOUTH AMERICAN

Alexander, Ellen. *Llama and the Great Flood: A Folktale from Peru*. New York: Thomas Y.
  Crowell, 1989.
  A llama has a dream that the sea overflows and floods the world. He becomes sad,
stops eating, and frustrates his owner. The llama tells the man and advises him to bring
his family and food to the top of the highest mountain. There, they see animals of every
species. The flood comes, wiping out all other people and creatures. The water reaches
the fox's tail, turning its tip black to this day. Compare this flood re-creation myth to
The Tree That Rains, The People of Corn, and other flood stories. Told simply in large
typeface, this tale can be read by second or third graders.

Belting, Natalia M. *Moon Was Tired of Walking on Air*. Illustrated by Will Hillenbrand.
  Boston: Houghton Mifflin, 1992.
  A collection of 14 creation myths of South American Indians. Selected tales would
be effective as short read-alouds, especially as tales to compare to other origin stories.
Titles that would make interesting comparisons include "Moon Was Tired of Walking
on Air" (the creation of earth), "The Traveling Sky Baskets" (Sun and Moon's path
across the sky), and "What Happened When Armadillo Dug a Hole in the Sky" (the
coming of people from the sky world to the earth world). Because of the unusual and
comparison-worthy tales, this collection is useful.

Brusca, María Cristina, and Tona Wilson. *When Jaguars Ate the Moon and Other Stories
  About Animals and Plants of the Americas*. Illustrated by María Cristina Brusca.
  New York: Henry Holt, 1995.
  A collection of 31 single-page tales of the origins of plants and animals and their
characteristics, arranged A–Z. A strong point of this book is its diversity of lesser-known
animals, especially of South and Central American species. Some notable tales include

"Why the Quetzal Is the Most Beautiful Bird," "Star Girl Brings Yucca from the Sky," and "The Flood and the Howler Monkeys."

Crespo, George. *How Iwariwa the Cayman Learned to Share*. Illustrated by the author. New York: Clarion Books, 1995.

This Yanomami myth explains how the animals obtained fire and also why animals' shining eyes gather at a distance to watch fire at night. The animals of the rain forest eat their food raw, not knowing about fire. But they find out that the cayman (alligator-like reptile) and his wife have flames and smoke and delicious-smelling food. The cayman keeps the fire hidden in a basket in his mouth. The animals devise a trick to make the cayman laugh and lose the basket. A relay race ensues to bring fire into their possession, and the animals win the right to use fire. This delightful pourquoi/trickster tale is accessible to middle-grade readers. Give students help pronouncing the long Yanomami names, using the guide in the book. Compare to Jonathan London's *Fire Race*.

Ehlert, Lois. *Moon Rope: A Peruvian Folktale/Un Lazo a la Luna: Una Leyenda Peruana*. Illustrated by the author. New York: Harcourt Brace Jovanovich, 1992.

In this bilingual pourquoi/trickster tale, Fox tricks Mole into going to the moon with him by convincing him there are lots of worms to eat there. Mole's disgraceful fall is the reason he hides under the ground to this day. Some say that Fox's face can be seen on the full moon. Large, easy text and large, stylized illustrations make this accessible for primary grades.

Flora. *Feathers Like a Rainbow: An Amazon Indian Tale*. Illustrated by the author. New York: HarperCollins, 1989.

In text readable by primary students, this tale explains how the birds of the Amazon rain forest got their colors. All the birds used to have dark feathers. The mother Jacamin, a gray-winged trumpeter, helps her son investigate the secret of the multicolored Hummingbird. Hummingbird kisses the brilliant flowers, taking a bit of each color and putting it in her bowl. The other birds cannot do the same; their beaks are too big and they are too heavy. Mother Jacamin steals the bowl of colors for her son, but all the birds rush and dive into the colors. By the time Jacamin tries, he just gets a bit of purple for his breast, plus an ashy-colored back from his exasperated mother. To this day, all the birds have the colors they stole, but only Hummingbird has all the rainbow colors. Bright, well-researched illustrations add to the appeal of this simple tale.

Gerson, Mary-Joan. *How Night Came from the Sea: A Story from Brazil*. Illustrated by Carla Golembe. Boston: Little, Brown, 1994.

African slaves brought with them their religious beliefs, including their stories of Iemanjá, the sea goddess. According to the legend, at the beginning of time, there is only daylight. Iemanjá's daughter wants to marry an earth person. The daughter loves her husband, but the constant daylight hurts her eyes and fatigues her; she misses the night she knew in the sea. The husband sends his servants down into the sea to find night. They get night in a bag from Iemanjá and carry it back. The daughter meets and welcomes the night, the stars and the moon, and the night creatures. She can now rest and become refreshed. In gratitude, Iemanjá's daughter makes three gifts: the morning star, the rooster's crow, and the birds' songs to herald the day. The text is readable by second or third graders.

Stiles, Martha Bennett. *James the Vine Puller: A Brazilian Folktale*. Illustrated by Larry Thomas. Minneapolis, MN: Carolrhoda Books, 1992.

As the author's note explains, this tale shows a combination of traditions from the Arawak people (native peoples in Brazil who were forced to work as slaves on Portuguese plantations) and Africans who were brought to Portugal as slaves. James the turtle is brutishly challenged by an elephant who claims he is the king of the jungle and the coconuts are all his. So James tries eating food from the ocean, where a whale tells him that he is the king of the ocean and James may not eat there either. James challenges the elephant to a vine-pulling contest; the loser must leave the jungle. Then he challenges the whale for rights to the ocean. He ties one end of the vine to the whale and the other to the elephant and gives the signal tug. The two beasts struggle all day, never seeing each other. James goes back to each, proposing that, since no one won, they must live side by side and share. Although the tale does not clearly state it, this is an Arawak pourquoi tale explaining the reason for the ocean tides. Typeface and text make this accessible to primary grade readers.

Troughton, Joanna. *How the Birds Changed Their Feathers*. Illustrated by the author. New York: Peter Bedrick Books, 1986.
   In easy-to-read text, this South American Indian tale recounts not only the origin of colorful feathers but also why people have since hunted birds and stolen their feathers. Long ago, all birds used to be white. A boy hunts them despite warnings to stop this cruelty. The boy finds some brightly colored stones, which turn him into a huge, harmful Rainbow Snake. The people and animals have a meeting, and Cormorant is the only volunteer to go after the snake to kill it. He is successful and is rewarded with the colorful snakeskin, which he shares with all the other birds, getting only the color black for himself.

MANY CULTURES (in a collection)

Adler, Naomi. *The Dial Book of Animal Tales from Around the World*. Illustrated by Amanda Hall. New York: Dial Books for Young Readers, 1996.
   A useful collection of nine stories for reading aloud or for independent reading by middle grades. "Grandmother Spider" (Cherokee) tells how several animals try to bring the sun, leaving them marked as they are to this day; only Grandmother Spider succeeds. "The Rabbit in the Moon" (Asian Indian) reveals the selfless generosity of the rabbit, who is rewarded by a heavenly spirit. "The Dragon and the Cockerel" (Chinese) explains how Dragon gets his antlers and why Cockerel continues to complain about it. In the trickster tale "Never Trust a Pelican" (Thai), fish and crabs learn to avoid pelicans. In "Magic in the Rain Forest" (Brazilian Native American), Snake plays a trick on Jaguar, stealing Jaguar's eyes. Harpy Eagle then tricks Snake for Jaguar's benefit, and ever since, Jaguar has left a portion of his kill for Harpy Eagle. A mood of mysticism, drama, and tragedy pervades the beautifully told "Sedna and King Gull" (Inuit), which explains the origin of sea creatures. Sedna loves King Gull, who transforms himself into a man; Sedna's father agrees to their marriage. One day, King Gull sees hunters killing birds needlessly, and in an effort to stop the hunters, he himself is mortally wounded. His dying wish is to have his body thrown into the deep ocean. When Sedna does this, King Gull transforms into a whale, and Sedna's tears transform into sea creatures: seals, dolphins, walruses, and more. Sedna becomes queen of the deep sea and makes a law that hunters may take only as much as they need or she will make storms.

Cohn, Amy L., comp. *From Sea to Shining Sea: A Treasury of American Folklore and Folk Songs*. Illustrated by eleven Caldecott artists. New York: Scholastic, 1993.
   A large, extensive collection found in many children's libraries. This book has many uses and many potential curriculum tie-ins. The first of 15 chapters is titled "In the Beginning" and contains four pourquoi tales plus two songs and three poems. Stories include "Raven Brings Fresh Water" and "Coyote Helps Decorate the Night."

Ganeri, Anita. *Out of the Ark: Stories from the World's Religions*. Illustrated by Jackie Morris. San Diego: Harcourt Brace, 1996.
   A broad collection of 37 stories arranged by categories, including "Creation Stories," and "Flood Stories." Other religious topics are also included, such as "Lives

of Religious Leaders." A strong point of this collection (as an elementary school tool) is that the tellings are straightforward without trying to accomplish too much in the way of explanations or mystical/religious background. However, each section does include a useful introduction to set the cultural background. Very usable for selected read-alouds or for additional material, especially for creation stories and flood stories.

Hamilton, Virginia. *In the Beginning: Creation Stories from Around the World.* Illustrated by Barry Moser. San Diego: Harcourt Brace Jovanovich, 1988.
Twenty-five creation tales spanning African, Native American, Chinese, Russian, Australian, Greek, and other cultures. Selected stories are suitable for reading aloud to older grades. Notable stories include the following: "The Woman Who Fell from the Sky," featuring the earth-diver motif; and "The Pea-Pod Man," featuring Raven.

Hoffman, Mary. *Earth, Fire, Water, Air.* Illustrated by Jane Ray. New York: Dutton Children's Books, 1995.
This colorful collection is a sampling of traditions, beliefs, mythical wonders, poems, and natural phenomena associated with the four elements. None of the topics are explored in depth but rather give the reader a taste of the many belief systems and lore that have evolved around the elements. Only a few folktales are found here. The book serves best as an enjoyable browse as a take-off point for further investigations or as brief background material for an investigation. Some examples from the "Air" section include "Thunderbirds and Starpeople," "Hurricanes and Tornadoes," "Winged Creatures," and "The Home of the Gods." Sources are not cited.

Lester, Julius. *How Many Spots Does a Leopard Have?* Illustrated by David Shannon. New York: Scholastic, 1989.
This collection of 12 folktales is found in many libraries, and it contains three strong pourquoi stories. Told in an easy, conversational style, they make good read-alouds. "Why the Sun and the Moon Live in the Sky" is the same story line as the same title by Daly. "Why Dogs Chase Cats" and "Why Monkeys Live in Trees" are humorous.

Mayo, Margaret. *Mythical Birds & Beasts from Many Lands.* Illustrated by Jane Ray. New York: Dutton Children's Books, 1996.
Ten well-told stories about creatures such as the unicorn, dragon, and mermaid. Four contain pourquoi elements. "The Green-Clawed Thunderbird" (Blackfoot Native American) explains the source of rainstorms. In "The Fish at Dragon's Gate" (Chinese), the Golden Dragon becomes the rain god, and he creates the path of the Yellow River. In the humorously told "Jamie and the Biggest, First, and Father of All Sea Serpents" (Scandinavian/Orkney Islands), Jamie defeats the huge serpent by riding a boat into the serpent's mouth and setting the serpent's liver ablaze with a glowing peat pot. The serpent's thrashing creates the straits between Denmark and Sweden; his teeth become the Orkney, Shetland, and Faroe Islands; and his dead, burning body becomes Iceland. "How Music Came to the World" is an Aztec tale. In "Three Fabulous Eggs" (Burma), a white crow fails his mission, and as a punishment, all crows are scorched black. In addition, three eggs hatch, explaining why crocodiles and tigers are found in Burma. The other stories in this collection, although not pourquoi stories, are useful and captivating tales.

———. *When the World Was Young: Creation and Pourquoi Tales.* Illustrated by Louise Brierley. New York: Simon & Schuster Books for Young Readers, 1996.
Ten tales told in a lively, cheerful tone with background notes at the end. Several stories offer opportunities for comparisons with other tellings. "Catch It and Run" features Coyote stealing fire with an ensuing relay race similar to London's *Fire Race* and others. "Māui and His Thousand Tricks" is a telling of how the Polynesian trickster harnessed the sun to keep it from setting too fast. "The Girl Who Did Some Baking" explains the differences in people's skin color. "Tortoise's Big Idea" explains why

humans and creatures must die but rocks live forever. "Raven and the Pea-Pod Man" tells the story of Raven and the sun, but with a lot more plot elements than McDermott's telling. This very accessible, well-illustrated collection is a must for a study of pourquoi tales.

McCarthy, Tara. *Multicultural Fables and Fairy Tales: Stories and Activities to Promote Literacy and Cultural Awareness.* New York: Scholastic Professional Books, 1993.

In the format of a professional teacher's resource book, this collection contains many short, accessible tellings of four folktale genres to read aloud. Each tale is accompanied by one page of preparatory suggestions and one page of student activities. The sections include seven pourquoi tales, five trickster tales, and six fairy tales that include some transformations. Notable pourquoi tales include "The Five Water-Spirits," describing the origin of Niagara Falls, and "How the Beetle Got Her Colors."

Milord, Susan. *Tales Alive! Ten Multicultural Folktales with Activities.* Charlotte, VT: Williamson, 1995.

Two of the 10 tales in this collection are pourquoi tales, and four are transformation tales. The Australian Aboriginal tale "Lighting the Way" is a moving story of a girl who is sad that her two closest friends are leaving the Island of the Dead. There is no way she can travel with them. She asks a magician to turn her into a star so she can follow her friends' canoe. After careful consideration, it is decided that she will become the morning star, for early morning is the time when they will most need light. In "Why Hare Is Always on the Run," Hare's rude mischief motivates the animals to use a sticky-sap trap (a "tar baby" motif) to catch him. This collection is a good source for read-alouds for middle and upper grades.

——. *Tales of the Shimmering Sky: Ten Global Folktales with Activities.* Illustrated by JoAnn E. Kitchel. Charlotte, VT: Williamson, 1996.

An excellent collection of well-told tales, each accompanied by hands-on activities and related information presented in a child-friendly format. All the stories are pourquoi tales about the sky and include "The Division of Day and Night," "The Twelve Months" (weather), "The Great Bear" (the Big Dipper and related constellations), and stories about the moon, the rainbow, clouds, the wind, and thunder. This book would not only be a valuable resource for pourquoi tale study or science teaching units but also provides an array of related activities for recreational programs. Useful for children of all ages.

Moroney, Lynn. *Moontellers: Myths of the Moon from Around the World.* Illustrated by Greg Shed. Flagstaff, AZ: Northland, 1995.

On each double-page spread, there is a brief legend explaining the image or face on the moon, accompanied by cultural information and a large illustration. Use these 12 tales as read-alouds or for additional moon stories for comparisons.

Pellowski, Anne. *Hidden Stories in Plants: Unusual and Easy-to-Tell Stories from Around the World Together with Creative Things to Do While Telling Them.* Illustrated by Lynn Sweat. New York: Macmillan, 1990.

A resource for teachers or recreation programs for storytelling, reading aloud, and craft activities. Science classes would enjoy many of these brief plant stories. Interesting tales include "Why Most Trees and Plants Have Flat Leaves," "Why Carrots Are the Color of Flame," and "Why Some Leaves Are Shaped Like the Human Hand."

Philip, Neil. *The Illustrated Book of Myths: Tales & Legends of the World.* Illustrated by Nilesh Mistry. New York: Dorling Kindersley, 1995.

A comprehensive reference collection of world mythology for teachers and advanced students. Six categories of myths include stories of gods from many cultures. Of particular use in the study of pourquoi tales are the sections "Creation Myths" and "Beginnings," totaling 24 stories. The book includes "Who's Who in Mythology" and an index.

Pourquoi Tales. Boston: Houghton Mifflin, 1989.

Schools that have purchased the Houghton Mifflin literary readers series for reading instruction may have copies of this anthology. Intended for the middle grades, its three tales are "The Cat's Purr," "Why Frog and Snake Never Play Together" (both African folktales by Ashley Bryan), and "The Fire Bringer" (a Paiute tale retold by Margaret Hodges).

Riordan, James, comp. *Stories from the Sea: An Abbeville Anthology.* Illustrated by Amanda Hall. New York: Abbeville Press, 1996.

A collection of nine tales, including pourquoi and transformation tales, good for reading aloud to all ages or for independent reading by fourth grade and up. "The Flood" (Squamish Native American) depicts an oncoming flood; the people construct a huge canoe to save the children and the strongest young adults. When the waters finally recede, they see the tip of Mount Baker, British Columbia, which still bears the markings of the great canoe. In the Finnish tale "Why the Sea Is Salty," a poor fisherman and his family are starving, and his rich brother gives him only a cow's hoof, telling him to go to the devil. This he does, getting advice from the Heesi's (the devil's) woodcutters on the way. Following their advice, the fisherman asks Heesi for his millstone as a reward for the visit and the cow's hoof. Heesi tells him magic words that cause the millstone to produce food. When the rich brother sees the millstone, he takes it for himself, using it to produce the salt he needs to preserve his day's catch of fish. He does not know the words to stop the millstone, however, and it continues to grind out salt, sinking the boat; it is making salt still. "Sea Wind" is a wistful, enchanting love story between a woman and the Sea Wind, who can take the shape of a man or other creature. He comes to Aminata's village and marries her but never stays for long, for he has much to do on the sea. He must move the boats and make the sea breezes. They have three children: Sea Breeze, Flower Wind, and Breath of Mercy. Aminata dies, and Breath of Mercy provides comfort to the sad. "The Old Man of the Sea" (Siberian) explains the source of fish and storms.

Rockwell, Anne. *The Acorn Tree and Other Folktales.* Illustrated by the author. New York: Greenwillow Books, 1995.

A collection of ten illustrated tales for young listeners. One, "Owl Feathers," is a pourquoi tale explaining why Owl hides in a tree until dark. Owl has nothing to wear to the ball, so Hawk borrows feathers from the other birds to help Owl. Not only does Owl not thank his benefactors but at the end of the ball, Owl doesn't want to return the feathers. So Owl hides all day from the other birds and comes out only at night to dance all alone. Hawk never again has helped anyone.

Rosen, Michael. *How the Animals Got Their Colors: Animal Myths from Around the World.* Illustrated by John Clementson. San Diego: Harcourt Brace Jovanovich, 1992.

A collection of nine pourquoi or creation myths accompanied by bright illustrations and background information. Some stories are easier to follow than others.

Rosen, Michael, ed. *South and North, East and West: The Oxfam Book of Children's Stories.* Illustrated by numerous artists. Cambridge, MA: Candlewick Press, 1992.

A collection of 25 tales including trickster, pourquoi, and ghost stories. Useful as a read-aloud resource or for additional material for comparison studies. Pourquoi stories include "Why Do Dogs Chase Cars?" in which three animals ride in a taxi; the dog gets cheated at the end of the ride. In "Ears, Eyes, Legs, and Arms," the body parts used to move around separately. After an antelope hunt, the body parts argue about whose job was the most important in killing the antelope. On the advice of a mosquito, a wise chief is consulted. The chief joins all the parts together into one body. And this is why all the body parts go after a mosquito. Compare this mosquito story to *Why Mosquitoes Buzz in People's Ears.*

Swanson, Diane. *Why Seals Blow Their Noses: North American Wildlife in Fact and Fiction*. Illustrated by Douglas Penhale. Stillwater, MN: Voyageur Press, 1994.

Chapters about ten animals present substantial factual information, as well as three short folktales about the animal. Many of the stories are pourquoi tales. Animals include whales, owls, bats, bears, beavers, salmon, eagles, and wolves. The information sections are quite useful for third to fifth grade research. This large-format paperback is useful to classes comparing folk and scientific knowledge about animals.

Thornhill, Jan. *Crow & Fox and Other Animal Legends*. Illustrated by the author. New York: Simon & Schuster Books for Young Readers, 1993.

Nine tales from six continents. Each tale is about two animals, and as the author notes, many are variant tellings of the same motif found in several cultures. Seven tales are trickster tales, and five tales have pourquoi elements. "Tortoise and Crane," from China, features tortoise "flying" by holding on to a stick held by two flying cranes; he can't keep his silly mouth shut, so he falls and cracks his shell (also found in Native American, Russian, Mexican, and other variants). In "Fox and Bear" (Northern Europe), Bear is tricked into fishing with his long tail in a hole in the ice, and it gets frozen off. "Bear and Coyote" (Canada) explains why we have day and night. "Crane and Crow" (Australia) tells why the crane has a croaky voice. Each tale is one or two pages of solid text accompanied by one or two full-page illustrations. A useful collection.

Walker, Paul Robert. *Giants! Stories from Around the World*. Illustrated by James Bernardin. New York: Harcourt Brace, 1995.

A collection of seven stories accompanied by detailed commentary and source notes. The Hawaiian tale, "Kana the Stretching Wonder" describes the works of Kana. Kana is a kapua, a hero who is part divine and part human, who may have extraordinary powers or the ability to change shape. One day, the princess Hina is kidnapped on a floating hill. Kana is asked to help rescue her. The various exploits leading to her rescue are successful, thanks to Kana's ability to stretch taller and higher, until he is as thin as a spider web. The floating hill is actually a giant turtle. After Kana rescues Hina, he steps on the turtle's back and breaks it into little pieces. These pieces become the turtles seen in Hawaii to this day.

———. *Little Folk: Stories from Around the World*. Illustrated by James Bernardin. New York: Harcourt Brace, 1997.

A collection of eight stories about "little people," leprechauns, fairies, and Menehune, accompanied by detailed source notes and commentary. "The Capture of Summer," from the Wabanaki people of northeast North America, tells how Glooskap kidnaps a fairy, the queen of Summer, and brings her to the giant of the north, thus bringing summer to the north.

ORIGINAL POURQUOI STORIES

Berry, James. *First Palm Trees: An Anancy Spiderman Story*. Illustrated by Greg Couch. New York: Simon & Schuster Books for Young Readers, 1997.

Despite its classification as a folktale, the author's note states that he used folk elements to create this original story. The priest tells the king of a dream he has had, of a wondrous new tree, a palm tree. The king announces a reward for the one who can make this dream come true. Anancy the trickster is there, scheming. Anancy starts by enlisting the help of the Sun-Spirit; together they can split the reward. The Sun-Spirit agrees to help but states he must include his partner. Partner? Anancy wants no more partners to split the reward, but he finally relents. The Sun-Spirit vanishes, and Water-Spirit is now before Anancy. The same conversation transpires, and Water-Spirit says he does not work in isolation; he must bring in his partner. Partner? Anancy tries to flatter Water-Spirit out of it but finally agrees. The same sequence happens with Earth-Spirit and Air-Spirit. The deal done, Anancy waits and waits, but no sign of palm trees. Finally one day, everyone is gathered at the king's grounds to view the new palm trees. Many people step forward to claim credit. The king decides to reward everyone equally with a feast. Anancy is portrayed as a relentless schemer, and the illustrations do an intriguing job of showing Anancy as both spider and human. For middle and upper grades.

Davol, Marguerite W. *Batwings and the Curtain of Night*. Illustrated by Mary GrandPré. New York: Orchard, 1997.
    At the world's beginning, the Mother of All Things creates many things: flowers and grasses, trees, sunlight, mammals, birds, and a night curtain so they can rest. After some days and nights, the night animals complain that night is too dark. The bats team up with other animals to fly to the sky and pull back the curtain slightly to let a little light in. The best they can do is hang upside down from the sky, with owl. When they flutter down and look back up, they see that their claws have made little holes in the curtain and that the owl's talons made a large hole. Now they have the stars and moon to see by at night.

——. *How Snake Got His Hiss*. Illustrated by Mercedes McDonald. New York: Orchard, 1996.
    Snake's appearance and ego used to be all puffed up. His encounters with other animals cause the hyena to have spots, the lion's mane to stand out, the ostrich to run, the monkey to jump about, and crocodile's back to have ridges. Elephant stomps and sneezes on Snake. Now he is so skinny, all he can say is "hiss." The story has the feel of a folktale in language and illustrations. It provides students with examples of animals' traits as a model for their own original writing of pourquoi tales.

Hadithi, Mwenye. *Hot Hippo*. Illustrated by Adrienne Kennaway. Boston: Little, Brown, 1986.
    An original story with the feel of an African folktale. Hippo asks Ngai, the god of Everything, if he can be a water creature because he is so hot. Ngai is concerned that Hippo will eat all the little fishes. Hippo promises to open his mouth often to show Ngai there are no fish and to eat grass so that he is not hungry for fishes. To this day, Hippo cools himself in the water, holds his breath and wags his tail, and opens his mouth wide. Another original pourquoi tale by the same author is *Awful Aardvark* (1989), which explains why Aardvark sleeps during the day and eats termites at night. Both are suitable for independent reading by primary grades.

——. *Hungry Hyena*. Illustrated by Adrienne Kennaway. Boston: Little, Brown, 1994.
    This original trickster/pourquoi story explains why Hyena no longer runs fast but slinks along. Hyena tricks Fish Eagle out of the fish he just caught. Fish Eagle plans revenge, getting all the hyenas to stand on each others' backs to reach the moon for the sweetest meat. They fall and slink away in embarrassment. This story has the feel of an African folktale and is suitable for independent reading by primary grades.

How the Sun Was Born/Cómo El Sol Nació. Written and illustrated by third-grade art students of Drexel Elementary School in Tucson, Arizona. St. Petersburg, FL: Willowisp Press, 1993.
    After learning about the Aztecs' concepts of the sun and studying the yarn art of the Huichol Indians of Mexico, third-grade students wrote this original pourquoi story in simple text. A dinosaur lays five eggs; four hatch. After volcanoes erupt, the sand gets hotter, and the fifth dinosaur egg hatches and turns into a ball of fire. It becomes the sun. This book makes a fine model for students writing their own pourquoi explanations.

Kipling, Rudyard. *The Beginning of the Armadillos*. Illustrated by John A. Rowe. New York: North-South Books, 1995.

The classic *Just So Stories* (1902) are well-known original pourquoi stories. The literary language and complex sentence structure may be challenging for students. A skilled read-aloud can unlock the humor in this story. A Painted Jaguar is instructed by his mother on the eating of tortoises and hedgehogs. Painted Jaguar finds Stickly-Prickly Hedgehog and Slow-and-Solid Tortoise in the forest. The two friends' quick wits and the Jaguar's slow mind combine for some funny conversations that totally befuddle Jaguar. The Hedgehog and the Tortoise practice taking on each other's characteristics to further confuse Jaguar and keep him at bay. Hedgehog and Tortoise end up looking like some other creature, which Jaguar's mother calls "Armadillo."

———. *The Elephant's Child: From the Just So Stories*. Illustrated by Tim Raglin. New York: Alfred A. Knopf, 1986.

This picture book edition has been adapted for a book-on-tape audiocassette and a video, both narrated by film star Jack Nicholson. In the early times, elephants did not have trunks. Elephant's Child has such curiosity about "why things are" that his incessant inquiries often get him spanked. He goes on a quest to find out what Crocodile has for dinner. His adventures bring him to Crocodile, who entices Elephant's Child to get close enough to grab Elephant by his nose. Elephant's Child pulls back, stretching Elephant's nose, aided by Bi-Colored-Python-Rock-Snake. In the aftermath, Snake points out to Elephant all the advantages of having a trunk. The tape and video have intriguing musical accompaniment by Bobby McFerrin. Audiocassette: Rabbit Ears Productions and Random House Home Video, 1986. Videorecording: Random House Home Video, 1986.

———. *Just So Stories*. Illustrated by Barry Moser. New York: Books of Wonder, 1996.

A new edition of 13 stories accompanied by 10 color plates painted in Moser's unique, dramatic style.

Knowlton, Laurie Lazzaro. *Why Cowboys Sleep with Their Boots On*. Gretna, LA: Pelican, 1995.

Each night after a hard day of cowboy toil, Slim Jim Watkins would take off his duds and lie down to sleep under the stars. Each morning, one article of clothing would be missing. The illustrations provide the clues. Each night, Slim Jim decides to keep one more article of clothing on until he keeps his boots on, too. A short, humorous tale suitable for reading by primary grades.

MacDonald, Amy. *The Spider Who Created the World*. New York: Orchard, 1996.

MacDonald uses folk elements of creation, sun, moon, and air to fashion an original story. When the sky is new, a spider, Nobb, is looking for a place to lay her egg. Her friend, Air, offers herself, but Nobb wants something firmer. Nobb asks Moon, Sun, and Cloud but is refused. Clever Nobb weaves a web and catches Moon, Sun, and Cloud. She takes a bite out of each, and from these three bites, she makes Earth. Sun is the fire inside, covered by a layer of Moon, and the rivers are made by Cloud. She never forgets that her only true friend is Air, so that is why spiders hang in the air to this day.

Richardson, Judith Benét. *Old Winter*. Illustrated by R. W. Alley. New York: Orchard, 1996.

Contemporary setting and dialog provide the backdrop for this brief story about the old man who brings winter and the young mom who brings spring. Old Winter overhears people complaining about being tired of winter weather. He grumpily decides he's not about to fly south and bring winter there if people don't appreciate it. He falls asleep in the meat locker of the P & J Supermarket for two months and awakens to find people still struggling against winter. A young mother (Spring) with two children drives up and is surprised to find Old Winter still there. She speaks gently to him and helps him on his way. Spring brings relief to the town, and then she continues on her drive north. Compare this light story to the Native American account of winter and spring, *Peboan and Seegwun*, by Charles Larry.

Wood, Nancy. *The Girl Who Loved Coyotes: Stories of the Southwest.* Illustrated by Diana Bryer. New York: Morrow Junior Books, 1995.

Twelve original stories reflecting the three cultures of the Southwest: Native, Hispanic, and Anglo. The stories contain folk elements and pourquoi elements, including "How Coyote Got His Song," "How Eagle Learned to See," and "The Coyote Who Became a Star."

Index